Harlem at War

Harlem at War

The Black Experience in WWII

Nat Brandt

Syracuse University Press

First Paperback Edition 1997
97 98 99 00 01 02   6 5 4 3 2 1

Except when noted, all photographs are courtesy of UPI/Bettman.

Use of verse from *The Panther and the Lash* by Langston Hughes is gratefully
acknowledged. Copyright © 1951 by Langston Hughes. Reprinted by permission of
Alfred A. Knopf, Inc.

Epigraphs for chapters 13, 15, 17, and 18 from poems by Claude McKay are taken
from *Crossing the Danger Water: Three Hundred Years of African-American Writing*, edited
by Deirdre Mullane (New York: Doubleday, 1993). Used by permission of the
Archives of Claude McKay, Carl Cowl, administrator.

This book is published with the assistance of a grant from the John Ben Snow
Foundation.

The paper used in this publication meets the minimum requirements
of American National Standard for Information Sciences—Permanence
of Paper for Printed Library Materials, ANSI Z39.48-1984. ∞™

Library of Congress Cataloging-in-Publication Data
Brandt, Nat.
Harlem at war : the Black experience in WWII / Nat Brandt.
p.   cm.
Includes bibliographical references and index.
ISBN 0-8156-0324-X (cloth : alk. paper) / ISBN 0-8156-0462-9(pbk.: alk. paper)
1. Harlem (New York, N.Y.)—Race relations.   2. Riots—New York (N.Y.)—History
—20th century.   3. New York (N.Y.)—Race relations.   4. World War, 1939–1945—
Afro-Americans.   5. Afro-Americans—New York (N.Y.)—History—
20th century.   I. Title.
F128.68.H3B65   1996
305.896'07307471—dc20   95-39044

To the memory of Sara D. Jackson of the National Archives

A journalist by profession, Nat Brandt has been a newswriter for CBS News, a reporter on a number of newspapers, an editor on the *New York Times,* managing editor of *American Heritage,* and editor-in-chief of *Publishers Weekly.* Since 1980, Mr. Brandt has been a free-lance writer, chiefly in the area of American history. He is the author of *The Man Who Tried to Burn New York; The Town That Started the Civil War,* a Book-of-the-Month Club and History Book Club selection; *The Congressman Who Got Away with Murder; Con Brio: Four Russians Called the Budapest String Quartet; Massacre at Shansi;* and with John Sexton, *How Free Are We? What the Constitution Says We Can and Cannot Do.*

Looky here, America,
What you done done—
Let things drift
Until the riots come.

Now your policemen
Let the mobs run free;
I reckon you don't care
Nothing about me.

You tell me that hitler
Is a mighty bad man.
I guess he took lessons
From the ku klux klan.

You tell me mussolini's
Got an evil heart.
Well, it musta been in Beaumont
That he had his start.

Cause everything that hitler
And mussolini do
Negroes get the same
Treatment from you.

You jim crowed me
Before hitler rose to power
And you're STILL jim crowing me
Right now, this very hour.

Yet you say we're fighting
For democracy.
Then why don't democracy
Include me?

I ask you this question
Cause I want to know
How long I got to fight
BOTH HITLER AND JIM CROW.

—Langston Hughes, "Beaumont to Detroit: 1943"[1]

Contents

Illustrations

Preface

I was a youngster, living in Brooklyn, when the United States entered World War II. I remember how committed my family, my friends, and my neighbors were to the struggle against the Germans and the Japanese. Everyone who had a son serving in the armed forces proudly displayed a little American flag in his or her parlor window. We had two: one for my brother who served in the navy, the other for my brother who was a marine. My mother and her sister, my aunt, joined the Volunteer Ambulance Corps. The money I earned for doing household chores was paid in twenty-five-cent Victory stamps, and when I amassed seventy-five of them in a little booklet, I went to a local bank and exchanged them for a twenty-five dollar war bond. The movies my friends and I went to on Saturday afternoons extolled the commitment and unity of purpose all Americans felt about the war.

It never dawned on me that anyone felt otherwise. I was totally unaware that there were several million Americans who did. Not that they weren't patriotic. If anything, they wanted to serve their country on the same terms as other Americans. But except for a few combat units, they were relegated to play a secondary role, and even then they were treated—to use their words—as "second-class citizens."

The experience of blacks during World War II was visually confirmed during the fiftieth anniversary of D-Day in 1994. One saw only white faces in the film documentaries of the invasion of France or of the wartime assembly lines in airplane, tank, and ship plants. The black troops that participated in the Normandy invasion were supply troops and labor battalions who landed after the beaches were taken. They were never shown. The black men and women who worked in defense plants for the most part wielded brooms and mops, not lathes and welding machines. They, too, were invisible. From an American perspective, it was evident that World War II was a white man's war.

Moreover, as a youngster, I never heard—whether from my parents or over the radio or at the movies—about the racial disorders that occurred frequently throughout the country, about the clashes between blacks and whites vying for the same jobs in boomtown defense-plant cities, about the treatment that northern black draftees encountered at training camps in the South, indeed about the incidents that became all too common wherever black troops were trained or stationed, be it in America or overseas. The rage surfaced frequently, was suppressed, but was not extinguished.

The War Department tried to keep a tight lid on information about troubles at military bases, and newspapers other than the black press gave little space to news that seemed of little importance to the country's war effort. Young Americans were dying in the Pacific, in North Africa, in Italy, in France. The British were fighting for their very existence. French, Dutch, Belgians, Norwegians, and Danes were shackled under Nazi domination. German troops had advanced to the outskirts of Moscow. Japanese armies controlled the Philippines and the Pacific west of Hawaii and north of Australia. This was a war for the very survival of democracy around the world.

I knew about that struggle, believed in it completely. What I didn't realize was that there was a fight for democracy at home, too, in America.

The focus of this book is on one of a number of racial disturbances that occurred during the war, a riot in Harlem, a section of Manhattan in the city of New York. But the context is the entire country.

Acknowledgments

I am grateful for the candor displayed by all those individuals who permitted me to interview them about their experiences growing up in Harlem as well as about their actions and reactions on August 1–2, 1943: St. Clair T. Bourne, Marvel Cooke, Evelyn Long Cunningham, Dr. James Jones, Frederick Douglass Mays, Arnold de Mille, Virginia Delany Murphy, Evelyn Hunt O'Garro, Foster Palmer, Doris Saunders, Jack Scarville, Walker Smith, and Allen Worrell. I am in debt also to insights provided by Edward Dudley, Madison S. Jones, Ernie Smith, and Maj. Arthur A. Tritsch (U.S. Army, Ret.).

Ernie Smith also graciously shared with me the transcription of an oral-history interview he conducted with dancer Norma Miller as well as the transcription of Robert P. Crease's interview with lindy-hop dancer Frankie Manning, both of which are part of the Smithsonian Institution's Jazz Oral History Project, "The Swing Era." He also screened for me two short films—"Pathe Harlem Newsreel 1930" and "Life in Harlem 1940"—that are part of the Ernie Smith Jazz Collection at the National Museum of American History. They bear the archival numbers 491.12 and 491.13, respectively.

I wish to thank my wife, Yanna, whose editing skills vastly improved this manuscript.

It is currently fashionable to use the term "African American." However, I do not. Most of the blacks I interviewed resented this form, which they felt was white-inspired and, in a sense, demeaning. As one woman in her seventies put it, "I don't want to go back to Africa. I don't want to go to Africa at all. I am an American."

New York City   Nat Brandt
August 1995

xv

Harlem at War

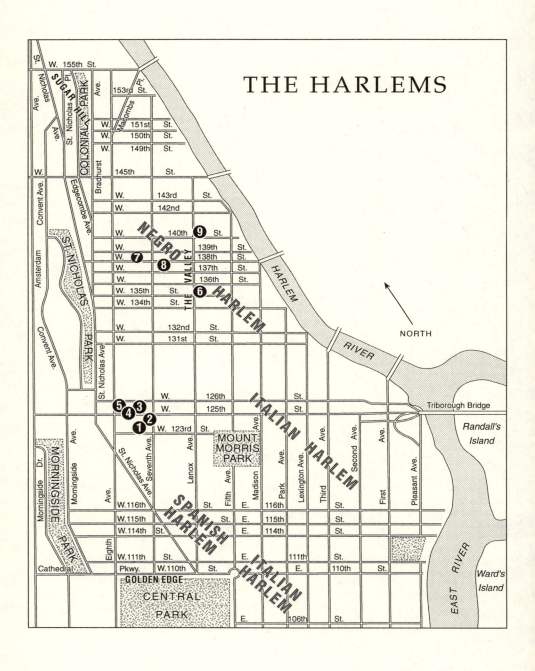

THE HARLEMS

Prologue

New York City, midsummer 1943. You could sense the new confidence in New York City that Sunday despite the sweltering heat and humidity. August has arrived in sultry fashion, with hardly any breeze stirring the air. It is the kind of day that city dwellers spend by open windows or on fire escapes, drinking beer and cold sodas, fanning themselves as they watch children play in the streets below. Or they take advantage of the shade under the trees in Central Park to spread blankets and picnic. Or, if they can, they escape by subway to the beach; a record-breaking 1,825,000 people flee to the Rockaways by midafternoon, to swim in the refreshing Atlantic, when the temperature rises to eighty-seven degrees and the humidity level stands at eighty.[1]

Opposite: Pertinent landmarks at the time of the Harlem riot in 1943: (1) 28th Precinct station house on West 123rd Street. (2) Theresa Hotel, (3) Sydenham Hospital and (4) Apollo Theater on West 125th Street. (5) Braddock Hotel on West 126th Street and Eighth Avenue. (6) Harlem Hospital on Lenox Avenue at 135th Street. (7) Strivers' Row, which includes both 138th and 139th Streets. (8) Abyssinian Baptist Church on West 138th Street off Seventh Avenue. (9) Savoy Ballroom on Lenox Avenue at West 140th Street. Lenox Avenue is now called Malcolm X Boulevard, Seventh Avenue is Adam Clayton Powell Jr. Boulevard, Eighth Avenue is Frederick Douglass Boulevard, and 125th Street is Dr. Martin Luther King Jr. Boulevard. Mount Morris Park has been renamed Marcus Garvey Park. *Source: New York City Guide.* Copyright © 1939 by the Guilds' Committee for Federal Writers' Publications of the WPA.

The good news is that the tide of the war has changed. Up until recently, ever since Pearl Harbor in December 1941, America and its Allies had been on the defensive. But now, for the first time, they are on the attack. American Liberator bombers based in North Africa have reached the Ploesti oil fields in Rumania, source of 90 percent of the German Air Force's gasoline. The Russian Army has stopped the Germans in the Donets Basin. The British Eighth Army is advancing in North Africa. American forces control most of Sicily, and the new Badoglio government on mainland Italy is already considering Allied terms for surrender. The recent downfall of Mussolini is, in Franklin D. Roosevelt's words, "the first crack in the Axis."

The president is nevertheless quick to temper his words. The war will not end this year, he cautions. Then he quickly adds that on the other hand the war will not last until 1949. "July," the *New York Times* crows, "was probably the best month of the war for the Allies."

The talk that day in the city is not about the war or the weather, but about baseball. In the most incredible trade New Yorkers can remember, the Brooklyn Dodgers have sent their star first baseman, Dolph Camilli, to their archrivals, the New York Giants.

Both those teams are playing out of town this day. The city's third major league team, the Yankees, is taking on the Tigers in a doubleheader in the Bronx and a large crowd is expected. For those who cannot make it to Yankee Stadium or to the beach, there is Times Square. Eight Broadway theaters, all proudly boasting that they are air-conditioned, have Sunday performances, and midtown movie houses, also air-conditioned, are featuring a number of star-studded films: Cary Grant in *Mr. Lucky* is playing at Radio City Music Hall; *Stage Door Canteen*, now in its sixth week, is at the Capitol, and the Roxy is showing *Stormy Weather* with Lena Horne, Bill (Bojangles) Robinson, and Cab Calloway.

Several miles north, in Harlem, *Stormy Weather* is also playing at the RKO Alhambra on Seventh Avenue, and around the corner on 125th Street the popular "growl trumpet king" Cootie Williams and his band headline the show on stage at the Apollo.

On the surface, the ebullience of midtown Manhattan is reflected uptown. Sunday is always a special day in Harlem, a day for promenading after church services, the heat and humidity notwithstanding.

There is something special to cheer about, as well. The *Amsterdam News* is running two photographs on its front page of the launching of the destroyer-escort *Harmon* at the Bethlehem Steel Company's shipyard in Quincy, Massachusetts. The ship is named in honor of Leonard Ray Harmon, mess attendant first class, who was killed in action in the battle of Guadalcanal in the Solomon Islands. It is the first time in history that a warship has been named for a black man.

And yet, behind the smiles and joviality as family meets family and stops to chat and gossip, as young men exchange banter, flirting with the young women who walk by, there is—if you are black yourself or can sympathize—a sense of profound anger and frustration. Because next to the photographs of the launching of the *Harmon* is a story about the execution in Georgia of a black sergeant who had gotten into a fight with a state policeman. And if you read beyond page one of the *News*, or glance through Harlem's other weeklies, the *People's Voice* and *New York Age*, there are articles about job bias in war industries, about the black longshoremen loading explosive munitions at a New Jersey dock who were refused admittance to a nearby restaurant, about complaints of being called "nigger" and "boy" at an air force training base in Minnesota, about the advertisement placed by the Ku Klux Klan in a South Carolina newspaper, about the beating of a black clergyman by a train conductor outside of Atlanta because the minister refused to leave an observation car reserved for whites. The feature editorial in the *Amsterdam News* is calling on the Federal Bureau of Investigation to do something about lynchings in Mississippi and Indiana. And, in answer to a threatening letter from a KKK leader, the city's lone black councilman, Adam Clayton Powell, Jr., warns that New York's blacks cannot be bullied: "There is a different kind of a Negro here."

Sometime shortly after seven o'clock, about an hour before dusk —when the temperature remains in the eighties and Harlem's streets are still crowded with giggling children playing on stoops and its boulevards are filled with friendly adults ambling down the wide sidewalks—a soldier with his mother on his arm steps through the open doors and into the lobby of the Hotel Braddock, at the corner of 126th Street and Eighth Avenue. They disappear inside for a moment when suddenly a sound rare in Harlem then—a gunshot—rings out. No sooner is the shot heard on the sidewalk outside the hotel than a crowd forms and a rumor spreads with the speed of a brushfire: a black soldier has been killed by a white policeman.

Within minutes, the quiet streets of the nation's largest black community resemble a battleground. People of both sexes and all ages, but especially young men, begin to race through the area, screaming and shouting: "White man kill black soldier! Get the white man! Get the white man! He's to blame!"[2]

The news spreads along 125th Street, both east toward Seventh and Lenox Avenues and west toward St. Nicholas Avenue, then up those boulevards and Eighth Avenue as well as on side streets as far north as 155th Street. Mobs form quickly everywhere. Roving bands of people holler and shout as they run this way and that on 125th Street and then up the avenues, smashing windows, their targets the many stores in Harlem owned by white proprietors. The rioters overturn peddlers' carts, set fire to cars, break streetlights. Some on the roofs of apartment houses drop cans and bricks at the few scattered policemen who are on duty. The rage spent, the vandalism and violence turn to looting. Boys, girls, men, and women risk being cut by broken panes to squirm inside grocery shops, furniture stores, haberdasheries, and pawnshops. They come out with their arms filled with foodstuffs, chairs and tables, clothing and jewelry.

The air is filled with noise: yelling, the "pop pop" of gunfire, police cars and fire engines racing through the area, their sirens going full blast. In their wake, ambulances rush from street to street, their corpsmen propping up the wounded on benches inside so they can jam as many as eight persons into each vehicle.

Before long, the floor of the emergency ward at Harlem Hospital is "a flood of blood."[3]

ONE

E Pluribus Unum

But can a people live and develop for over three hundred years simply by reacting?

—Ralph Ellison[1]

They were called Negroes or colored then, and one of the first surviving written references to them in New York dates back to February 1644 when eleven blacks, once slaves in the service of the West India Company, petitioned for and were granted conditional freedom. They formed a tiny community of free blacks, the first in the northern tier of colonies in America. They owned farms in what was then the frontier of a tiny Dutch settlement, a swampland stretching roughly from present-day Canal Street to Fourteenth Street. Portions of the so-called negro frontier in what became Greenwich Village would remain a black enclave for nearly two hundred years.

By 1644, the Dutch had been trading in the area for thirty-three years, ever since Henry Hudson sailed up what was for several centuries called the North River. Their settlement on the tip of Manhattan, founded officially in 1625 as New Amsterdam, was then but one outpost in the vast colony known as New Netherland. It included a fort with four bastions, two windmills, and numerous houses close to the shoreline built in the image of the colonists' homes in Holland. Vessels making their way up the Narrows to the island would haul in their sails as they edged toward a wharf where a crane for unloading and weighing cargo towered above the ships. Next to it was a gallows.[2]

The freed blacks—with names such as Paul d'Angola and Simon

Congo—had once been "Company's Negroes," brought to New Amsterdam in 1626 by the Dutch West India Company to cut timber, clear land, build roads, and erect dwellings and forts. They worked also as servants and farm workers. They were joined two years later by three black women—"Angola slaves, thievish, lazy and useless trash."[3] Although the Dutch opposed the legal marriage of slaves, the women became in fact the wives of some of the men. After laboring eighteen or more years in the service of the Company,[4] the eleven blacks and their wives were freed. Their manumission, however, was conditional on paying a yearly tax in the form of a hog and crops,[5] and their children remained slaves until the former slaves could earn enough to purchase their freedom.[6]

The manumission of those eleven men and their wives might, on the surface, appear to have heralded a spirit of antislavery, but nothing was further from the fact. Two years later, in May 1646, a vessel arrived from Brazil with what is considered the first cargo of black slaves ever sold in the colony of New Netherland.[7] The slaves, most of whom were from the Dutch colony of Curaçao, were sold for "pork and peas."[8] Nine years later, in 1655, the first cargo of slaves imported directly from Africa arrived in Manhattan.[9] Because of the shortage of skilled craftsmen in the colony, some of the slaves were trained as caulkers, carpenters, bricklayers, and blacksmiths.[10]

Although greatly in demand, black slaves were apparently relatively few in number at first and were only a small part of a conglomeration of merchants, trappers, artisans, soldiers, sailors, indentured servants, laborers, and apprentices from all parts of Europe who resided or traded in New Amsterdam. A French Jesuit was astonished to learn that the "four or five hundred men of different sects and nations" on and about the island spoke eighteen different languages, a Babel-like atmosphere that remained a characteristic of the city.[11]

Threatened by a squadron sent by Charles II, the Dutch meekly surrendered New Amsterdam to the Crown in 1644, and the city, then of some fifteen hundred souls, officially became New York. One reason the Dutch gave for surrendering without a fight was that they could not withstand a British siege because three hundred newly imported slaves had devoured all the surplus food stores.[12]

With the English in control, the slave population rose rapidly. White labor remained in short supply, so as the colony of New York grew, the demand for slave labor increased markedly. By 1711 there were so many slaves—they represented nearly one-fifth of the population[13]—that a new market house at the Wall Street Slip was appointed the official site "where Negroes and Indians could be bought, sold, or hired."[14]

If anything, the status of blacks changed from bad to worse once the English wrested the area from the Dutch. The British enforced a policy of segregating blacks from whites in the fear that allowing them to intermingle would militate against keeping the blacks enslaved. Slaves were not permitted to testify against a freeman in any criminal or civil case. Slaves who carried weapons could be punished with ten lashes. To prevent runaways, slaves were prohibited from traveling beyond forty miles north of Saratoga, and in a treaty the British negotiated with the Six Nations, the Indians agreed to return any slaves who sought refuge with them.[15]

Unlike slaves reared in bondage in colonial America, those who came from Africa were not docile, and to make unruly ones obedient, their masters resorted to whipping and torture to punish them for insubordination. Queen Anne in London received so many reports of the ill-treatment of slaves and indentured servants that she decreed that any master willfully killing a slave would be executed. Despite the queen's attempt to alleviate the slaves' treatment, her cousin, Lord Cornbury, whom she had appointed governor of the colony, took a different tack. Slaves in the colony were not allowed to congregate. As early as 1683, it had been forbidden for more than four slaves to meet together, and the number was reduced to three in 1702. Four years later, Cornbury issued a proclamation permitting officers to "fire upon . . . kill or destroy" any blacks who "shall be found to be assembled" and who refused "to submit."[16]

Despite the possibility of such harsh punishment, a number of angry, desperate blacks met one day in 1712 in an orchard in Maiden Lane, near the Wall Street Slip, and set fire to an outhouse. As nearby residents ran to put out the flames, the slaves, who had gotten hold of hatchets and knives, attacked them, killing nine men and wounding six others. It took two weeks to bring the insurrection under control. Six blacks committed suicide rather than face capture; twenty-one others were executed. Among the latter were three men identified as the ringleaders: one was broken on the wheel, a second was hanged in chains, and the third burned alive.[17]

Deeply troubled by the actions of the slaves, the British enacted even more restrictive laws. One prohibited any freed "Negro, Indian, or Mulatto" from owning a house or land within the New York colony. To discourage masters from manumitting their slaves, the British required that a master who freed a slave to pay the huge sum of two hundred pounds a year to the freed man for life.[18] A later law prohibited slaves from being seen on the streets after nightfall without a lighted lantern or candle. And those who sold fruits and other produce at the Catharine Market off the East River in lower Manhattan as well as the entertainers that the market attracted were to be whipped if, "after the ringing of three bells and the proclamation made for silence," they did not disperse.[19]

The insurrection in 1712 was only a foretaste of a more serious conspiracy that took place in 1741, when the "Great Negro Plot" to burn the city—which by then held upwards of eleven thousand residents—occurred. At the time, only Charleston, South Carolina, outranked New York in British North America as an urban center of slavery. One in every five New York inhabitants was black, and all but a few were slaves. A series of robberies and fires was traced to a number of slaves. There was also evidence that a group of them often met in a remote place off lower Broadway and discussed regaining their freedom by force and avenging themselves on their masters. The English got wind of it, and between May 11 and August 29, 1741, they tried, convicted, and burned thirteen blacks at the stake; they hanged seventeen more, all for their role in the plot.[20] The English deported seventy-one other troublemakers to Africa.[21] In addition, they hanged two white men and two white women for aiding the blacks in planning the aborted rebellion.[22]

That frightening conspiracy did little to stem the importation of black slaves, though an effort was evidently made to reduce the number of those from Africa. A traveler reporting to the royal governor in 1749 on the proliferation of trade and commerce in New York noted that Negroes were being imported "from British Colonies," as well as "from the African Coast," although "now less than formerly" from Africa.[23]

There is no record of exactly how many blacks, slave and free, lived in the city then. In fact, the history of blacks in New York for almost the first two hundred years, from Dutch times to after the American Revolution, is spotty, and even after then what efforts were made to record their life were lean and erratic until modern times. Historians were astonished when a "Negros Burial Ground," recorded on a map drawn up in 1755, was uncovered in the early 1990s in the Foley Square area west of the Brooklyn Bridge. The actual age of the cemetery is unknown, but it was in use as early as 1712. Excavation for a new federal office building uncovered part of the huge cemetery, which covered more than five acres. The burial ground that was unearthed yielded the remains of more than four hundred slaves. More—perhaps as many as ten thousand, according to the estimate of archaeologists—are believed to be still buried under existing streets and buildings.[24]

At the time, blacks could not bury their dead in church cemeteries. Other restrictions limited their funeral processions and services at graveside to no more than twelve persons, and a slave required a pass to travel to the cemetery, which then was about a mile from the town proper. No burials were allowed at night, although many African tribal rituals customarily took place then.[25] As an English naval officer noted, "The laborious people in general are Guinea Negroes who lie under particular restraints from the attempts they have made to massacre the inhabitants for their liberty."[26]

The English may have been pleased that travelers all thought New York was the gayest of its colonial communities in North America, but they were dismayed by the number of foreigners that the city attracted, so many that one wrote, "Our chiefest unhappyness here is too great a mixture of Nations, & English ye least part."[27] By 1771, blacks were the most visible segment of that mixture, not only because of their pigmentation but also because they still made up almost a sixth of the population. European visitors unaccustomed to slavery were shocked by how many there were. "It rather hurts an Europian [*sic*] eye to see so many negro slaves upon the streets," a Scottish visitor wrote.[28] New York's growth as a city of commerce and trade had by then limited the demand for cheap black labor to domestics. Numerous blacks, an English physician noted, worked as servants in "handsome Spacious Houses" on lower Broadway.[29]

Ostensibly, the American Revolution brought little change for blacks in New York City, which the British occupied for the duration of the war. The blacks continued to occupy a low position, as one

German mercenary officer stationed with the British forces discovered. He complained about the cost of "foodstuffs, wages for labor and personal services," saying that, for one thing, "a royal chimney-sweep" who looked after army quarters "keeps a half-dozen negroes, each of whom can sweep at least twenty chimneys a day, and often must clean more; and for each chimney his master, who sits quietly at home, is paid two shillings York money (twenty-eight coppers). The negroes get nothing out of it save coarse food and rags."[30]

The end of the war, however, saw a surge in the number of free blacks. More slaves gained their freedom, either earning it or being manumitted by their owners, and a sense of commonality spread. New York City was then both the capital of the nation and the capital of the state. Free blacks were able to find work as stevedores, bakers, carpenters, blacksmiths, tailors, and seamstresses as well as household servants. Some thirty black members of the John Street Methodist Episcopal Church formed their own congregation in 1796, the first of its kind in the city.[31] A few years later, other blacks organized the Abyssinian Baptist Church.

By 1807, a traveler from Canada reported that there were some four thousand "negroes and people of colour" in the city, and twenty-three hundred of them were free blacks: "These people are mostly of the Methodist persuasion, and have a chapel or two of their own with preachers of their colour; though some attend other places of worship according to their inclination."[32]

A year later, in 1808, Congress banned the importation of slaves from abroad. In 1809, freedmen in New York were granted the right to receive and hold estates and all marriages in the state between slaves were declared legal.[33] At almost the same time, the number of free blacks in the city multiplied considerably. The city contained so many that during the War of 1812 a thousand black males volunteered when New York authorities called up all available militiamen, fearing that the city, like Washington, would be invaded by the British. One patriotic "Citizen of Colour" took out a notice in the *Evening Post*, saying that

> it becomes the duty of every coloured man, resident in this city, to volunteer. . . . Under the protection of her laws we dwell in safety and pursue our honest callings, none daring to molest us, whatever

his complexion or circumstances. . . . We have now an opportunity of shewing that we are not ungrateful . . . but are willing to exert ourselves . . . for the protection of our beloved state.[34]

The "Citizen of Colour" made a point of remarking that the state legislature had indicated that "there is a fair prospect of a period not far distant, when this state will not contain a slave."[35]

That "period" was not far off, though the road to it was long and complicated. At first, in 1785, the New York legislature prohibited the sale of slaves in the state but not the ownership of them. It was not until fourteen years later that the legislature granted freedom to the children of slaves. Finally, in 1817, the lawmakers provided that slavery itself would be totally abolished in ten years, on July 4, 1827.

Shortly before emancipation, the Duke of Saxe-Weimar-Eisenach, who was considering settling in America, passed through the city. He became particularly interested in the staffing of households, noting "Americans have a great abhorrence of servitude." Servants, he discovered, were generally "negroes and mulattos," who were "abundant" but "generally rank low, and are labourers." If white, servants were usually Irish.

One day, the Duke watched as a parade wended its way through lower Broadway in celebration of the forthcoming end of slavery in the state. Few whites were among the celebrants. "Scarcely any but black faces were to be seen," the duke wrote. The parade, as well as a dinner and ball afterward, were sponsored by "an African club," the Wilberforce Society. "The coloured people of New York, belonging to this society," said the duke, "have a fund of their own, raised by weekly subscription, which is employed in assisting sick and unfortunate blacks."[36]

In spite of the abolition of slavery in New York State, blacks continued to be viewed and treated as inferior even by the law. They had won freedom from slavery, but most—like, at first, poor whites who were propertyless—could not vote. A major reason for the blacks' disenfranchisement was the struggle between Federalists, who favored emancipation, and Jeffersonian Democrats. New York's Tammany Society was a particularly vigorous opponent of black voting rights. One of its leaders, warning of the "dangerous importance of the Negro," said that "a few hundred Negroes of the city of New

York, following the train of those who ride in their coaches, and whose shoes and boots they had so often blacked, shall go to the polls of the election and change the political condition of the whole State."[37]

Since the adoption of the state's first constitution, drafted in 1777, restrictive covenants made it virtually impossible for blacks and lower-class whites to vote. The first constitution based suffrage upon qualifications that virtually no black man could meet: the ownership of property worth one hundred pounds. Still, in the election of 1813 three hundred blacks had voted and provided the balance of power to the Federalists.[38] The Democrats swept them out in the next election and a second state constitution, adopted in 1821, dropped the property qualification for whites, but not for blacks. That year, only 163 blacks voted and in 1824 that number dropped to fifteen.[39] However, in the spirit of "no representation, no taxation," a black who did not possess property worth in excess of $250—and thus could not vote—could not be taxed. Framers of yet a third state constitution, which was debated in 1846, maintained the property qualification after engaging in a particularly ugly discussion of black rights. One upstate delegate said, "The Almighty had created the black man inferior to the white man"; a New York City delegate declared unequivocally, "Negroes are aliens."[40]

It took fifty years after state emancipation, and the adoption of the Fifteenth Amendment following the Civil War, before a male black voter was finally put on equal footing with a male white voter. Yet New York State was not among the two-thirds of the nation's states to ratify the amendment.[41]

By the mid-1830s, the nation was growing rapidly, pioneers bursting out from the thirteen original states, headed westward, opening new lands to farming and industry. New waves of immigrants passed through New York, most pausing only momentarily on their way, others forming little communities within the city. Capt. Basil Hall, a Scot who had served in the Napoleonic wars, noted that store signs were written in English, "but the language we heard spoken was different in tone from what we had been accustomed to." Hall was taken by the "more or less of a foreign air in all we saw." He especially noticed the "Negroes and negresses" who were "in abundance on the wharfs."[42]

Looking back at that time, one is struck by how quickly newcomers from Europe prospered in the New World, whether they were Dutch, English, French, Germans, Irish, Italians, Poles, Russians, or Swedes. Each immigrant group found a place on the island at one time or another, and a number of them—Irish, Germans, and Italians, in particular—created their own ethnic communities in the ever-expanding city. Often they did so by pushing blacks from one neighborhood to another northward from lower Manhattan.

Before the turn of the century, when New York was no longer the capital of the nation or of the state, the city had become America's business capital. The city and its residents, both whites and blacks, thrived; no beggars were to be seen. Many blacks still worked as servants, coachmen, and laborers, but others had learned trades and were prospering as craftsmen, barbers, and shopkeepers. English tourists always had a word to say about the "sable cast" of the city's residents. "One striking feature" that Henry B. Fearon found in the "street population," he said, "consists in the number of blacks, many of whom are *finely* dressed, the females very ludicrously so, showing a partiality to white muslin dresses, artificial flowers, and pink shoes."[43] Both Frances Trollope and Sarah Maury also remarked on the "smartly" attired but showy black women with their "gallant" escorts who promenaded along with others on Broadway.[44]

But the racial balance of the New York's population was slowly changing, and, as it changed, blacks became superfluous to the city's economic life.

TWO

Urban Migrants

Nigger, Nigger never die.
Black face, shiny eyed.

—Irish chant[1]

As visible as blacks were because of their skin—a visibility that continued to prompt comments from European observers—they were becoming overwhelmed by the huge influx of immigrants from Europe. The newcomers, fighting for work and places to live, steadily forced blacks out of jobs and neighborhoods. The result was that blacks became migrants, moving from one section of Manhattan to another. Eventually, there were few areas of the island that blacks had not resided in, and been pushed out of, exiles in their own city.

In 1790, immediately after the Revolution, blacks had made up nearly 10 percent of the population. There were 3,262 of them counted in the census then. By 1840, fifty years later, there were 16,358 blacks in the city, but they now accounted for only 5 percent of the population.[2]

A reverse pattern was true for European immigrants. Aliens had made up 11 percent of the population in 1825. By 1845, they accounted for 35 percent.[3]

Moreover, newly arrived immigrant groups competed for the same cheap-labor jobs that blacks held, and, concomitantly, they quickly adopted antiblack attitudes that other whites held about blacks. Until 1827, and the abolition of slavery in the state, even free blacks were not allowed to work beside white persons in any single trade. And whether free or slave, white workers objected to blacks

16

learning trades. As a result, many blacks had little skill or training and their plight worsened. Work barriers against them existed with federal jobs as well; blacks were not allowed to handle or carry mail until 1825.[4] The resentment of white workers extended to individuals who favored nationwide emancipation. Riots against abolitionists broke out once the Anti-Slavery Society of New York was founded in 1833. Further riots occurred in 1834; one disturbance went on for eight days.[5]

Even after slavery was abolished in the state, visitors commented on the discrimination against people of color in churches and theaters. Black children attended separate public schools. When a dark-skinned Mexican legislator, later vice president of the Republic of Texas, arrived in 1830, he could not procure a hotel room and had to stay in a black's home.[6]

Slowly, over the years, blacks were pushed farther uptown. Many of those who had lived along the waterfront in lower Manhattan had by 1820 moved into the notorious Five Points section, a neighborhood of old, miserable tenements and narrow alleyways near the heart of today's Chinatown. By 1840 it was regarded as the most dismal slum area in America.[7] More than a thousand blacks and Irish lived in one building alone, a rundown five-story brewery that had been converted into a dwelling. One of its rooms was known as the Den of Thieves; another room, fittingly, was called Murderers' Alley. For more than fifteen years a murder a night was committed within the building.[8]

Five Points was close to the huge cemetery where blacks in the eighteenth century had buried their dead, and also near the site where the British had executed the slaves involved in the Great Negro Plot of 1741. Blacks were living in Five Points, which later became a stronghold for Irish gangs, when Charles Dickens visited the city in 1842.[9] Dickens found the area "rife" with "Poverty, wretchedness, and vice," and "reeking everywhere with dirt and filth." He said he walked down a "squalid street," off of which were "lanes and alleys with mud knee-deep," until he came upon the steps leading to an "assembly-room of Five-Point fashionables" called Almack's. "Heyday!" Dickens exclaimed, "the landlady of Almack's thrives! A buxom fat mulatto woman, with sparkling eyes, whose head is daintily ornamented with a handkerchief of many colors."[10]

The city's black population actually shrank in the years between 1840 and 1860, though the reason is unclear. Outbreaks of yellow fever had swept through New York in 1803 and 1819, taking a heavy toll in lives, but no serious epidemics had occurred since then.[11] In fact, by 1850, New York's total population had grown to more than half a million people, a leap of two hundred thousand in ten years.[12] Manhattan's population grew even more in the next ten years. In 1860, on the eve of the Civil War, the city counted 814,000 residents, and the lower end of the island, as far north as Fourteenth Street, was densely built over and populated.[13] But there were only 12,472 blacks by then, a decline of nearly four thousand in the intervening twenty years. Still, Isabella Bird, the twenty-three-year-old daughter of an English missionary, discovered in 1854 that, in one part of New York at least, the city was "a negro town."[14]

Bird was apparently referring to the west side of Broadway below Houston Street. There, blacks predominated in two political wards, the fifth and the eighth, neighborhoods that are now known as Soho and Tribeca. One contained 1,396 black men, women, and children, the other 2,918. Some fourteen hundred more lived farther uptown, in the rapidly growing Twentieth Ward above West Twenty-sixth Street.[15] Each of the neighborhoods was near or abutted the North River, where wharves, warehouses, and factories meant jobs to be had, for there were still some black shipbuilders, trimmers, riggers, coopers, caulkers, engravers, printers, and pharmacists. Many others ran eating places. One black writer noted, "All the caterers and restaurant keepers of the high order, as well as small places, were kept by colored men."[16]

But, almost daily, as ships from Europe arrived in New York, spilling their human cargo of cheap labor onto the streets, black New Yorkers began to find that they were no longer needed. Their chief rivals after the late 1840s, immigrants fleeing a devastating potato famine in Ireland, were laborers without any experience in running their own businesses who competed for the same low-paying jobs and for housing in the same poor neighborhoods. The antiblack Tammany Society found the Irish ready adherents. From the time in 1854 that Isabella Bird made her observation, organized Irish dockworkers began openly fighting in the streets with blacks for stevedore jobs. The situation grew worse during the Panic of 1857, when the unemployed marched through the city demanding work and bread, and the militia had to be called out to handle disorderly mobs of the jobless.[17]

That same year, a small, working-class enclave of blacks numbering perhaps two hundred in all, were uprooted from their homes in Seneca Village. The otherwise desolate section of Manhattan contained three churches and at least one school. Blacks who had been denied or could not afford property elsewhere were able to build respectable multistory frame houses there and laid out flower and vegetable gardens. Of the one hundred black New Yorkers eligible to vote in 1845, ten lived in Seneca Village. One in five of the seventy-odd black property owners in the city in 1850 resided there. But the once-thriving community, which extended westward from Seventh Avenue between seventy-ninth and eighty-sixth Streets, was lost to history until the mid-1990s, when research sponsored by the nearby New-York Historical Society uncovered the village. Nearly 140 years earlier, in 1857, Seneca Village's black residents had been forced to leave and their homes were demolished because they stood in the way of the construction of Central Park.[18]

Perhaps by then it was clear to blacks that, although New York was a northern metropolis, it was far from a haven. For one thing, the city had many financial ties with southern cotton growers and merchants and identified itself with them. Its leading politicians and newspaper publishers included Peace Democrats known as Copperheads. Before the Civil War they had seriously discussed seceding from the Union and declaring New York a free port of trade. Twice— in the presidential elections of 1860 and 1864—the city's white citizens voted against Abraham Lincoln by two-to-one margins.

The culmination of years of ethnic rivalry and racial discord came on the eve of a national conscription in the middle of the Civil War, in July 1863. The Irish, convinced that the draft would take a disproportionate number of Irishmen and that the emancipation of slaves proclaimed by Lincoln would lead to more blacks coming to New York and competing for jobs, erupted in a violent riot. More than 105 persons, mostly black, were killed. The rioters, chiefly young unmarried males liable to be drafted, beat blacks, shot blacks, and hanged blacks from lampposts. Mobs targeted homes of racially mixed couples and white women who socialized with black men. A major tragedy was averted when more than twelve hundred children escaped through the back door of the Colored Orphan Asylum, between Forty-third and Forty-fourth Streets on Fifth Avenue, as rioters broke through the front door of the building, set fire to it, and burned it down.

Another foreign visitor, a young Frenchman who passed through the city afterwards, chanced upon the area between Broadway and the North River, finding "a dirty and ragged section inhabited by Irishmen and colored people." He thought that "Nothing could be more depressingly miserable than these wooden hovels, these long, muddy streets, and this impoverished population." As he walked the neighborhood, a horse car passed him bearing, to his amazement, the inscription: "This carriage for colored people." A New Yorker would have understood the sign. Even though the state supreme court had ruled in 1855 that it was unlawful for common carriers to deny carrying passengers no matter what their race, drivers and conductors had continued the practice of segregated transportation. The Frenchman was indignant:

> Are there laws against Negroes? Are they outside the common law? No; but public prejudice persecutes them more tyrannically than any law. They are denied omnibuses, are excluded from the churches. That's how these democrats interpret equality, and these Puritans, Christian charity.[19]

As might be expected, that summer after the draft riots, many blacks fled New York, fleeing either across the North River to New Jersey, or across the East River to the city of Brooklyn. Yet, amazingly, at the same time, two regiments of blacks were organized in the city and fought Confederate forces in South Carolina. Of the eighty thousand black troops who died in the Civil War, 877 were from New York.[20]

Meanwhile, many of the blacks who moved out of the city to settle elsewhere left, the *Tribune* reported, "with the intention of never returning to it again."[21] Those who remained could not get near the docks to work, and omnibus drivers still kept them from boarding public vehicles. White gangs continued to beat blacks.

The only safe place, it seemed, was the old negro frontier of

Dutch days, now called Greenwich Village, a Republican stronghold, where blacks had resided for two hundred years. Blacks there armed themselves and fought back as a unit. In the years after the war, blacks continued to live there as well as along the river south of Thirty-second Street and in an old neighborhood of theirs, "Little Africa," a section that included wretched hovels on Thompson Street, south of Houston Street and Greenwich Village. But fresh waves of immigrants continued to press them north. By the 1880s, the latest newcomers—and the newest rivals of blacks—were Italian immigrants, who successfully elbowed blacks out of "Little Africa." It became "Little Italy."

Those who were pushed out joined blacks, most of them employed as waiters, coachmen, bootblacks, and hairdressers, living in the Hell's Kitchen district west of midtown Broadway, which became the center of the city's black population by 1880. Seventh Avenue from the twenties to the fifties became known as Black Broadway.[22]

Other blacks had chosen the upper East Side, in the Yorkville area around Eighty-sixth Street where Germans predominated. Reformer Jacob Riis drew up an imaginary map of New York, with so many colors designating nationalities that it "would show more stripes than on the skin of a zebra." The city on his map was divided into two great halves—one, the West Side, occupied by the Irish; the other, on the East Side, occupied by Germans. Caught in the middle of both were the blacks. Riis described how blacks were making "a stand at several points along Seventh and Eighth Avenues; but their main body, still pursued by the Italian foe, is on the march yet."[23]

Through the latter half of the nineteenth century, some blacks, a minority within a minority, achieved economic and social status. They were an elite of sorts—black teachers, black doctors, black lawyers, black realtors, and prosperous black headwaiters. And they could be as snobbish as their white counterparts. The Society of the Sons of New York was so exclusive that it admitted only blacks born in New York; southern blacks could only become associate members with no say in the organization's deliberations.[24] Always a small fraction of the city's large black community, the achievers were numerous enough to support one of the city's longest-lived black newspapers, the *New York Age*, a weekly that began publishing in 1886. Blacks had their own lodges, fraternal organizations, and women's auxiliary groups, as well as churches and their concomitant charity societies. One block alone on West Fifty-third Street contained the offices of numerous black professionals, a black Young Men's and Young Women's Christian Association, three black hotels, and three black churches.[25] West Fifty-third Street was also the center of the neighborhood's arts and entertainment life and was known as Black Bohemia. The achievers were among the "well-to-do Negroes" residing in the Tenderloin district, just east of Hell's Kitchen, who impressed José Martí. The Cuban patriot, who lived in New York from 1880 to 1895, said the blacks spoke of "the minister's sermons, the happenings at the lodge, the success of their lawyers, or the achievement of some Negro student . . . just graduated from a medical school."[26] All seemed to testify, in Martí's words, to the chances for advancement that blacks were enjoying.

By the end of the Spanish-American War, a number of blacks who lived on the West Side had again moved, this time to the higher ground north of Sixtieth Street and west of what is now the Lincoln Center area. Many of its residents, a study revealed, were poor blacks who had been born in the South, lured, as blacks had been lured since the Civil War, to the north. Others were from the West Indies and had come to industrialized America seeking work. One block, comprised of 5.4 acres, held more than six thousand blacks by the turn of the century. Originally called Columbus Hill, the neighborhood became known as San Juan Hill, though why is a matter of dispute. Some say the nickname was given in deference to black veterans who had served in the Spanish-American War; others say it was coined by an onlooker watching policemen charging up the streets during a racial disturbance.[27]

In 1900, two seemingly unconnected events occurred that presaged yet another black migration north. The first happened on March 24, when, in a ceremony in City Hall Park, ground was broken for the Lenox Avenue portion of the West Side IRT, which would open up suburban-like upper Manhattan north of Central Park to further development.[28] Anticipation about the line had already set off a frenzy of land purchases and construction by speculators and builders eager to take advantage of the new area that the subway line would make easily accessible. Expecting large profits, they purchased unimproved lots above 125th Street near Lenox Avenue as well as

undeveloped marshes and garbage dumps. A building boom resulted, but the speculators overextended themselves.

The second event occurred in Hell's Kitchen on the night of August 12, when a police officer, Robert J. Thorpe, who was in civilian
clothes, arrested a woman—identified variously as the wife of Arthur
Harris or his girlfriend[29]—for soliciting at the corner of Forty-first
Street and Eighth Avenue. Harris, a black man, was in a tobacco store
purchasing a cigar at the time. When he came out, he saw the woman
being manhandled and did not realize that Thorpe was a policeman.
He tried to rescue her. Thorpe struck Harris with his club, where-
upon Harris pulled out a penknife and mortally wounded the officer.
Four days later, when Thorpe's funeral was held, fellow officers of
the Twentieth Precinct swore vengeance, and their outspoken vindic-
tiveness stimulated gangs of whites, all apparently of Irish extraction,
to race through Hell's Kitchen and the Tenderloin, beating and club-
bing men and women. According to a citizens' protective organization formed as a result of the riot, the West thirty-seventh Street
station house soon resembled "a field hospital in the midst of battle"
as bleeding blacks sought shelter there.[30] Even though the city's police chief lived in the neighborhood—or perhaps because he did; the
chief was Irish—numerous policemen reportedly joined in the furious attacks, using their nightsticks. Afterwards, blacks protested
against the brutality but, the Citizens' Protective League reported,
"not a single complaint" was made "against any police officer for
brutality or neglect of duty during the riots."[31]

Together, the two events—the new subway line and the riot on
the West Side—proved the incentive that spurred blacks in Manhattan to move again, this last time in an exodus five miles north to a
section of the island that dated back to 1637, when a Dutchman
named Hendrick de Forest settled there. Twenty-one years later the
village that had grown up around his property was officially founded.
Ironically, to promote its settlement, Governor Peter Stuyvesant offered the Dutch West Indies Company's "Negroes" to help turn the
Indian path that led to the village into a wagon road that later became
known as Broadway.[32]

The village was named after a city in Holland, Haarlem.[33]

THREE

Negro Harlem

Some are coming on the passenger,
Some are coming on the freight.
Others will be found walking,
For none have time to wait.

—Anonymous[1]

Harlem, in the 1940s, was divided into three neighborhoods—a racial mirror of the kind of ethnic and religious separation that occurred in every borough of the city. Italian Harlem stretched from 106th Street to 125th Street on the east side of Manhattan; Spanish Harlem just to the west covered a smaller area reaching only to 116th Street; and then there was Negro Harlem.

Although it overlapped the other two neighborhoods in many places, the bulk of Negro Harlem was bounded by the Harlem River on the east, St. Nicholas Avenue on the west, and reached as far north as 155th Street. Its main artery was West 125th Street, and its heart, depending on whom you spoke to, was either Seventh Avenue and 125th or Seventh and 135th. At either intersection, on any day in any season, numerous street peddlers sold their wares from pushcarts, and orators astride soapboxes or on the back of trucks harangued passersby, shouting political slogans, urging religious piety, voicing opinions about anything and everything.

Negro Harlem was a community unlike any other, "a city within a city,"[2] the largest black neighborhood in the country, covering in its three and a half square miles[3] close to four hundred city blocks.[4]

24

Within its environs, poor and rich dwelled together, shopped together, played together, and prayed together. It was, in a sense, a
bedroom community. Most of those with jobs worked outside Harlem, either downtown or in the Bronx, and commuted to work on the
subway or in buses.

Black writer Claude McKay called Harlem "the Negro capital of
the world."[5] To another black writer, James Weldon Johnson, Harlem
was not a fringe area, nor a slum or a " 'quarter' consisting of dilapidated tenements." Instead, he said, it was

> a section of new-law apartment houses and handsome dwellings,
> with streets as well paved, as well lighted, and as well kept as in
> any other part of the city. Three main highways lead into and out
> from upper Manhattan, and two of them run straight through Har-
> lem. So Harlem is not a section that one "goes out to," but a section
> that one goes through.[6]

The city's mayor, Fiorello La Guardia, spoke of the area as a place
where "as nowhere else in the world . . . the people of all races,
religions, creeds, and color can live as neighbors."[7] But that was an
exaggeration. By the time La Guardia made that remark, in the mid-
1940s, each ethnic group had carved out its territory and did not stray
into its neighbor's. And the "new-law tenements and handsome
dwellings" of James Weldon Johnson's Harlem had begun to deterio-
rate into the nation's largest slum.

Then, too, when one spoke of Harlem, one did not think of the
Italians or the Puerto Ricans, or even of the Irish who occupied the
area hugging the river west of St. Nicholas Park. If you were going to
hear jazz in Harlem, you were going to Negro Harlem. If your maid
came from Harlem, she was from Negro Harlem. The waiter, the
shoeshine boy, the elevator operator who said he was from Harlem
meant Negro Harlem.

It had begun with a fluke.

For almost two centuries after its founding in the seventeenth
century, Harlem remained a quiet, neatly laid out community of
country estates and farms. Its peaceful environs attracted a number
of wealthy families of diverse European backgrounds. In the early
nineteenth century, Alexander Hamilton built a country home, the

Grange, which still stands. But the soil in Harlem was exhausted by the mid-1840s and Irish squatters occupied the land. At one point, so many hogs roamed parts of 125th and 126th Streets that the area earned the sobriquet Pig's Alley. Its lower section was known as Goatville.[8]

Harlem escaped becoming a perpetual backwater when New York City annexed it in 1873 and drained some of its marshlands for new housing. The subsequent erection of an elevated railway revitalized the area, and once-abandoned land took on the aspects of a well-planned and well-groomed town. Its boulevards were wide, the side streets quiet, middle-class residential byways. Medians ran down both Lenox and Seventh Avenues, the one on the latter boulevard covered with trees and shrubbery. Fancy apartment buildings were no more than five or six stories high; a seven-story one was a rarity. The white brick Hotel Theresa, erected later at the corner of 125th Street and Seventh Avenue, stood out dramatically because of its height, though it was only twelve stories high. The lack of tall buildings and the broad avenues combined to create an unusual sense of space. Equestrians liked to ride their horses down the avenues, or play polo on what became the home of the New York Giants, the Polo Grounds. It was an idyllic ambience, so unlike Manhattan south of Central Park, with its busy streets, crowded thoroughfares, and increasing number of architectural innovations called skyscrapers.

Harlem was, at the turn of the century, a white enclave with a mixed ethnic character that was part German, part Irish, and part Eastern European. Its religious structures reflected the diversity: St. Paul's German Evangelical Lutheran Church on West 123rd Street, which was completed in 1898; St. Thomas the Apostle Roman Catholic Church on West 118th Street, an imposing edifice built in neo-English Gothic style that could seat a thousand parishioners; and Temple Ansche Chesed on Seventh Avenue at 114th Street, designed by the noted architect Edward I. Shire.

An even more famous architect, Stanford White, was responsible for the rows of graceful houses that lined West 138th and 139th Streets, some of which sported wrought-iron balconies in the style of the Florentine Renaissance. Stables lined the back of the houses, and gates off the streets bore signs warning drivers to slow their horses.

On other cross streets, imposing brownstones dating from the 1880s and 1890s stood cornice to cornice.

Jews for the most part then operated the stores along its main shopping thoroughfare, 125th Street. There Blumstein's and Koch's department stores vied for shoppers, and retail chains such as A. S. Beck Shoes and restaurants such as Child's had branches, too. For entertainment there was the Hurtig and Seamon Theater down the block, a burlesque house that became a vaudeville theater.

The change in Harlem's complexion was swift. At the time the Lenox Avenue portion of the West Side IRT was completed in 1904, the nation was plunging into a major depression. The many new apartment houses that had been built sat virtually empty. There were just too many of them, and not enough whites could be persuaded to move up to Harlem to occupy them.

The bellwether for the black invasion of Harlem was a black man, Philip A. Payton. A college graduate from North Carolina, Payton had managed to survive by finding odd jobs. He had done everything from cutting hair to working as a slot machine attendant in a midtown department store and as a porter in an apartment house. It was seeing all the "For Rent" signs on the new apartment houses that gave Payton an idea. He approached the manager of an apartment house on West 133rd Street where a murder had been committed. Tenants were fleeing the building. Payton was able to convince him to permit black families to move into the building. For one thing, he assured the manager that blacks would pay a five dollar premium to live in an apartment in the building.

At first, there was a trickle of blacks, then a steady stream as owners saw a chance to turn disaster into largesse. Rental signs sprouted: "For Respectable Colored Families Only." A city survey in 1900 had reported only three hundred black families in the area, most of them located on six streets; ten years later, the same section held nearly forty-five hundred black families.[9]

A reporter for *The New York Times* expressed amazement one Saturday when he witnessed Harlem's transition from white to black. He had come upon a street clogged with horse-drawn moving wagons, many of which had to wait around the corner until they were able to get into the street: "A constant stream of furniture trucks loaded with the household effects of a new colony of colored people who are invading the choice locality is pouring into the street. Another equally long procession, moving in the other direction, is carrying away the household goods of the whites from their homes of years."[10]

In the beginning, the black newcomers were confined to specific streets, such as 119th between Seventh and Eighth Avenues, or to the relatively small rectangle created from 130th to 140th Streets between Fifth and Seventh Avenues. Although they often lived side by side with white residents, they were rarely welcomed. Some whites formed associations and drew up restrictive lease agreements. One such group, the Property Owners' Protective Association, which was organized in 1913, charged that blacks were not only poor tenants but also destructive ones, and caused real estate values to decline.[11] But one by one, landlords, faced with the desertion of white tenants, surrendered to the inevitable and took in black families.

All the unspoken barriers came down when one of the best-known black churches, wealthy St. Philip's Protestant Episcopal Church, moved from midtown Manhattan into a new edifice on West 133rd Street in 1910. The next year, St. Philip's purchased a row of apartment houses occupying all of the north side of 135th Street between Lenox and Seventh Avenues.

Inexorably, as whites fled the area, blacks took over street after street, fanning out in all directions. On the one hand, the move into Harlem appeared to finally answer the black quest for a stable, unified neighborhood that they could call their own. But it was, on the other hand, a grim period for them. The move into Harlem coincided with another massive wave of European immigrants coming into the city, this time from the Mediterranean region. By the turn of the century, only 20,395 black males were gainfully employed, a mere eighteen for every thousand blacks in the city. And despite their overall total, blacks in Manhattan were so outnumbered by whites in 1910 that they represented only 2 percent of the island's population, and, as one black businessman wrote, immigrants "occupy every industry that was confessedly the Negro's." Italians, Sicilians, and Greeks "have the bootblack stands, the news stands, barbers' shops, waiters' situations, restaurants, janitorships, catering business, stevedoring, steamboat work, and other situations occupied by Negroes."[12] Blacks had become even less of a significant factor in New York's economic life.

Black economic decline could be measured in the occupations to which they were relegated. As in the past, blacks made up an overwhelming proportion of New Yorkers holding the most low-paying of jobs—servants, stewards, and waiters.[13] They were numerous as hostlers, porters, and store helpers, too, and some worked as draymen and messengers. Blacks were well represented in the clergy, as musicians, and as professional showmen. But few, if any, were journalists, lawyers, or government workers,[14] nor were there many black salesmen, boatmen, railway employees, foremen, clerks, and bookkeepers. None were bankers or investment brokers.[15] Blacks were barely represented in factories as steamfitters, tailors, machinists, printers, and steelworkers; they were not represented to any appreciable extent as blacksmiths, butchers, carpenters, and masons.[16]

The influx of blacks into Harlem, the lack of work, the exorbitant rents that landlords realized they could charge, the negligence of landlords in providing repairs and services, the unhealthy conditions spawned by congestion—all contributed to an incredible death rate among New York blacks as early as 1908: 28.9 in every thousand, almost twice that of the white death rate. Most of those deaths were attributable to two diseases, tuberculosis and pneumonia.[17] One block—from Lenox Avenue to Seventh, between 142nd and 143rd Streets—soon became known as "lung block" because of the high death rate among its residents from tuberculosis.[18]

Nevertheless, Harlem continued to serve as a magnet for blacks. Waves of southern blacks from the Carolinas, Georgia, and Virginia streamed into the area, so many coming that by 1910 only some 14,300 of the city's more than sixty thousand blacks had been born in Manhattan.[19] Harlem's attraction reached almost feverish pitch during World War I. Because of the war, the massive European emigration to America came to an abrupt halt and seemed to foreshadow increased job opportunities for blacks. Southern blacks came north, eager to find work in defense plants and adding to Harlem's decidedly southern accent. So many came that by the end of the war, 70 percent of all the blacks living in Manhattan resided between 118th and 144th Streets.[20] Nearly half of them, an Urban League survey found, were spending more than 40 percent of their monthly income on rent,[21] and to survive, most families held rent parties to raise money, took in boarders, or sublet at least one room in their homes.

The density of black population per acre in Manhattan by 1925 was half again as much as it was for whites.[22]

And yet they continued to come, dreaming of a better life that seemed tantalizingly close. W. E. B. Du Bois, a prime mover in the National Association for the Advancement of Colored People, had urged blacks to "close ranks" with whites in support of the war effort. Racism, he was convinced, would diminish.[23] After all, when given the opportunity, blacks in the 369th Regiment had distinguished themselves in battle. Though part of a segregated army, the regiment, known as Harlem's "Hellfighters," had gone off to Europe, fought under the French flag, compiling, after 191 days in the trenches, the longest service record of any American regiment, and earning for itself the croix de guerre. The returning regiment's victory march up Fifth Avenue and into Lenox Avenue drew cheers from thousands of proud Harlem residents.[24]

Blacks believed that their support of the war would be rewarded. Returning doughboys anticipated new work opportunities and a chance to better themselves. Du Bois spoke of a "Talented Tenth," an educated middle class that would lead the entire black community into full integration with whites. The war, as one black educator noted, had stimulated the black man's "hopes and ambitions that he would enter as a full participant in the fruition of that democracy which he was called upon to sustain and perpetuate."[25]

Disillusion set in quickly when there was so little progress in jobs, schooling, and housing.

At first, it seemed as though whites and blacks could live together in Harlem in harmony in an integrated community, but that was illusion, too. What was actually going on resembled a revolving door, with whites exiting and blacks entering. The two races did exist together for a while, into the 1920s, but that was because the whites still maintained a presence. It was a diminishing one, however. One day after another, a white family moved out and a new black household moved in.

Oddly enough, as blacks moved in, another fantasy took hold, prompted by fanciful, optimistic, and erroneous estimates made by blacks themselves. They believed they owned virtually all of Negro Harlem; that three-fourths of the area's real estate was in black hands. As a result, blacks got the impression that they controlled their own economic destiny and that Harlem was a self-supporting community. In truth, blacks owned less than 20 percent of Harlem's businesses.[26] As reality surfaced, Harlemites became increasingly frustrated at the lack of employment opportunities in white-owned stores and businesses. And Harlem was becoming a vast slum.

Seen from the distance of three-quarters of a century, the immediate postwar era in Harlem seems schizophrenic. On one hand, there was the crowding, the families struggling to make ends meet, the despair over the lack of opportunity, the daily obsession with playing the numbers game hoping to strike it rich—a Harlem of men and women who were "ordinary, hardworking people," busy, said James Weldon Johnson, with "the stern necessity of making a living, of making ends meet, of finding money to pay the rent and keep the children fed and clothed."[27]

Another writer noted in 1928:

> Fifth Avenue begins prosperously at 125th Street, becomes a slum district above 131st Street, and finally slithers off into warehouse-lined, dingy alleyways above 139th Street. . . . The tenement houses in this vicinity are darkened dungheaps, festering with poverty-stricken and crime-ridden step-children of nature. This is the edge of Harlem's slum district; Fifth Avenue is its board-walk. Push carts line the curbstone, dirty push carts manned by dirtier hucksters, selling fly-specked vegetables and other cheap commodities.[28]

On the other hand, the 1920s were also Harlem's Camelot of sorts, its Renaissance, when writers and poets such as McKay, Johnson, Countee Cullen, and Langston Hughes gave blacks throughout the United States a sense of their history and tradition, and voiced their yearnings. It was the period when, as Hughes put it, "the Negro was in vogue."[29] To a great extent, the writers as well as the artists and photographers of the Renaissance concerned themselves with esthetic and cultural matters rather than political goals. Those were left to militant black nationalists such as Marcus Garvey who, exasperated by the inequalities, advocated black independence. Black pride and self-reliance became catchwords. Irreverent New Negroes, as black socialist radicals called themselves, pooh-poohed the Old Negroes—accommodationists like Booker T. Washington, even protesters like Du Bois.

The 1920s were also the Jazz Age, and jazz reigned supreme in Harlem. By day, Harlem was a working person's community, but at night it was a playground for whites, or, in the words of *Collier's* magazine, "a national synonym for naughtiness" and "a jungle of jazz."[30] White men and women cabbed up to see the lavish shows at nightclubs such as the Cotton Club, the so-called "Aristocrat of Harlem," where blacks were barred and the only ones to be seen on the premises were either in the chorus line or the band. The whites danced at huge ballrooms like the Savoy, or they listened to jazz and swing at the old Hurtig and Seamon vaudeville house on 125th Street, which had been renamed the Apollo Theater.

By 1930 and the start of the Depression, when whites were still "slumming" in Harlem, the Renaissance had run its course. Appraising it realistically, Langston Hughes said, "All of us knew that the gay and sparkling life . . . was not so gay and sparkling beneath the surface." Hughes acknowledged that he had had a "swell time while it lasted. But I thought it wouldn't last long. For how long could a large and enthusiastic number of people be crazy about Negroes forever?" Besides which, he added, "ordinary" blacks "hadn't heard of the Negro Renaissance. And if they had, it hadn't raised their wages any."[31]

Few whites remained in what was becoming known as Negro Harlem. Blacks inhabited almost the entire district, some even reaching out farther south into Spanish Harlem, others pushing west toward Broadway, still others finding a home near Washington Heights to the north. By then, nearly all black churches had followed St. Philip's and moved to Harlem, as had black fraternal organizations such as the Masons, Elks, Pythians and Oddfellows.

Like all of Harlem, Negro Harlem was itself divided, not only geographically but also socially and economically. Even color—the variety of shadings of skin tone—was a factor. Dark-skinned blacks looked down on light-skinned ones, whom they called "high yallers." Part of their attitude might have been prompted by jealousy, because many light-skinned blacks could pass for white. Northern-born blacks snubbed the southern-born, who were often illiterate and displayed a subservience to whites that was expected in the South. The exact opposite to the southern blacks were West Indian immigrants, who made up almost a fifth of the area's population and as many as a third of its professionals. As a national magazine noted, the West Indians lacked "the Southern Negro's diplomacy," were outspoken about their rights, and were "very quick to go to court—the last place on earth the Southern Negro seeks." Because they were better schooled and more aggressive as business people, West Indians were referred to by other blacks as "Black Jews." Many West Indians flew the British flag, and about five thousand of them attended a ball in May 1937 to celebrate the coronation of King George VI.[32]

Another phenomenon, a black sociologist found, was that Harlem's small but upper-class group of doctors, dentists, lawyers, businessmen, teachers, social workers, government employees, and successful actors and musicians "attempt to identify themselves culturally with upper-class whites." They tended in general to look down on lower-class blacks, regarding them as "black, boisterous, stupid or sexually promiscuous." In return, lower-class blacks accused "the big shots" of "snobbishness, color preference, extreme selfishness, disloyalty in caste leadership ('sellin' out to white folks'), and economic exploitation of their patients and customers."[33]

Separate, distinct neighborhoods grew up as blacks of all economic classes and backgrounds settled in Harlem's environs. Many of the elite—professionals and clergymen who were descendants of old New York families—lived in the Stanford White homes on 138th and 139th Streets. Poorer Harlemites nicknamed the blocks Strivers' Row.

Some other upper-class blacks lived nearby. Harlem's first "millionaire," Mme. C. J. Walker, who made her fortune with a hair-growing concoction, shared with her daughter, A'Lelia, a splendidly furnished residence on 136th Street that was a focal point of the community's high society.

Other professionals lived in apartments along the Golden Edge, 110th Street facing Central Park, in apartments that had been the residences of Jewish families.

Well-to-do and successful entertainers preferred to live in a section that was once part of Washington Heights but that blacks had renamed Sugar Hill. It was on a high bluff that ran north from 145th to 155th Street west of Colonial Park. One of its most prestigious addresses was 580 St. Nicholas Avenue, where the singer and actress

Ethel Waters and other entertainers lived.[34] Another, 409 Edgecombe Avenue, a luxurious apartment house with a marble lobby built originally for whites, was the home to "smart people with small incomes,"[35] among them three members of the NAACP: Walter White, Roy Wilkins, and Thurgood Marshall.

Sugar Hill overlooked the Valley, a slum area extending from 130th to 140th Street east of Seventh Avenue, where most of Harlem's poor lived. But the Valley was also the center of Harlem's cultural life, a rich conglomeration of churches and community centers, dancehalls and nightclubs, schools and bookstores, theaters and businesses.

There was one area that god-fearing blacks disdained: The Market, a strip of Seventh Avenue that ran from 110th to 115th Streets. It was so named because of the number of streetwalkers who frequented the blocks. Otherwise, north of that, Seventh Avenue—"the Great Black Way"[36]—was where, on a Sunday, the Harlemite, whether well-off or poverty-stricken, promenaded. Promenaded, not walked, as James Weldon Johnson put it. A promenade was an adventure:

> One puts on one's best clothes and fares forth to pass the time pleasantly with friends and acquaintances and, most important of all, the strangers he is sure of meeting. One saunters along, he hails this one, exchanges a word or two with that one, stops for a short chat with the other one. He . . . takes part in the joking, the small talk and gossip . . . is introduced to two or three pretty girls who have just come to Harlem.[37]

But to Claude McKay, the scene in Harlem smacked of something else. It "is like the glorified servant quarters of a vast estate. It has that appearance, perhaps, because the majority of Aframericans are domestics, who live in imitation of their white employers, although upon a lower level."[38]

To those who lived there, Harlem was ultimately a state of mind.

FOUR

"Nigger Heaven"

*That's what Harlem is. We sit in our places in the gallery of this
New York theatre and watch the white world sitting down below
in the good seats in the orchestra. Occasionally, they turn their
faces towards us, their hard, cruel faces, to laugh or sneer, but
they never beckon. It never seems to occur to them Nigger Heaven
is crowded, that there isn't another seat, that something has to be
done.*

—Carl Van Vechten[1]

Negro Harlem was a study in contrasts. The bubbling night life,
with music filtering into the avenues where cabs disgorged zoot-
suited hipsters, differed sharply from the humdrum daily life of most
of its citizens. The wide, open-sky vistas were marred by the silhou-
ettes of rundown tenements. And for every beaming smile and burst
of laughter, there were a dozen frowns. To live in Harlem was to
navigate between joy and pain.

To Walker Smith, who was born and raised in the 1920s in rural
West Virginia, where schools, restaurants, and parks were segregated, Harlem was a place where he could feel "comfortable."[2]

The sight of a police officer named Lacy—"a big black giant"—
who directed traffic at the intersection of 125th Street and Seventh
Avenue, "making white folks stop and go at his bidding," was symbolic of the sense of empowerment blacks experienced in Harlem.
Many residents, like Elton Fax of Baltimore, had come from places
where "there was no black authority or authoritative figure who commanded respect."[3]

For those born and bred in Harlem, there was a special pride,

35

even a feeling of superiority. Foster Palmer was "led to think that we were special because we came from New York—superior to everybody else."[4] For Allen Worrell, "There was no reason to feel different."[5]

To Evelyn Hunt O'Garro Harlem meant a sense of what she calls "family."[6] Doris Saunders "knew everybody—the milkman, the postman, the garbageman. And everybody knew everybody's name, white or black."[7]

Above all, Harlem was a "state of mind." For Dr. Herman Warner, a Jamaican by birth, it "just had so much to offer, sociologically and psychologically. It was the place to live."[8] And for Sadie and Bess Delany, two sisters from North Carolina, "Harlem was as close to Heaven as we were going to find on this Earth."[9]

And yet, in the same breath, while extolling the virtues of Harlem, its residents were quick to see its underside.

In spite of the symbolic triumph of a black policeman directing white motorists, Elton Fax, for one, still realized that the exercise of such authority was "superficial."[10] There were only 155 black policemen on a force that totaled nearly eighteen thousand officers.[11] Many Harlemites resented the black policemen as much as they did the white officers. One of the few black patrolmen, six-foot-three, 280-pound Benjamin (Big Ben) Wallace, was known as "Mr. Terror."[12] When blacks used the term "police brutality," they did not necessarily mean physical violence. They meant something much more pervasive and insidious—intimidation. An editor on the *Amsterdam News* says he heard about many incidents involving blacks and the police, about half of which, upon investigation, turned out to be true. "You'd be less than human," he adds, "if you didn't begin to wonder, why is it always this way—people coming in to me with stories, complaining?"[13]

The intimidation could be subtle, as when Walker Smith was standing around with friends on a street corner, chatting, and was told to move on.[14] Or it could be oppressive, as when respectable black people, for no reason other than the color of their skin, were picked up and questioned because they happened to be in the vicinity where a crime had been committed.

Entering an apartment house, Dr. Herman Warner says, it was not unusual to find that the "indoor aviator"[15]—the elevator operator

—had a doctorate. "It was a common thing—a Ph.D. who couldn't get work."[16] All Americans were experiencing a job crisis in the 1930s, but in Harlem the problem was exacerbated by continuing large-scale discrimination. The traffic manager of the New York Telephone Company freely acknowledged that none of Manhattan's forty-five hundred operators was black; blacks were not hired, he said, because they were incompetent.[17] Similarly, the New York Edison Company had ten thousand workers, but only sixty-five were blacks, all of whom worked as porters, cleaners, and hall men. The same was true of the Consolidated Gas Company; only 213 of its ten thousand workers were blacks, and all of them were porters. Among the ten thousand employees of the Interborough Rapid Transit Company were 580 black messengers, subway porters, and cleaners. The Fifth Avenue Coach Company's policy of excluding blacks from operating its buses, a government report declared, "assumed the aspects of a caste system."[18]

It also bothered Evelyn Hunt O'Garro that few blacks owned the stores she and others patronized. "It was the white man's world, entirely the white man's world. The white man pay you with one hand, and you come home and he take it with the other hand."[19] Typically, although the Theresa Hotel had an exclusively black clientele, it was white-owned. So, too, were virtually all its famous nightclubs, although as a result of Prohibition the proprietors were now Italians rather than Irish.[20] Because white chain stores could charge less than could black shopkeepers, blacks tended to buy from them rather than the black-owned businesses. As a result, of twelve thousand retail stores operating in Harlem in 1930, only 391 were owned by blacks and 172 of them were groceries.[21] There *was* one black-owned cinema, and seventy-five black-owned saloons,[22] but otherwise black enterprises were limited to small groceries, insurance agencies, hair salons,[23] and funeral parlors. One writer cynically quipped that "the only businesses which are still left to the Negro are those of pruning himself and burying himself."[24] There was, however, one flourishing industry that was unlisted: the numbers game, what whites called "the nigger pool" or "nigger pennies."[25]

Particularly irksome was the fact that all the white-run stores on 125th Street, whose customers were for the most part blacks, refused outright to hire blacks as salespersons or in any positions other than as porters and cleaning people. At first, Blumstein's even refused to hire black elevator operators.[26] Of two thousand employees in 258 stores in Harlem in 1930, when the Depression began, only 163 were black and, almost without exception, they all held menial positions.[27]

Doris Saunders recalls the time her aunt, a college graduate, applied for one of the few jobs that became available downtown. But she did not get it because she was black. A friend who happened to accompany her, a light-skinned woman who could pass for white, was offered the job. "I thought that was so terrible."[28]

Worrell became aware of discrimination when he entered high school, where blacks and whites sat separately in the lunchroom. He learned, he says, not to go into "certain" areas, "like by the river, because the Irish boys were there. You stayed in your neighborhood."[29]

Foster Palmer still feels shortchanged by the education he received. "The school system cheated us of a lot of things we could have had. I think we were already considered failures."[30]

Sadie Delany, a graduate of Columbia University, became the first black to teach domestic science in a public high school, but she got the assignment by purposely avoiding a personal interview and just showing up on the day classes started. Her sister, "Dr. Bessie," a dentist, bemoaned that "there was little respect from white people, no matter how accomplished you were. It was like you were invisible. It was so strange to be so respected among Negroes, but to white people you were just some little pickaninny."[31]

Such widespread lack of respect could be as demoralizing as job discrimination. "Negroes like to be addressed by the customary titles of polite and civil society, Mr., Mrs., Miss," wrote six black men in a letter to the *New York Times*. Situations that "most often offend the feelings of Negroes," they said, included a "dislike" for being "called 'boy,' 'girl,' 'aunty,' 'uncle.' " In addition, "A sentimental tale about one's 'old black mammy' will prevent or destroy rapport with a Negro audience." Blacks, they added, "want to be treated like ordinary human beings. Paternalism is almost as deadly a sin as deliberate mistreatment."[32]

If anything, the great movement of blacks out of the South and into the North, Midwest, and West Coast aggravated existing situations in the cities to which they went. First of all, between 1900 and

1940, the nation's black population increased more than 45 percent. Concomitantly, the number of counties with black majorities decreased dramatically in Alabama, Arkansas, Florida, Georgia, Louisiana, Mississippi, Tennessee, Texas, and the Carolinas.[33] Continuing a great migration that reached unprecedented numbers during World War I, blacks were moving to urban areas where, they hoped, work was available, wages were higher, schooling was better, and conditions in general more palatable—in the main, Chicago, Detroit, Pittsburgh, and New York. In Chicago alone, their number increased 150 percent in the decade after 1910.[34]

New York City had a special appeal because New York State prohibited racial discrimination in, among other things, jury service and school admissions, and equal protection of state laws could not be denied—at least theoretically—to anyone "because of race, color, creed or religion."[35] The protagonist of Rudolph Fisher's short story "City of Refuge," a rural southern black, arrives in New York, steps out of the subway at Lenox Avenue and 135th Street and exclaims, "Done died an' woke up in Heaven." Looking about, he says, "In Harlem black was white. You had rights that could not be denied you; you had privileges, protected by law."[36] In the 1930s, more than 145,000 blacks, chiefly from the South, came to New York City.[37]

Between 1910 and 1935, Harlem's population alone increased 600 percent[38] and rivaled that of the population of cities such as Atlanta, Dallas, and Portland, Oregon.[39] By then, one tenement block in Harlem had a density of more than seven hundred residents per acre, and eight other blocks had six hundred per acre.[40] A federal study estimated that more than ten thousand blacks lived in dungeon-like cellars and basements that had been converted into makeshift flats.[41] Others who resided in tenements lived "without exception" in buildings that were "filthy and vermin-ridden," with only one toilet serving a floor of four apartments.[42]

Blacks in Manhattan now represented nearly 15 percent of the borough's population. Of the 7.45 million people living in it and the city's four other boroughs by 1940, more than 458,000 were blacks; they represented slightly more than 6 percent of New York's total population.[43]

The Harlem of Smith, Fax, Warner, O'Garro, Saunders, Worrell, Palmer, and the Delany sisters was the Harlem of the Depression. No section of New York was harder hit by the nationwide economic downturn. Long before the terms "underprivileged" and "underclass" became catchwords, their meanings would have accurately portrayed the existence most blacks were experiencing. The combination of the explosive growth of population there and neglect on the part of city administrations turned Harlem into the largest slum in the country. Only Hispanics, chiefly Puerto Ricans who were neighbors to Harlem's blacks, suffered comparably, primarily because their problems were complicated by their struggle with the English language.

The statistics from the 1930s are sobering. Even at a time when breadlines were common in every city, when men and women tried to eke out a living selling apples on street corners for a nickel each, when the plea "Brother, can you spare a dime?" echoed throughout the nation, the conditions in Harlem always seemed a bit worse. It was a situation upon which socialists and communists tried to capitalize, though their appeals never attracted sizeable memberships in Harlem.

During the Depression, well over six out of ten black married women worked to help their families make ends meet, a figure four times higher than that for white married women.[44] Yet what they earned—most worked as domestics for twenty-five cents an hour— was hardly enough to feed, clothe, and shelter a family.

In 1933, nine months after the establishment of the Home Relief Bureau, more than twenty-five thousand families in Harlem, representing almost half of all the families there, were receiving unemployment relief. Three years later, in 1936, one in five families on the city's relief rolls were black.[45] Because the city's welfare bureau allotted only eight cents a meal for food, it was not unusual to see a family foraging in garbage cans for leftovers.[46] It was also common to see a sidewalk strewn with the belongings of a family thrown out of its apartment for failing to pay its rent. Even A. Philip Randolph's Brotherhood of Sleeping Car Porters, the first organized black union to successfully win decent wages and work conditions for its members, was evicted from its national headquarters on 136th Street for nonpayment of its lease.[47]

When the Depression began, there were more black children in New York than in any other city in the world—more than seventy-five thousand under the age of fifteen, some forty-seven thousand in Manhattan alone.[48] Yet, while the city sought nearly $121 million in federal funds for new school buildings, only $400,000 was earmarked for schools in which blacks made up the majority of students.[49] And while 255 new playgrounds were opened throughout the city during the 1930s, only one of them was in Harlem. Riverside Park on the upper West Side of Manhattan was widened with landfill, but only up to 125th Street.[50]

Alarmingly, as the Depression continued, one in four Harlem families broke up, a result, many blacks charged, of the ban on relief to any family with a male wage earner. At the same time, the number of black youngsters arraigned in Childrens Court, which had nearly tripled in the decade before, more than doubled again afterwards. In 1938, black youngsters represented a fourth of all cases, which ran the gamut of serious crimes, such as stealing, to minor offenses, such as hitching rides on trolleys and selling newspapers after 7 P.M.[51] The high degree of delinquency, a federal study stated, "undoubtedly covers up many cases of abandonment due to family and economic reasons." The Childrens Court determined in one five-year period alone, from 1931 through 1935, that more than thirty-two hundred black children were neglected. There were few services to help them. Only six out of the thirty-four Protestant agencies in the city that cared for children would accept black ones.[52]

No one questioned that most Harlem residents were law-abiding, but adult crime statistics were equally high and also affected by the economic situation of blacks. One in every five persons arrested in New York State in 1936, for example, was black. During the first six months of that year in Harlem, almost a third of all arrests were for possessing numbers game policy slips. Among women arrested, 80 percent were charged with soliciting.[53] One street, in particular, was notorious: 133rd between Lenox and Seventh Avenues. Called "Beale Street" because of its similarity to the thoroughfare of that name in Memphis, Tennessee, it was a place "where a knife blade is the quick arbiter of all quarrels, where prostitutes take anything they can get."[54]

Health problems continued to plague the area. A sample survey in 1934 found that 3 percent of Harlem's residents suffered from pulmonary tuberculosis,[55] but most hospitals that treated the disease refused to admit black patients or only offered a limited ward service.[56] In the previous five years, the rate of venereal disease—more than three thousand cases for every hundred thousand blacks—was twice that of the white ratio.[57]

Health care did improve comparatively in the late 1930s. Until 1920, there were no black doctors in city hospitals, and until 1922 no black nurses. By 1940, fifty of the two hundred doctors working in Harlem Hospital were black, and black nurses and trainees numbered 350.[58] Still, other city hospitals refused to take in black cases. In one much-publicized incident, the wife of W. C. Handy, composer of "St. Louis Blues," lay critically ill in an ambulance for more than an hour while officials of Knickerbocker Hospital discussed whether to admit her.[59]

Harlem Hospital was evidently the most congested hospital in the city. Its 642 beds were always filled, and patients were forced to sleep on the floor, on mattresses, and on benches, even in the maternity ward.[60] In one year alone during the Depression, there were 19,579 inpatients and 461,768 outpatients. Only Bellevue Hospital downtown, with nearly two thousand beds and more than 475,000 clinic patients, had a comparably huge caseload.[61] But the death rate at Harlem Hospital was substantially higher: twice as many patients died in Harlem Hospital than in Bellevue in 1932, and twice as many black women died in childbirth as white women did.[62] Blacks feared to go to Harlem Hospital, which they dubbed the "morgue" or the "butcher shop."[63]

Beyond the employment, housing, and health problems were the persistent humiliations and social discrimination that blacks experienced in their daily lives. A black woman shopping in Blumstein's or Koch's on 125th Street was not permitted to try on a dress within the store; she had to purchase it and take it home to see how it looked on her and if it fit.[64] White-run stores also refused to allow black patrons to use toilet facilities reserved for customers.[65] Black moviegoers could only sit in the balcony at Loew's Victoria on 116th Street.[66] Those who wanted to attend Hurtig and Seamon's, before it became the Apollo Theater, had to go around to a back stairway and sit in what the management euphemistically called the upper mezzanine. Blacks called it "nigger heaven."[67]

Restaurant owners could be capricious, if not outright hostile, to black customers. Blacks could not get into most restaurants downtown. A *New York Times* reporter remembers interviewing jazz pianist Fats Waller, who was appearing in a show in the Broadway theater district. The reporter wanted to meet him in a nearby restaurant, but Waller said no establishment in the district would seat him.[68]

In Harlem, the discrimination took another form. Siding with the owner of a restaurant on West 113th Street, a Municipal Court judge ruled that the owner, a white man, was within his rights when he refused to serve blacks who wanted to dine with two white friends. The judge said that as long as the restauranteur was willing to serve blacks at their own tables he was in compliance with state law.[69]

Harlemites became so sensitive to prejudice, whether blatant or subtle, that the slightest rebuff or negative connotation was seen as antiblack. Their accumulation of grievances, economic and social, real and imagined, came to a head one day in 1935.

FIVE

Dress Rehearsal

A crust of bread and a corner to sleep in,
A minute to smile and an hour to weep in,

A pint of joy to a peck of trouble,
And never a laugh but the moans come double
And that is life.

—Paul Laurence Dunbar[1]

The riot broke out over a seemingly minor incident. During the afternoon of March 19, a sixteen-year-old Puerto Rican black named Lino Rivera strolled into the Kress five-and-dime store on 125th Street. Rivera, who ran errands for a local movie house, passed a counter displaying hardware and saw a ten-cent penknife that struck his fancy. He slipped it into his pocket; but a clerk saw him and took the knife away. The clerk then grabbed Rivera by the arm and began to push him out of the store. The youth fought back, biting the thumb of the clerk, who shouted that he would "beat the hell" out of him. Together with another employee, the clerk took the boy into the store basement, while a fellow worker called the police. After the police showed up, it was decided to let Rivera go. They let him out from a back door. Rivera immediately ran home.

In the meantime, crowds of blacks had formed both inside and outside the store. When a rumor spread that the boy had been beaten so severely that an ambulance had to be summoned, a brick crashed through the Kress window. Just then, a hearse appeared on the

44

street. People were now convinced that Rivera had indeed been killed. The riot that followed was fueled by leaflets distributed by both the Young Communist League and the Young Liberators, a radical black organization. Before it was over, one black had been killed and more than a hundred wounded.[2]

The outbreak stunned Americans, but not because of the violence or the loss of life. Race riots were not a new phenomenon: there were major riots in Atlanta in 1906; in Springfield, Illinois, in 1908; and no less than twenty-two race riots in the period 1915–19,[3] when the terrorist antiblack Ku Klux Klan was revived in both the South and the North, attracting millions of members and vying for political power in localities and states extending from Georgia to Indiana. In the bloodiest riot of all during World War I, as many as forty blacks and three whites were murdered by mobs in July 1917 in East St. Louis, Illinois.[4] (Three weeks later, in silent protest over the slaughter of the blacks, fifteen thousand Harlem residents marched down Fifth Avenue.) During the "Red Summer" of 1919, mobs murdered seventy-eighty blacks—ten of them war veterans still in uniform[5]—and rioters clashed in the streets not far from the White House in Washington as well as in Chicago, where forty people were killed.[6] Sporadic outbursts of race hatred broke out in, among other places, Lexington, Kentucky; Ocoee, Florida; and Tulsa, Oklahoma. KKK opposition to black voting spurred the riot in Ocoee, which took place on election day in 1920; as many as thirty-two blacks were believed to have been murdered. The alleged rape of a white girl by a black youth set off the Tulsa outbreak in the spring of 1921; estimates were that between 150 and 200 blacks and fifty whites were killed during the horrifying two-day riot.[7] In all, between 1865 and 1940, more than five hundred blacks were killed in eruptions of race hatred. But in those riots, whites were the aggressors. If blacks took to the streets, it was in retaliation. The Harlem riot in 1935 represented the first time that blacks initiated the violence.[8]

New York authorities and leaders were quick to advance all sorts of theories to explain the outburst. Many whites, including District Attorney William C. Dodge, believed that it had been instigated by "Reds."[9] But black leaders were vociferous in disputing that. Channing Tobias, black field secretary of the YMCA, declared:

It is erroneous and superficial to rush to the easy conclusion of District Attorney Dodge and the Hearst newspapers that the whole thing was a Communist plot. . . . [W]hat gave them their opportunity? The fact that there were and still are thousands of Negroes standing in enforced idleness on the street corners of Harlem with no prospect of employment while their more favored Negro neighbors are compelled to spend their money with business houses directed by white absentee owners who employ white workers imported from every other part of New York City.[10]

Noting that the riot was "variously diagnosed as a depression spasm, a Ghetto mutiny, a radical plot and dress rehearsal of proletarian revolution," Alain Locke, the first black Rhodes scholar and head of Howard University's philosophy department, declared:

Whichever it was, like a revealing flash of lightning it etched on the public mind another Harlem than the bright surface Harlem of the night clubs, cabaret tours and arty magazines, a Harlem that the social worker knew all along but had not been able to dramatize, a Harlem, too, that the radical press and street-corner orator had been pointing out but in all too incredible exaggerations and none too convincing shouts.[11]

Roy Wilkins, editor of the NAACP's magazine, *Crisis*, attributed the outbreak to discrimination "in economics, employment and justice, and living conditions."[12]

White merchants, said Rev. William Lloyd Imes, pastor of St. James Protestant Episcopal Church, were "reaping a harvest that they had sown."[13] To George W. Harris, publisher of the *Amsterdam News* and the city's first black alderman, "colored people have been denied a decent economic opportunity . . . [and] the result is a magazine of dynamite which it is only too easy to set off."[14]

One of Harlem's up-and-coming political leaders, Adam Clayton Powell, Jr., of the influential Abyssinian Baptist Church, saw the outburst as

an open, unorganized protest against empty stomachs, over-crowded tenements, filthy sanitation, rotten foodstuffs, chiseling landlords and merchants, discrimination on relief, disfranchisement, and against a disinterested administration. It was not caused by Communists.[15]

New York's mayor, Fiorello La Guardia—a liberal known for his espousal of minority causes—appointed a special biracial commission to look into the situation. When the commission finally turned in its report a year later, it was highly critical of the directors of some city agencies and, in particular, of the city's police. A commission subcommittee reported that "the insecurity of the individual in Harlem against police aggression is in our judgment one of the most potent causes of the existing hostility to authority. Various witnesses testified as to illegal searches of their persons and property by the police . . . the rights of Negroes [are] now flouted."[16]

La Guardia suppressed the report. The *Amsterdam News*, however, got hold of the thirty-five-thousand-word document and published it on July 18, 1936. The riot, the commission had concluded, was the result of "the smouldering resentments of the people of Harlem against racial discrimination and poverty in the midst of plenty."[17] A state commission concurred, saying that the disturbance was "a spontaneous and an incoherent protest by Harlem's population against a studied neglect of its critical problems."[18]

There were signs of improvement afterwards. A women's pavilion was opened at Harlem Hospital; a district health clinic in congested central Harlem was begun; plans for two new schools in Harlem were made part of the city's 1937 budget; and ground was broken that year for a housing project in the area for some 575 low-income families.

Speaking at the ground-breaking ceremony for the housing development, La Guardia cautioned, "We cannot be expected to correct in a day the mistakes and omissions of the past fifty years. But we are going places and carrying out a definite program. While the critics have been throwing stones, I have been laying bricks."[19]

Alain Locke, however, insisted,

The only answer is to eliminate the evils. . . . The blame belongs to a society that tolerates inadequate and often wretched housing, inadequate and inefficient schools and other public facilities, unemployment, unduly high rents, the lack of recreation grounds, discrimination in industry and the public utilities in the employment of colored people, brutality and lack of courtesy by police. As long as these conditions remain, the public order can not and will not be safe.[20]

"Discrimination and injustice," Locke said, "are the causes, not radicalism. But to neglect the symptoms, to ignore the grievances will be to spread radicalism.

"Violence," he warned, "will be an inevitable result."[21]

Calls for change rang out not only in Harlem, but also in every black community across the nation. A few weeks after the riot in Harlem, four thousand delegates representing twenty-six states as well as nations as diverse as Germany, Japan, Mexico, and Cuba gathered in New York for the first American Writers' Congress. The opening session was addressed by Langston Hughes.

There were "practical things American Negro writers can do," he said, to expose the "lovely grinning face of Philanthropy—which gives a million dollars to a Jim Crow school, but not one job to a graduate of that school; which builds a Negro hospital with second-rate equipment . . . or which, out of the kindness of its heart, erects yet another separate, segregated, shut-off, Jim Crow Y.M.C.A."

Hughes expounded a litany of complaints—about labor unions that refused to take in black workers; about the "Contentment Tradition of the O-lovely-Negroes school of American fiction, which makes an ignorant black face and a Carolina head filled with superstition"; about the "colored American Legion posts strutting around talking about the privilege of dying for the noble Red, White and Blue, when they aren't even permitted the privilege of living for it. Or voting for it in Texas. . . . Or even rising, like every other good little boy, from the log cabin to the White House":

> White House is right! . . .
> We want a new and better America, where there won't be any poor, where there won't be any more Jim Crow, where there won't b[e] any lynchings, . . . where we won't need philanthropy, nor charity, nor the New Deal, nor Home Relief.[22]

Almost a year later, in February 1936, A. Philip Randolph took a more militant stand. Randolph was a radical socialist who had viewed

America's involvement in World War I as a capitalist ploy. He considered the NAACP—whose founders, at its inception in 1910, were, in the main, white liberals—a moderate, if not futile, organization that was wedded to the interests of the small black middle class. Randolph did have in common with the NAACP a repugnance to the philosophy of accommodation with whites long espoused by Booker T. Washington, and a belief in the legality of retaliatory self-defense. He was also highly critical of the Roosevelt Administration's New Deal programs. They were "no remedy," he said, because they failed "to change the profit system."

An impressive speaker, Randolph was scheduled to give the keynote address at the founding convention of the National Negro Congress. The organization, which he would head for the next four years, claimed to represent 585 black groups in twenty-eight states that had a combined membership of 1.2 million. But Randolph was ill and could not attend the meeting in Chicago. Instead, his speech was read for him:

> Black America is a victim of both class and race prejudice and oppression. Because Negroes are black they are hated, maligned and spat upon; lynched, mobbed, and murdered. Because Negroes are workers, they are browbeaten, bullied, intimidated, robbed, exploited, jailed and shot down. Because they are black they are caught between the nether millstones of discrimination when seeking a job or seeking to join a union.
>
> Thus voteless in 13 states; politically disregarded and discounted in the others; victims of the lynch terror in Dixie, . . . unequal before the law; jim-crowed in schools and colleges throughout the nation; segregated in the slums of ghettos of the urban centers; landless peons of a merciless white landlordism; hunted down, harassed and hounded as vagrants in the southern cities, the Negro people face a hard, deceptive and brutal capitalist order.[23]

Led by Randolph and influential clergymen such as Imes and Powell, Harlem's blacks discovered a new method of change: mass protest. Randolph and Powell, for example, were instrumental in the formation of the Greater New York Coordinating Committee for Employment, which claimed it represented more than two-hundred organizations that had fifteen thousand members.[24] The difficulty, however, was that sometimes other groups vied for the support of Harlem residents in antibias campaigns and diluted their impact. Adherents of Marcus Garvey, whose "Back to Africa" philosophy attracted widespread support in the 1920s, formed the African Patriotic League, which was primarily concerned with making blacks self-sufficient. An offshoot, the Harlem Labor Union, picketed both stores and utilities. Still other demonstrators staged rent strikes against landlords for raising rents or took part in boycotts of stores along 125th Street, carrying signs that read "Don't Buy Where You Can't Work."

The demonstrators were helped, in part, by a Supreme Court decision in 1938. A lower court injunction had barred a potpourri of protesters, organized as the New Negro Alliance, from demonstrating for jobs outside the A. S. Beck shoe store on 125th Street because they were not an organized labor union. The high court, however, ruled that blacks could engage in boycott activities against racial discrimination.

Powell subsequently organized the picketing of the Empire State Building to force officials of the New York World's Fair to hire blacks, and when that failed five hundred demonstrators showed up to embarrass President Roosevelt and New York governor Herbert H. Lehman at the official opening of the fair, dedicated to "Building for a Better Tomorrow," in April 1939.

In time, one group or another, or groups working together, were able to make some headway. But the gains they made were token. The Consolidated Edison Light Company finally agreed to hire some trainees, and two city bus lines likewise agreed to train blacks as bus drivers. The telephone company opened operator positions to blacks. Blacks finally filled about seven hundred positions at the World's Fair, but that was out of a work force of seven thousand and most of the jobs were menial.[25]

Up in Harlem itself, Koch's department store took on one or two blacks, as did several other shops as well as Child's restaurant. Eventually, Koch's and Child's abandoned the street altogether. Kress's was the last to accede to hiring blacks. Often, however, light-skinned people were preferred to those who were darker, or West Indians to American-born blacks because they were believed to be more industrious. Virginia Delany Murphy, a niece of the Delany sisters, was one of the few blacks who worked at Woolworth's and later landed a job at Blumstein's. She got the job at the latter store through the influence of the father of a white high school classmate. But even though Virginia was a student at the prestigious Hunter High School, she was relegated to sorting stock in a back room, and was not allowed to use the employees' bathroom or to eat lunch with other Blumstein workers.[26]

Two years after the 1935 riot, the Bureau of Labor reported that the "poorer half of the colored population must live on an income which is only 46 percent of that achieved by the poorer half of the white population."[27]

Despite all their complaints, hurts, and humiliations, Harlem residents grudgingly admitted that they had it good—that is, relatively, considering the temper of the times. A black lived in Harlem without fear of being lynched, or having a cross burned in his front yard. Biases against him, or her, existed, but were subtle. There were few outward symbols of discrimination, no "Whites Only" or "Colored Only" signs. A black could sit anywhere he or she liked in a bus or a subway. Public schools may have been crowded and de facto segregated, but, unlike the South, where books, teachers, and facilities were in desperate short supply, a determined black youth in Harlem could get an education. True, there were areas where a black did not feel wanted, and where police confronted any black stranger, but there were no night riders to scare or intimidate; there was no reason to have a shotgun resting beside the front door, as in the South. Weapons, in fact, were almost unknown in Harlem.

A black cleric who felt "never wanted" in the Southern city of his youth said, "In New York I am tolerated."[28]

"When you got out of New York City, discrimination was just as bad if not worse than in the South," says Arnold de Mille, who worked for a variety of black newspapers in Harlem. "The city was a little better. In fact, the city was a helluva lot better."[29]

Blacks in the 1930s voted in New York, served on juries, and could protest without fear of retaliation. Although confined to a ghetto like every other black community in the country, Harlem's citizens, all in all, still had a measure of freedom not shared by most blacks in most other cities in most other states.

All blacks did share, however, in suffering the ill effects of the

Depression. When the decade began, there were some 11.9 million blacks in the United States. Of those, 5.5 million were reported employed, the greater number—3.5 million—as domestics and in agriculture. By 1932, 1.5 million blacks were *un*employed, and two years later, the figure rose to between two and three million. That meant that in 1934, half of the black working population of the nation was without work, at a time when unemployment among whites was between 20 and 25 percent.[30]

In October 1933, six months after Franklin D. Roosevelt first took office as president, more than 1.2 million blacks were on relief throughout the country. They represented close to a fifth of the total black population. Nearly two years later, despite the New Deal recovery measures that the Democratic administration instituted, that figure rose to 3.5 million blacks. Almost one in every three blacks was now on relief.[31] The median income of blacks by 1939 was less than half of what it was for whites.[32]

Blacks, in the main, were supporters of Roosevelt—had, in fact, deserted the party of Lincoln for the first time and voted overwhelmingly for the Democratic president when he ran for reelection in 1936. In Harlem alone, the president received 84 percent of the vote.[33] Roosevelt's wife, Eleanor, was an outspoken advocate of minority rights and a compassionate crusader for righting wrongs. Often as a result of her urging, the president had named a number of blacks to roles in his New Deal programs, and those who were his advisers became known as the "Black Cabinet." His secretary of the interior, Harold Ickes, was a champion of black causes.

But discrimination remained rampant throughout the nation, especially in the South, where almost three out of every four blacks lived.[34] There, a system of racial intolerance known as "Jim Crow" existed that was based on local and national laws and enforced by states through their courts and police. The term symbolized the segregation in schools, transportation, parks, and other public facilities protected by the "separate but equal" decision handed down by the Supreme Court in 1896. As insidious were the poll taxes and other requirements that in twelve southern states kept the number of qualified black voters down to only 2 percent of those otherwise eligible to vote.[35]

Efforts to rectify the inequalities that existed were successfully blocked by the political clout of southern congressmen of the ilk of

Theodore G. Bilbo and James O. Eastland of Mississippi, Allen J. Ellender of Louisiana, Ellison DuRant (Cotton Ed) Smith of South Carolina, and John H. Bankhead of Alabama. Many of them were senior members presiding over important committees. Congress had not passed a federal civil rights bill since 1875, and in 1940 there was only one black member in both houses.[36]

Worse than the legal barriers was the terror that was omnipresent. Beatings, horsewhippings, torture, and house burnings were common in the South for the slightest sign of "comeuppance." More than three thousand blacks were lynched between 1882 and 1935,[37] an average of more than fifty-six a year. Yet, typically, southern senators effectively filibustered against antilynching bills that had been introduced repeatedly in Congress since 1919 and passed by the House each time. Roosevelt explained to Walter White of the NAACP in the midst of the Depression that he could not endorse an antilynching campaign because he had "to get legislation passed by Congress to save America." Southerners that controlled key committees in both the Senate and the House, he said, "will block every bill I ask Congress to pass to keep America from collapsing. I just can't take that risk."[38]

Perhaps the most insidious legacy of the slavery system that had prevailed for two hundred years was the vicious feeling of inferiority that whites impressed upon their slaves. Considered chattel without any legal rights or protection whatsoever, a black, before the Civil War, was powerless. The do's and don't's black children learned were strictures related to what they could or could not do in relation to their masters. Whiteness came to personify wisdom and adequacy, while blackness meant ignorance and subservience. Many blacks came to adopt the attitudes of their masters, in effect acquiescing to the contention that they were inferior.

Pearl Buck, a white novelist who had grown up in China and understood what it meant "to be hated because of my color and my race,"[39] put herself in the position of being a black. Speaking in New York in 1933, Buck declared:

> Our greatest tragedy is that this is our country. We are not foreign-
> ers here. We belong here—we have nowhere else to go. . . . I say
> this is our greatest tragedy. Sometimes I think there is one still
> greater. It is that in ourselves we are afraid we are not really quite

so good as the white man. We cannot forget that our fathers were
slaves. . . .

To some of us life becomes increasingly intolerable. We either
shrink from going to places where we fear slights or else we find
ourselves with a sort of pride going stubbornly on and receiving the
slights, and so the suffering mounts in us and the soreness increases. Some day it will break into crisis, inevitably. . . .

The truth is we have two problems to solve. We have the actual
fact that we are discriminated against as a race. . . .

But our more serious problem . . . is within ourselves. . . . That
is, we must believe in our own selves.[40]

Abroad, world events were about to overtake the minds and hearts
of the country, blacks included. War was brewing, a righteous war,
and with the invasion of Poland in 1939, the United States started to
gear up to the possibility that, despite strong and vocal isolationist
sentiments, the nation might be dragged into the conflict. Inevitably,
a key issue attracted attention in the black community: would blacks,
caught up in economic and social discrimination at home, support
America's involvement?

Answers came in the form of questions. "Am I a Negro first
and then a policeman or soldier second," asked sociologist Horace
Clayton, "or should I forget in any emergency situation the fact that
. . . my first loyalty is to my race?"[41]

C. L. R. James, a West Indian active in both American and British
Trotskyist movements, summed up a ten-part installment in the *So-
cialist Appeal* by asking: "Why should I shed my blood for Roosevelt's
America, for Cotton Ed Smith and Senator Bilbo, for the whole Jim
Crow, Negro-hating South, for the low-paid, dirty jobs for which
Negroes have to fight, for the few dollars of relief and the insults,
discrimination, police brutality, and perpetual poverty to which Ne-
groes are condemned even in the more liberal North?"[42]

In spite of such negative sentiments, many blacks looked upon
world events with a certain optimism. Perhaps there might be a
chance for work for everyone. Perhaps there would be the opportunity to serve their country and prove patriotism. Perhaps they finally
had good reason to hope that things were going to get better.

SIX

The Black Dilemma

How would you have us, as we are?
  Or sinking 'neath the load we bear,
Our eyes fixed forward on a star,
  Or gazing empty at despair?

—James Weldon Johnson[1]

To blacks, the president and his wife were heroes, she especially. Her dedication was a remarkable turnabout. Reared as a child in a southern household—grandmother Martha Bulloch's family had owned slaves in Georgia—Eleanor had first referred to black members of her household staff in Washington as "darkies and pickaninnies." But as soon as Mrs. Roosevelt became aware of the injustices, mortifications and struggles that blacks experienced, she fought to right the wrongs. When the Daughters of the American Revolution refused to let black soprano Marian Anderson sing in Constitution Hall, Mrs. Roosevelt resigned from the organization. When she went to Birmingham, Alabama, to participate in a program, she was told that a local ordinance barred her from sitting with blacks whom she knew and regarded. So she got herself a folding chair and sat in the middle aisle between the white and black sections of the audience.

Mrs. Roosevelt was a persistent advocate, the channel through which black complaints got to the president. Roosevelt's New Deal program discriminated subtly against blacks, but when she heard about black tenant farmers in the South being victims of the federal crop-reduction program or that blacks were paid less than whites under the National Recovery Act, Mrs. Roosevelt pressed for reforms. It was she who got the president to issue an executive order that barred discrimination in contracts let by the Works Progress Administration. Blacks who worked on WPA projects, or in National Youth Administration training programs could thank her for the opportunity. Whatever advances blacks achieved in New Deal programs, or whatever shortcomings were rectified, were her doing. She even amplified the president's famous "Four Freedoms." Roosevelt had enunciated them in his annual message to Congress in January 1941: freedom of speech, freedom of worship, freedom from want, and freedom from fear. To them, she added four more freedoms: equality before the law, in education, in jobs, and in voting. She dealt with "that old bugaboo, intermarriage," Roy Wilkins of the NAACP said admiringly, by saying that "people should marry whom they choose."[2] Mrs. Roosevelt's name became synonymous with black aspirations. In return, blacks loved her—and white southerners hated her.

But there was a limit to what she could accomplish. Mrs. Roosevelt was an idealist. The president was a pragmatist who was known as a gradualist in racial matters. To accomplish his programs, he was forced to wheel and deal with a group of conservative southern Democrats who wielded a great deal of power and influence in Congress. The president's stance became even more difficult after the 1938 off-year congressional elections, when Republicans doubled their representation in the House, winning eighty-one seats, and joined their conservative Democratic counterparts in a coalition that stymied liberal legislation.

In spite of Mrs. Roosevelt's persistent, stubborn, and prolonged fight for black rights, the truth was that Washington was a killing ground for their hopes and desires. The gains they achieved, in great measure through her help, were relative—critical in tempering black frustrations, but often token. Washington, the nation's capital, was hostile to blacks, whether on a political, social, or economic level. The *Amsterdam News* characterized the city as "Washington, J.C. (Jim Crow)."[3]

As in New York City, many of the District of Columbia's major employers, including the transit and telephone companies, would not hire blacks except as menial laborers. And almost no restaurant outside the black ghetto would serve blacks. But there resemblances between the two cities ended. Washington was a wholehearted southern, segregated metropolis, as it had always been. Until the Compromise of 1850, the city, situated between two slave states, Virginia and Maryland, was the center of domestic slave traffic in the United States; there were at least four slave pens in the city proper. Even after 1850, when trafficking in slaves was banned, it was still legal to own slaves in Washington; there were more than seventeen hundred of them in the city on the eve of the Civil War. Free blacks then—there were about nine thousand of them—were forbidden to hold public meetings without the mayor's permission. There was a 10 P.M. curfew for all blacks, slave and free.[4]

In the 1930s, southern Democrats in Congress—they were called Dixiecrats—dominated the committees that governed the district, and, as a result, funds to make improvements beneficial to blacks were virtually nonexistent. Washington's schools were separate but hardly equal; while white students studied in half-empty buildings, black youngsters had to cope in old schools, a number of which were so overcrowded that they were on double and triple sessions. The federal Department of the Interior once tried to transfer ownership of golf courses and swimming pools to the District's Board of Education, but it refused because the pools would have had to be desegregated.[5]

Some observers commented that there were no worse slums in America than in the black section of the nation's capital. Malcolm Little (he later changed his name to Malcolm X) worked briefly in the late 1930s as a "fourth cook"—"a glorified name for dishwasher"— on the Colonial, a train that ran between Boston and the capital. In his spare time on his first trip to Washington, he went sightseeing downtown. Little was "astounded" to discover, "just a few blocks from Capitol Hill, thousands of Negroes living worse than any I'd ever seen in the poorest sections of Roxbury." He said he had "seen a lot, but never such a dense concentration of stumblebums, pushers, hookers, public crapshooters, even little kids running around at midnight begging for pennies, half-naked and barefooted."[6]

Gordon Parks, who worked as a photographer for the Farm Security Administration, had the same reaction the first day he arrived in Washington. He walked about "in a hurry and with enthusiasm," reveling in the big, cloudless blue sky. "Everything seemed so pure, clean and unruffled." But his pleasure was "short-lived." Within an hour's time, Parks, who had grown up the son of a tenant farmer in Kansas amid bigotry and hopelessness, realized that "racism was busy with its dirty work. Eating houses shooed me to the back door; theaters refused me a seat, and the scissoring voices of white clerks at Julius Garfinckel's prestigious department store riled me with curtness." Parks, who later became a photographer for *Life* magazine as well as a writer, composer, and painter, felt as if he was experiencing "a bad dream":

> In a very short time Washington was showing me its real character. It was a hate-drenched city, honoring my ignorance and smugly creating bad memories for me. During that afternoon my entire childhood rushed back to greet me, to remind me that the racism it poured on me had not called it quits.
>
> Not only was I humiliated, I was also deeply hurt and angered to a boiling point. It suddenly seemed that all of America was finding grim pleasure in expressing its intolerance to me personally. Washington had turned ugly . . . even here in the nation's capital, the walls of bigotry and discrimination stood high and formidable.[7]

Nowhere was the legacy of prejudice more visible and more troubling than in the armed forces. After all, the armed forces were government-controlled and should, in the estimation of many blacks, be free of the constraints of ordinary society. And the armed forces provided a forum where blacks could prove their right to equality, their patriotism, and their allegiance to their country.

Blacks pointed with pride to the fact that the first person to die in the fight for liberty with England was a black man, Crispus Attucks, who was shot in the Boston Massacre in 1770. Once the Revolutionary War started, the British started encouraging the enrollment of escaped slaves into their army. In response, some rebel colonies abandoned their fear of armed blacks and promised freedom for those who served for three years or were honorably discharged. Some five thousand blacks signed up to fight on the American side. More than 175,000 blacks served in the Civil War, and twenty-four of them earned the newly created Congressional Medal of Honor.[8] After the war, Congress formally established the Twenty-fourth and Twenty-fifth Infantry and the Ninth and Tenth Cavalry as permanent black units. The latter were the Buffalo Soldiers who fought in the Indians Wars; eighteen of them won the Medal of Honor.[9] Five thousand blacks saw combat during the Spanish-American War, when infantry units fought alongside Teddy Roosevelt's Rough Riders at San Juan Hill in Cuba. But World War I left a festering wound.

Even before America entered the war, blacks were arguing against involvement in it. Socialist agitators who called themselves New Crowd Negroes asked what business blacks had in taking up arms. From soapboxes and stepladders in Harlem, at junctions such as the corner of Lenox Avenue and 125th or 135th Street, they decried the European conflict as a "capitalist" and "imperialist" war.[10] They complained about fighting alongside colonial countries such as Britain and France. Propaganda aimed at arousing American sympathy for the plight of Belgians met with indifference from blacks, who were all too aware of Belgian atrocities in the Congo. British rule over millions of Africans was as savage, they believed, as the German oppression of the Cameroons and in German East Africa. Rev. Adam Clayton Powell, Sr., urged that "the powers that be" provide blacks with "at least some verbal assurance that the property and lives of the members of our race are going to be protected from Maine to Mississippi." Powell said that it was "infinitely more disgraceful and outrageous to hang and burn colored men and boys and women without a trial in times of peace than it is for Germans in times of war to blow up ships loaded with mules and molasses."[11]

There were complaints, too, about the paucity of meaningful defense work open to blacks, about the fact that white officers had always commanded black units, and about the president, too. After all, hadn't Woodrow Wilson screened the film *Birth of a Nation* in the White House and approved of its virulent pro-Ku Klux Klan view of the tumultuous Reconstruction Period as "history written with lightning"?[12] Wasn't this the same president who turned his back on a black delegation, calling their words "insulting," when they came to the White House to protest a new, more encompassing segregation policy among federal workers?[13]

Blacks who argued against blacks serving in the military had an unexpected ally, Sen. James K. Vardaman of Mississippi. National conscription would mean, he said, that "millions" of blacks "will be armed. I know of no greater menace to the South than this."[14]

Despite the litany of complaints that militant blacks voiced, influential leaders in the black community were afraid that opposition to the war would be misconstrued to the detriment of black goals. W. E. B. Du Bois, then editor of the NAACP's magazine *Crisis*, believed it was the duty of blacks to "close ranks" and support America's policy.

The "millions" Vardaman had worried about became, in reality, a bit more than 300,000 blacks who were drafted; together with black regulars and National Guard members, they brought the number of blacks who saw service during World War I to 380,000. Their experience, in the main, bordered on the disastrous. Emmett Scott, a black who was a special assistant to Secretary of War Newton D. Baker, noted that because of its "immense Negro population, the South furnished the bulk of the colored men" who were called up for training. Their morale, he said, "was at times lowered to a degree that was little short of dangerous."[15]

Some of the problems blacks encountered would be echoed less than a quarter of a century later. All-white draft boards exempted white males with no dependents while blacks with families were taken. Southern governors, senators, and representatives violently protested the quartering of black troops in their states. There was discrimination in promotions, assignments, and working conditions. Blacks received inferior accommodations and frequently lacked medical care. There were restrictions even in the use of toilet facilities at depot restaurants and cafés. One infamous and especially onerous bulletin was issued at Camp Funston after a theater manager in nearby Manhattan, Kansas, refused to admit a black sergeant of the Ninety-second Division because his white patrons might object. The bulletin instructed "All colored members" of the division to "refrain from going where their presence will be resented."[16] In addition, white soldiers refused to salute black officers. And there were race riots at army bases.

"A flood" of complaints, Scott noted, reached the War Department in 1918 from many camps, charging that black soldiers "were being grossly mistreated by their officers, ofttimes physically assaulted, called by names that were highly insulting—such as 'nigger,' 'coon,' 'darkey,' and worse, and that the colored men were forced to work under the most unhealthy and laborious conditions."[17]

About two hundred thousand blacks served in France, but only one out of four of them went as a combat doughboy; the rest served in what Scott termed a "vast army of Stevedores."[18] Service overseas was also tainted by discrimination. The executive officer of the *Virginia*, Scott reported, requested that blacks assigned to be transported on his ship be *"removed on the ground that no colored troops had ever traveled on board a United States battleship."*[19] In France, troops of the Ninety-second Division were told not to speak "with or to French women."[20] The headquarters of the American Expeditionary Force issued an explanatory document on August 7, 1918, for the benefit of French officers in command of black doughboys. As evidenced by the "loathsome vice of criminally assaulting women," the blacks, Scott noted, "were referred to as a 'menace of degeneracy which had to be prevented by the gulf established between the two races.' " The French were called upon " *'not to treat the Negroes with familiarity and indulgence which are matters of grievous concern to Americans and an affront to their national policy.'* " The French army was advised to prevent intimacy between its officers and black officers—" *'not to eat with them, not to shake hands or seek to talk or meet with them outside of the requirements of military service.'* " French officers were asked " *'not to commend too highly the black American troops in the presence of white Americans.'* "[21]

It was no small miracle, then, that the first two American soldiers to receive the croix de guerre, Henry Johnson and Needham Roberts, were both blacks from the Fifteenth Regiment of New York's National Guard. Or that the entire Fifteenth, renamed the U.S. 369th Regiment, which served under the French flag, was also awarded the croix de guerre. Nicknamed the Harlem Hellfighters, the regiment took part in the Battle of the Meuse-Argonne and was the first Allied regiment to reach the Rhine River. Its 191 consecutive days on the frontline were the longest any American force served. Its men never gave up a trench, retreated an inch, or surrendered a prisoner.

But the 369th was the exception to the rule. W. E. B. Du Bois complained that black men were "allowed to volunteer only as servants in the Navy and as common laborers in the Army outside of the regular four Negro regiments."[22] Most blacks worked not only as stevedores loading and unloading supply ships, but also as laborers building roads and chopping wood for trenches and fires, as railroad hands, mechanics, and gravediggers. The ten thousand blacks who were in the navy were all mess attendants.

It was no surprise that the demoralizing conditions experienced by draftees, particularly those from the South who had had little if any schooling, created problems—and an extremely negative assessment of the value of black troops. In 1925, the Army War College issued a report on "Negro Manpower" that was devastating in its conclusions. Black officers in World War I failed under fire, and the troops under them "displayed entire inaptitude for modern battle," the report said. "Negro troops are efficient and dependable only so long as led by capable white officers." As for the black man as a soldier, "In the process of evolution, the American negro has not progressed as far as other sub species of the human family." The report said that the "cranial capacity" of a black was smaller than a white's, and that his psychology, "based on heredity derived from mediocre African ancestors, cultivated by generations of slavery, is one from which we cannot expect to draw leadership material." The report found the black man to be "jolly, docile, tractable, and lively," though if ill-treated he could become "stubborn, sullen and unruly." He did not have the physical courage of a white man, and, the report said, "he is most susceptible to 'Crowd Psychology.' He cannot control himself in fear of danger." In fact, the report added, "He is a rank coward in the dark."[23]

Twelve years later, in 1937, the personnel division of the War Department, in an attempt to avoid mistakes made in the use of black troops in World War I, came up with a secret guideline that would serve as the basis for the army's treatment of blacks throughout World War II. The plan included the inclusion of more blacks in the service and reserving the posts of warrant officers, chaplains, and reserve officers in black units for blacks. But it also called for confining black officers in the National Guard to positions already authorized, restricting the number of black officer candidates to the number actually required to fill positions in only all-black units, and limiting the number of blacks assigned to reception, placement, and training centers. In explaining the reason why the guideline should remain confidential, Maj. Gen. H. E. Ely, commandant of the Army War College, told Army Secretary Harry H. Woodring that otherwise its disclosure would provide time for "those seeking political capital, for points on which the War Department may be attacked, or embarrassed."[24]

Unaware of the army plan, that October Charles H. Houston, special counsel to the NAACP who was a veteran of World War I, urged Roosevelt to issue an executive order "to give Negro citizens the same right to serve their country as any other citizen, and on the same basis." The black community was loyal, he declared, but "the Negro population will not silently suffer the discrimination and abuse which were heaped upon Negro soldiers and officers in World War I."[25]

SEVEN

The Battle Before the War

What happens to a dream deferred?
  Does it dry up
  like a raisin in the sun?
  or fester like a sore—
  and then run? . . .
  or does it explode?

—Langston Hughes[1]

As the nation began to rearm in the summer and fall of 1940, blacks
—with the experience of World War I still in mind—repeatedly asked
themselves: why fight for democracy abroad when we don't have
democracy at home?

Preparing a memo for Gunnar Myrdal's classic study of the black
experience, *An American Dilemma*, Ralph Bunche wrote that there
were blacks "who, fed up with frustration of their life, here, see no
hope and express an angry desire 'to shoot their way out of it.' "
Bunche, who would one day represent the United States in the
United Nations, said that he had "on many occasions heard Negroes
exclaim, 'Just give us machine guns and we'll blow the lid off the
whole damn business.' "[2]

Columnist Ludlow W. Werner echoed black frustrations in the
New York Age:

> I am an American, but I cannot, if I want to, enlist in the United
> States Marine Corps. . . .
>   I am an American, but I cannot, if I want to, join the Navy
> except as a cook, messman or kitchen scullion. . . .

I am an American, but if I am drafted, I must be sent to a Negro regiment for service. . . .

I am an American, but if I live in the Southland, I cannot vote in primary elections and I must pay a poll tax. . . .

I am an American, but if I live in the Southland, I cannot go into a first class department store and try on a hat or suit of clothes . . . before I buy it.

I am an American, but if I live in the nation's capital I must go to a Negro school. . . .

I am an American, but if I live in the nation's capital I cannot go to a movie house. . . .

I am an American, but if I live in the nation's capital, I cannot attend concerts in the D.A.R. Hall. . . .

I am an American, but if I live in New York City, I pay higher rents and live in more squalid quarters than other citizens.

I am an American, but if I live in New York, I may not be employed . . . except as porter, elevator operator or in a menial capacity for the most part. . . .

I am an American, but if I live in New York City, I may take out membership only in the Negro Y.M.C.A.'s.

I am an American, but if I am a skilled worker, I may not become a member of any A.F. of L. Union except in a few rare instances.

I am an American, but if I am accused of a crime in the North, I am always guilty before I am tried.

I am an American, but if I am accused of a crime in the South, I may not even face trial—I may be lynched. . . .

I am an American, but I am a Negro.[3]

It was out of such despair that the "Fight for the Right to Fight" campaign, as it became known, was born. It was based on the blacks' hope that they could secure equality by proving themselves on the battlefield.

Part of the frustration blacks felt was prompted in no small part by the Selective Service Act, which Roosevelt signed into law on September 14, 1940. At the time, the peacetime army was some five hundred thousand strong. But little more than forty-seven hundred soldiers, less than 1 percent of the total roster, were blacks, and all, as was the custom since Civil War days, were in segregated units. There were only five black officers, three of whom were chaplains.

The other two were a father-and-son team, Col. Benjamin O. Davis, Sr., and Lieut. Benjamin O. Davis, Jr., The elder Davis had taken command of the 369th Regiment—the old Fifteenth Regiment—in 1939.[4] The navy counted four thousand blacks in its ranks, all mess attendants.

Almost immediately, blacks who wanted to enlist ran into obstacles. The black doctor or dentist who tried to volunteer was rejected because the army did not want blacks to treat white soldiers. Often, blacks were not called up because separate facilities did not exist. Trained black pilots who tried to join the Army Air Corps were bluntly told, "There is no place for a Negro in the Air Corps."[5] There had never been blacks in the Marine Corps, which had no intention of changing its policy. Mess attendants complained that they were refused other postings in the navy; when fifteen of them wrote an open letter to the *Pittsburgh Courier,* griping about conditions on board the USS *Philadelphia,* all were summarily indicted for conduct prejudicial to good conduct and dishonorably discharged.

In the summer of 1940, the NAACP was asked to join an interventionist group, the Committee to Defend America by Aiding the Allies, which had been set up to counter isolationist sentiment. The group's argument was that fascism threatened blacks, who had more opportunities in America than anywhere else. Its request was rejected outright by Thurgood Marshall, then the NAACP's legal counsel. Marshall, who would one day became an Associate Justice of the United States Supreme Court, said that the argument that "we must have national unity regardless of whether or not we have democracy at home" was directly "in conflict with our position."[6]

Walter White pointed out that few blacks wanted the Allies to lose, but all wanted white society to change. A. Philip Randolph cautioned that "before the war ends," many blacks "want to see the stuffing knocked out of white supremacy and of empire over subject peoples."[7]

A few blacks thought they understood why whites were so worried. It was a theme Mississippi Sen. James Vardaman had brought up at the outset of World War I: the menacing thought of blacks armed with guns. After a national conference in Chicago on the new conscription law, the Political Committee of the Socialist Workers Party issued a supplementary resolution. "The capitalists," it read, "fear that *no Negro trained to handle a gun would peacefully go back to the old life of discrimination, segregation, disfranchisement, and insult, after training in an army where he was treated as an equal with white soldiers."* [8]

On the surface, the new conscription law that Roosevelt signed appeared to finally emend inequalities and satisfy black complaints. It provided that all men between the ages of eighteen and thirty-six were eligible to volunteer in land and naval forces. It also included a pledge that black participation in the army would be increased to accurately reflect the ratio of blacks in the population, roughly 10 percent. Moreover, an amendment decreed that there would be no discrimination in the selection and training of men under the act. The amendment was introduced by Rep. Hamilton Fish of New York, who had served as a company commander in the 369th Regiment in World War I.[9] Fish also tried to include provisions for an all-black army division and the annual appointment of two blacks to West Point, but he failed to muster enough support for either proposal.

For all its seeming nondiscrimination, the new law nonetheless contained a loophole that gave the War Department the final say over who would be accepted: no one would be inducted unless "acceptable" to the army and "until adequate provision" was made for his "shelter, sanitary facilities, water supplies, heating and lighting arrangements, medical care and hospital accommodations."[10] In other words, the army was free to set up whatever physical and aptitude qualifications it desired and did not have to accept anyone who did not meet those prerequisites, nor did it have to accept any blacks unless it had separate barracks and other facilities to house and care for them.

Some blacks were willing to accept segregation and recruitment quotas. Among them were Charles Houston of the NAACP and Robert L. Vann, editor and publisher of the *Pittsburgh Courier*, who had prevailed upon Fish to introduce the antidiscrimination amendment. But other blacks were opposed. Walter White insisted that "segregation in public institutions always works to the disadvantage of the segregated group and must be resisted with all the united strength we can command." Roy Wilkins, editor of the *Crisis*, thought there was "no reason why we should not have Negro aviators or generals or admirals."[11]

Even before the president signed the conscription bill, White and

Randolph repeatedly tried, without success, to meet with Roosevelt to discuss it. But it was not until after he had signed the law that they were finally able to arrange a conference, thanks to Mrs. Roosevelt. T. Arnold Hill, former secretary of the Urban League and now adviser on black affairs for the National Youth Administration, was going to accompany them.

On the morning of the meeting, September 27, the three blacks held a conference of their own to plan strategy. They came up with an agenda that they thought offered a number of ways that blacks could be assimilated in the military services. Among them was the integration of black doctors and dentists, the selection of army officers regardless of race, opening posts other than that of messmen to blacks in the navy, the appointment of blacks to draft boards, the designation of centers where blacks could be trained in aviation, and the naming of blacks as assistants to the Secretaries of Navy and War.

Randolph, White, and Hill then went to the White House where they were met by the president, Navy Secretary Frank Knox, and Assistant Secretary of War Robert Patterson. Once the meeting got underway, Randolph told Roosevelt that blacks wanted to participate in defense preparations but felt unwelcome in the armed forces. Not so, the president responded. The government, he insisted, was not confining blacks to noncombat roles, as it had in World War I. "We're putting them right in, proportionately, into the combat services." That, he said, is "*something.*" [12]

Knox, though, was intransigent about integrating the navy, which, he said, had a "factor" that the army did not have. "These men live aboard ship. And in our history we don't take Negroes into a ship's company." [13]

Facetiously, Roosevelt remarked that things would be different if there could be such a thing as a northern ship and a southern ship. He then suggested assigning black martial-music bands on ships to get white sailors used to having blacks onboard.

The meeting ended on an optimistic note with the president taking the blacks' agenda under advisement and promising to discuss the issues with government officials and his cabinet. He would then get back to the three black leaders.

Nearly two weeks later, the president's press secretary, Steve Early, a southerner who resented Mrs. Roosevelt's intervention in

White House affairs, released to the press an official statement regarding the government's so-called new policy regarding blacks in the army and navy. The statement said that the traditional policy—that is, segregation—would be continued and that, except for already established black regiments, all future black units would be officered by whites. Moreover, the statement implied that White, Randolph, and Hill had endorsed the policy. The statement took them totally by surprise. They were shocked when they read it. Rather than abolishing segregation, the policy "actually extended it!" White exclaimed.[14]

The War Department was adamant. Whether it was called integration or desegregation, the time for change was not propitious. Its General Staff had advised Stimson that "every effort should be made by the War Department to maintain in the Army the social and racial conditions which exist in civil life in order that normal customs of white and colored personnel now in the Army may not be suddenly disrupted." The staff said that the army "can, under no circumstances, adopt a policy which is contrary to the dictates of a majority of people [because] to do so would alienate the people from the Army and lower their morale at a time when their support of the Army and high morale are vital to our national needs." Chief of Staff Gen. George C. Marshall espoused the belief that integration was "fraught with danger to efficiency, discipline, and morale."[15] He believed that the War Department could not "ignore the social relationships between negroes and whites which has [sic] been established by the American people through custom and habit."[16] As for Stimson, he thought the black problem in America was "insoluble" and that "foolish leaders of the colored race" were trying to seek social equality, which was impossible because it would mean intermarriage.[17] Assistant Secretary of War John J. McCloy felt "frankly" that he did "not think that the basic issues of this war are involved in the question of whether Colored troops serve in segregated units or in mixed units and I doubt whether you can convince the people of the United States that the basic issues of freedom are involved in such a question."[18] A navy board created specifically to analyze the relationship between the navy and blacks held three brief meetings before concluding that "the enlistment of Negroes (other than as mess attendants) leads to disruptive and undermining conditions."[19]

Knox told Roosevelt that he would have to resign if asked to desegregate the navy while also trying to create a two-ocean force. Stimson confided to his diary that during World War I black army officers had "made perfect fools of themselves." Then, echoing the War College's report of 1925, he wrote:

> Leadership is not embedded in the Negro race yet and to try to make commissioned officers to lead the men into battle is only to work disaster to both. Colored troops do very well under white officers but every time we try to lift them a little beyond where they can go, disaster and confusion follow. . . . I hope for heaven's sake they won't mix the white and colored troops together in the same units for then we shall certainly have trouble.[20]

Eventually, at Mrs. Roosevelt's prodding again, Early was forced to issue a retraction stating that the three blacks had not approved of the new policy. At her instigation, the president assured the black leaders that there was no rigid policy about having black officers command white troops in the future, only that "at this time and this time only" it would not be wise to "confuse the issue of prompt preparedness with a new social experiment, however important and desirable it may be."[21]

Though White and Randolph were mollified by Roosevelt's remarks, other blacks were not. There was a rally in Harlem to protest the War Department's policy, and there was talk that many blacks were thinking of voting for Republican Wendell Willkie in the coming presidential election.

To assuage black feelings, on the eve of national elections in the fall of 1940 Roosevelt announced three appointments. The elder Davis, Benjamin O., Sr., was promoted from colonel to brigadier general. He was eventually posted to the Inspector General's Office with the express assignment of monitoring the experience of blacks in the army. Davis was the first black to achieve such high rank. In addition, another black, Campbell Johnson, was named a special aide to the director of Selective Service.

The third appointment was the most notable, a man that Roosevelt had three years earlier named to the U.S. District Court in the Virgin Islands, making him the first black federal judge: William H. Hastie. Hastie had graduated Phi Beta Kappa from Amherst College in 1925, obtained two degrees from Harvard Law School, and worked as an assistant solicitor in the Department of the Interior before being appointed by Roosevelt to the federal bench in 1937. He left two years later to accept the deanship of Howard University Law School.

Hastie became Civilian Aide to Secretary of War Henry Stimson. His new boss, however, was not happy about the appointment. "Negroes," Stimson wrote in his diary, "are taking advantage of this period just before the election to try to get everything they can." Mrs. Roosevelt's "intrusive and impulsive folly" was responsible. Stimson said he "fully expected" on his next visit to the Navy Department with General Davis "to be met with a colored Admiral."[22]

What the appointments would engender—particularly that of Hastie—would not become clear for at least another year. In the meantime, Randolph and White had another battle on their hands.

EIGHT

Prewar Maneuvers

Freedom's not just
To be won Over there
It means Freedom at home, too—
Now—right here!

—Langston Hughes[1]

Roosevelt's transfer of fifty over-age destroyers to Britain in the summer of 1940 amply demonstrated the president's commitment to supporting her struggle against Germany. The Lend-Lease program that he initiated also made it clear that the United States could not avoid involvement in the war in Europe. American industry began gearing up to make the material needed to fight: ships, tanks, and planes as well as uniforms, parachutes, and tents. The massive retooling and expansion of assembly lines and plant capacity meant that tens of thousands of jobs would soon become available. The nation was coming out of the Depression as the result of a widening world conflict.

With the United States about to embark on what would be the greatest industrial mobilization in history, blacks had high hopes of bettering themselves as a result of the bounty of jobs it would provide. From the outset, though, the question was whether they would be allowed a meaningful share.

At one point before the Japanese attack on Pearl Harbor thrust America into the conflict in December 1941, the U.S. Employment Service asked industries around the country how many new jobs would be available in the coming six months. The total came to

282,245 work openings. But of that total, 144,583 jobs—slightly more than half of them—were barred from the outset to blacks, no matter whether the manufacturers were located in a northern or a southern state, or whether the jobs were considered skilled or unskilled.[2] The manufacturers simply would not consider hiring black workers.

The black press was already filled with stories of discriminatory hiring and training practices. Typical was the reaction of Vultee Air in California, which issued a statement saying "It is not the policy of this company to employ other than of the Caucasian race." A lone young black, with the best grades in his group, was the only one who was refused employment among a hundred trainees sent to work in an aircraft factory outside of Buffalo. Even in New York City, plants seeking skilled workers such as mechanics and tool-and-die makers openly advertised for white applicants only. Ads for porters, janitors, and cleaners were clearly earmarked for "colored" applicants.[3]

The list of plants that refused to employ blacks seemed endless to the executive secretary of the National Urban League, Lester B. Granger. Granger reported that the Curtiss-Wright and Bell aircraft plants in Buffalo did not hire blacks on any production jobs. He quoted a spokesman for Standard Steel of Kansas City, Missouri, as declaring, "We have never had a Negro worker in twenty-five years and don't intend to start now." North American Aircraft in Kansas City said blacks would be hired "only in custodial jobs."

Granger found similar discriminatory practices at Sperry Gyroscope in New York; Pratt and Whitney in Hartford; Budd Manufacturing in Philadelphia; the New York Shipbuilding Corporation in Kearney, New Jersey; the Buick, Chrysler, and Packard auto plants in Detroit and Flint, Michigan; Studebaker and White Motors of Chicago; Bethlehem Shipbuilding of Los Angeles; and both Julius Heil and A. O. Smith of Milwaukee. The same was true for Stewart-Warner, Majestic Radio, "and hundreds of other large manufacturers in every part of the country."[4] The Newport News Shipbuilding Company, a third of whose workforce was black, "refused to train their dark-skinned labor [for] such jobs as machinists."[5] And the reasons —"of infinite variety, often mutually contradictory"—seemed just as endless: the most common, he said, were "Negroes never applied; whites and blacks can't mix on the same job; haven't time or money to build separate toilets; no trained Negroes are available; they are racially unequipped for skilled work; the union won't have them; don't like Negroes and don't want them around; this is a rush job and we haven't time for experiments."[6]

According to the study Granger made, only Illinois and New York were making an effort to induce employers to hire black labor, and those steps were "usually tentative." Overall, he found that by the winter of 1940 the "employment gates of an estimated 75 per cent of defense industry were closed against all Negro labor."[7]

Corporate rigidity was due in no small part to union intransigence. Granger reported that eighteen unions—either independent or members of the American Federation of Labor—"still maintained constitutional or ritualistic restrictions against Negro membership." As early as the turn of the century, the AFL had purposely chosen to bar blacks so as not to contaminate its drive to sign up white workers. Its affiliates either excluded blacks entirely, admitted only a token few, or maintained segregated locals. The most important of them were the powerful Machinists and the Boilermakers, who between them represented about a third of all aircraft frame workers in the nation and more than a fifth of all the shipyard workers. The International Association of Machinists had closed-shop contracts with twelve major aircraft companies that excluded blacks. The Brotherhood of Boilermakers, Iron Shipbuilders and Helpers of America admitted blacks to segregated locals but denied them any voice in union policy.[8] The head organizer for Aeronautical Mechanics Local 751 of the Machinists defended the union's refusal to admit blacks for jobs at the Boeing plant in Seattle, saying, "Organized labor has been called upon to make many sacrifices for defense and has made them gladly, but this is asking too much."[9]

Black leaders were fully cognizant of the obstacles blacks faced for employment. They could not count on Congress taking action, if indeed it would take any, until after the end of the year at the earliest. The Senate had set up a committee under Harry S Truman of Missouri to look into discrimination not only in employment but in vocational training, and into the operation of local draft boards and segregation in the armed services. But Truman informed Walter White that its hearings would take at least six months.

The only recourse black leaders had left was to take their case to the White House, but repeated efforts to send a delegation to meet with the president were ignored. The problem was who had the time and resources to press the issue in Washington. None of the three major black groups seemed in a position to do so.

White's colleagues in the NAACP were already overwhelmed with fighting segregation cases in courts in the South and had neither the staff nor the time to lobby for quicker action. Typical of the time it took to litigate such matters was the case of Democratic Rep. Arthur W. Mitchell of Chicago. Mitchell, who was born in Alabama but had moved to Chicago in 1929, had attended Tuskegee Institute, Columbia University, and Harvard; he was a lawyer and had founded the Armstrong Agricultural School in West Butler, Alabama. In 1939, Mitchell was traveling from Chicago to Hot Springs, Arkansas, aboard a Chicago, Rock Island, and Pacific train. He held a first-class ticket and was sitting in a Pullman car when the train reached the Arkansas state line. A conductor forced him to leave the Pullman car and take, instead, a seat in a "filthy and foul-smelling" second-class car reserved for blacks.[10] Mitchell subsequently complained to the Interstate Commerce Commission, but the ICC dismissed his case on the ground that "because there was comparatively little colored traffic, the lack of equal accommodations was not unjust or undue."[11]

Undaunted, Mitchell pursued his case through the legal system, suing the state of Arkansas over its laws dealing with the segregation of whites and blacks on trains. With help from the NAACP, he appealed the case all the way up to the Supreme Court. Mitchell's determination sent a shockwave of fear through the South. Nine other states with similar laws—Alabama, Florida, Georgia, Kentucky, Louisiana, Mississippi, Tennessee, Texas, and Virginia—joined in preparing a friend-of-court brief to protest the review of Arkansas's Jim Crow laws. They feared that a ruling in Mitchell's favor would spread to other areas of segregation, affecting street cars, theaters, hotels, restaurants, and schools. "Such statutes," their joint brief read, "were enacted for the purpose of promoting the welfare, comfort, peace and safety of the people of both races."[12]

On April 28, 1941, some four years after the incident on the train took place, the Court ruled unanimously in Mitchell's favor, but its finding was limited to rail travel and upheld the "separate but equal" concept. Chief Justice Charles Evans Hughes, who wrote the decision, said that Mitchell's removal to a second-class car was a "palpably unjust" discrimination. "Colored persons who buy first-class tickets must be furnished with accommodations equal in comforts and conveniences to those afforded to first-class white passengers."[13]

Because he was a congressman, a case such as Mitchell's won headlines in newspapers around the country, but there were scores of others over the years—the appeals of convictions of blacks by all-white juries, attempts to bring lynching mobs to justice, peonage-like labor conditions—that went unheralded. "We had more work than we could handle," one attorney who worked for the NAACP at the time recalls. In addition, there was always the threat of violence. "Down below, you feared for your life."[14]

Overwhelmed, the NAACP was unable to take up every cause. Neither was either of the other two major black groups. Lester Granger's own National Urban League was basically a social service agency. Its main purpose was to work for health, social, and industrial improvements. It was not geared to take on political causes. That goal might have been taken up by the National Negro Congress, but its influence had waned since its founding in 1936 as it was gradually taken over by the Communist Party. The party, which tried to forge a beachhead in the Harlem community, never attracted any more than an estimated two hundred blacks at any one time,[15] though it was quick to take up black causes.

The vacuum was filled by A. Philip Randolph. Early in June 1941, as it became clear that the increase in jobs was, for all intents and purposes, virtually a whites-only bonanza, he called on blacks to participate in a March on Washington as an attention-getting protest against discrimination. It was a ploy that Randolph knew would bring the issue to a head. The demonstration, he said, would take place on Tuesday, July 1. Randolph even leveled a direct challenge to Roosevelt. About three weeks beforehand, Randolph wrote the president, asking him to address "a throng of 100,000 Negroes" from the steps of the Lincoln Memorial.[16]

Walter White of the NAACP, for one, thought that Randolph's estimate of the expected number of marchers was highly inflated and represented a clever ploy on his part. Whether such a massive turn-out would have resulted is speculative, but there was evidence that the total would be impressive. Randolph had quickly set up an organization with branches in eighteen cities. Special trains were already chartered to carry blacks to Washington from Chicago, Memphis, and Cleveland.

Randolph must have sensed that the march created a dilemma for the president. If Roosevelt permitted such a large, vocal demonstration to take place in Washington—where Jim Crow discrimination was openly practiced—it might lead to violence in the capital's streets and make a mockery of his appeals for national unity at a time of looming crisis. He would also incur the wrath of southern congressmen whose support he needed. On the other hand, if Roosevelt blocked the rally, his support among the nation's blacks would diminish considerably, and so many had moved north and registered as voters that they had already become a major factor in elections in several states.

There is some discrepancy as to who initiated what. One story has it that Eleanor Roosevelt appealed to Randolph directly to call off the march, telling him that she had spoken to the president but that, unfortunately, "one must face situations as they are and not as one wishes them to be." Persuasion, not coercion, was the answer, she believed. Industrialists could be appealed to. But Randolph was adamant. Nothing, he answered, had "gripped" black hearts more "than the girding of our country for national defense without according them the recognition and opportunity as citizens, consumers and workers they felt justified in expecting." It was at that point, so the story goes, that Roosevelt asked Aubrey Williams, the head of the National Youth Administration, to go to New York to get Randolph and White to cancel the rally. His wife was already in the city. "Get the missus and Fiorello and Anna [Rosenberg, regional director of the city's Social Security Board] and get it stopped."[17]

According to White, when word of the march reached Fiorello La Guardia of New York, the mayor immediately asked him and Randolph to a meeting at City Hall on Friday, June 13. When they showed up, they found that La Guardia had also invited several others to the gathering, including one unexpected guest, the president's wife.

However it happened, the president was clearly counting on her reputation as a champion of minority causes and La Guardia's friendship with White—the two men often met socially—to convince Randolph that the march would be self-defeating. The president's argument was that the purpose of the protest would backfire if violence erupted.[18] Mrs. Roosevelt hammered home that point, saying that she was especially worried about the reaction of Washington's police force, most of whom, she noted, were southerners. That fact "and the general feeling of Washington itself," she told them, "are such that I fear that there may be trouble if the march occurs."

But, White said, the march was the only alternative possible. Their repeated requests to meet with the president about "the steadily worsening conditions" had been spurned.[19] As White's colleague, Roy Wilkins, put it, White was too clever a politician to let the Roosevelts know that he could not talk Randolph out of the march. What he was seeking was a chance to meet face-to-face with the president at the White House.[20]

Which is what happened. After hearing White and Randolph out, Mrs. Roosevelt said she understood their point of view and promised to get in touch with her husband "immediately" because, she told the black men, "I think you are right."[21]

The conference with Roosevelt took place on Wednesday, June 18, 1941, with the scheduled march only two weeks away. Among those present in the Oval Office, besides Randolph, White, and La Guardia, were Williams; Rosenberg; two members of the Office of Production Management, Sidney Hillman and William S. Knudsen, who formerly headed the General Motors Corporation; and two men who had attended the conference with Randolph and White a year earlier that led to the executive order against discrimination in the armed forces, Assistant Secretary of War Robert P. Patterson and Secretary of the Navy Frank Knox.

With both Patterson and Knox present, White took the occasion to stress first the problems that blacks were encountering in trying to enlist and serve in the military. Both the army and navy, he pointed out, were "handicapped with inefficient and prejudiced Southern officers in the higher ranks," a circumstance that had developed because many of the southerners, who lacked "energy and ambition, stayed in the Army, where they found a ready-made career." The southerners, he continued, represented more than half of the top-ranking posts, the majority of whom "were neither able nor racially democratic in spirit or attitude."

Patterson acknowledged that what White said was true in the

army. Knox went further; he said that the estimate was "far too low for the Navy." Knox promised to look into the situation, though both White and Randolph got the "distinct conviction" that Knox "had no real interest" in correcting it.[22]

The president then asked Randolph what he wanted him to do. Randolph said that he wanted Roosevelt to issue an executive order mandating that blacks be allowed to work in defense plants.

He could not do that, the president responded. Indeed, he could not do anything unless the March on Washington was called off. "What would happen if Irish and Jewish people were to march on Washington?" Roosevelt asked. "It would create resentment among the American people because such a march would be considered as an effort to coerce the government and make it do certain things."

But Randolph refused to budge. He could not call off the march, he said. Roosevelt asked how many blacks Randolph expected. "One hundred thousand, Mr. President," the black leader answered.[23]

Was it possible that that many blacks would assemble in Washington, march to the Lincoln Memorial, hear speeches denouncing American democracy? Skeptical, Roosevelt turned to White and asked how many blacks would really march. Without hesitation, White echoed Randolph's figure. The president stared White in the eyes for a long time, then finally said to the two black men, "What do you want me to do?"

At this point, La Guardia chimed in, suggesting that everyone try to reach a settlement. The president agreed. He asked the blacks to retire to the Cabinet Room with La Guardia and the others and try to draft an executive order. Like the Roosevelts, Knudsen believed that an executive order was unnecessary, that "persuasion and education" were the answer. As for Stimson, the meeting was an annoyance, just "one of those rather harassing interruptions with the main business with which the Secretary of War ought to be engaged— namely in preparing the Army for defense."[24]

In the days following the White House meeting, Roosevelt made a last-ditch effort to dissuade Randolph from going ahead with the March on Washington without the promise of an order. He asked La Guardia to speak to the black leader again, but Randolph was adamant.[25]

On June 25, 1941, a reluctant Franklin Delano Roosevelt signed

Executive Order No. 8802. It stated unequivocally that "there shall be no discrimination in the employment of workers in defense industries or government because of race, creed, color, or national origin." All federal departments and agencies were to take "special measures to assure" that vocational and training programs were "administered without prejudice." Moreover, all government defense contracts were to be negotiated to include a provision "obligating the contractor not to discriminate." To help ensure that there would be no discrimination, the order established a five-member Fair Employment Practice Committee (FEPC) to "investigate complaints" and to "take appropriate steps to redress grievances which it finds to be valid."[26]

For his part, Randolph called off the protest. Roy Wilkins wondered if Randolph could have enlisted "enough marchers to make his point stick." As Wilkins knew, Walter White always "suspected" that Randolph "was bluffing, but what a bluff it was."[27]

The president's action was seemingly an impressive acknowledgement of minority rights to employment, and a personal triumph for Randolph, who hailed the order as a "second" Emancipation Proclamation. The *Amsterdam News* called it "epochal to say the least."[28] But a number of other blacks were skeptical about its efficacy. Roosevelt obviously had to downplay the order if he was to maintain any influence with southern congressmen, who were upset at what they considered a surrender to liberal interests. Some interpreted the president's attitude as feeling that the order was unimportant. Roosevelt, George Breitman said, "apparently" believed that the order was so insignificant that it was not worthy of comment. Writing in the Socialist Workers Party's newspaper, the *Militant*, Breitman—who was later the party's candidate in New Jersey for the Senate—noted that the document referred "only to 'defense' industries" and made no mention whatsoever about the armed forces or even federal departments.[29] Moreover, as Breitman was quick to point out, Roosevelt, who had become famous for his "fireside chat" broadcasts to the nation, "didn't speak about it over the radio; you won't see him reading the order in the newsreels; he didn't even hold a press conference on the matter, as he does on almost everything else, small or big."[30]

The White House's efforts to minimize the importance of the order was also evident in the comment made by Mark Ethridge, a southern white liberal who was named to the FEPC. It was "perfectly apparent," he said, that the order "is a war order and not a social document." Ethridge declared that there was "no power in the world —not even in all the mechanized armies of the earth, Allied or Axis —which could force the Southern white people to the abandonment of the principle of social segregation."[31]

Conservative white reaction was stronger. Gov. Frank M. Dixon of Alabama rejected a War Production Board contract for the cotton mills operated by the state's prison system on the ground that it was a "federal attempt to abolish segregation of races in the South." The black weekly *Pittsburgh Courier* quoted Hamner Cobbs, editor of the Greensboro (Alabama) Watchman, as saying that "90 percent of the white people of the South are in accord over the present system, and that's all we need to know." Cobbs raised the specter of a backlash against blacks in the South comparable to the one that occurred after the Reconstruction Period of the 1870s: "The night riders will be out again. There will be hangings, shootings, burnings."[32]

It soon became clear that Executive Order 8802 was ineffective. The FEPC had no teeth. It could investigate complaints, issue findings, and hope to reform union and corporate policies. But without enforcement powers, it could not compel manufacturers to hire blacks, or train them, or promote them; nor could it force unions to end their restrictive policies.

The FEPC's flaws became dramatically clear in its investigation of the railroad industry. Of thirty-one national unions that discriminated against blacks either by rules or practice, nineteen were railway brotherhoods. The so-called Big Four unions—the Brotherhoods of Railroad Trainmen, Locomotive Engineers, and Locomotive Firemen and Enginemen, and the Order of Railway Conductors—were the most notorious. Black train porters did braking work in addition to sweeping the coaches and handling the mail, baggage, and all passenger needs, yet were paid only half a brakeman's salary. On Pullman cars, where blacks often performed all the duties of conductors, they were categorized as "porter-in-charge" and paid a porter's wage. In dining cars, a black sometimes served as steward but was called "waiter-in-charge" and never received a steward's pay. "The only difference," said one black civil rights advocate, "was that the steward had a white face and black coat, while the waiter-in-charge had a black face and a white coat."[33]

In 1941, twenty railroads and seven unions in southeastern states joined in a secret agreement to exclude blacks. The FEPC learned about the compact and issued a directive saying they must cease discrimination. Its chairman, Malcolm Ross, said that testimony showed a sharp decline in blacks employed by railroads in all but the lowest categories during the past twenty years.[34] Four of the railroads complied. All the rest, and all the unions, ignored the order.[35]

The reality was that, for all that Randolph accomplished, Executive Order 8802 never lived up to its high-minded goals. Blacks would never participate in the nation's war effort on the same level as whites.

In mid-November 1941, within a few weeks of America's entry into the conflicts raging in the Pacific and Europe, the regents of the Daughters of the American Revolution, whose Washington chapter had kept Marian Anderson from appearing in Constitution Hall, entertained an unusual guest speaker at a meeting in the Waldorf-Astoria Hotel in New York City. She was Mary McLeod Bethune, president of Bethune-Cookman College in Daytona Beach, Florida, and head of the National Council of Negro Women.

Blacks, the doughty Mrs. Bethune said, believe the fight against fascism is their fight, too, that "for America it must be all-out or it is all over." They also realize that they would be worse off under Hitler, but, she continued, "we're not blind to the fact that the doors of democratic opportunity are not opened very wide to us." America, she added, had the "dual task of defeating Hitler abroad and Hitlerism at home."[36]

That same week, the *New York Times* published a long, impassioned plea from writer Pearl Buck. Her words were ominous for the future and global in impact.

Buck, who had been awarded the 1938 Nobel Prize for Literature, declared that the reason why blacks were compelled to live in ghettos was "the segregation to which race prejudice compels." Such prejudice, she said, "compels" blacks to "take what work they can get, . . . makes and keeps Negroes' wages low, . . . [and] alone is the root of the plight of people in greater and lesser Harlems all over our country." As a result, Buck continued, blacks throughout America are coming to a "very serious conviction":

They are coming to see that what they have been taught and have believed is not true—namely, that if colored people can be patient and good and show themselves obedient and humble they will inevitably prove themselves worthy citizens and will therefore receive the rewards of full citizenship. They are beginning to believe . . . that individual and even collective worth as human beings gains them nothing so long as they are Negroes. The hopelessness natural to their race is now changing to despair. Collored leaders are saying today that no amount of achievement will gain anything for the colored people as a whole, and that, moreover, they no longer believe the people of the United States will fight for democracy. . . .

When hope is taken away from a people more degeneration follows swiftly after. Young colored men and women today are giving up hope of justice or security in their own country. When this hopelessness reaches down to a certain strata in any society, outbreaks of crime are inevitable. We must expect it in many places besides Harlem.

Buck, whose ancestors were all southerners, wrote that she was familiar with race problems in the South, though, she said, she did not believe "in the familiar pattern, that the Negro is a childish creature, delightful enough in his place, who only wants to be taken care of and fed and sheltered and treated kindly." But, Buck went on, if the United States "is to include subject and ruler peoples, than let us be honest about it and change the Constitution and make it plain that Negroes cannot share the privileges of the white people." Only then, she added, will white Americans "be relieved of the necessity of hypocrisy and the colored people will know where they are. . . . With all the evils that Hitlerism has[,] at least it has one virtue, that it makes no pretense of loving its fellow-man and of wanting all people to be free and equal."

Buck said that it was critical to face up to the situation that existed between whites and blacks. She warned that

it is upon this rock that our own ship of democracy may go down first, and upon this rock, too, that all peoples may divide into the ultimate enmity. Everywhere in the world the colored peoples are asking each other if they must forever endure the arrogant ruling white race. . . . There is a deep, subtle, dangerous relationship between them. We are foolish if we do not realize it.

The hopelessness of educated black Americans, Buck said, "results not in simple crime but in a rejection of patriotism." And, she added, "until race prejudice is conquered and its effects removed, the bitter fact remains that the colored American knows he will not get a better job for being better educated and better housed or for having in his childhood more playgrounds." Prejudice "will still deny democracy to him."[37]

As urgent as Buck meant her words to be, they were drowned by the sounds of the approaching war. America had something else on its collective mind.

NINE

Priorities

The black has no rights which will be respected unless the black man forces that respect.

—A. Philip Randolph[1]

A black, a half century ago, must have felt that living in the United States was like riding a rollercoaster, if the pages of the newspapers he read are any indication. There was always good news, and there was always bad news. Ups and downs. Continually.

Often, the good news might appear trivial to a white reader—the selection of the first Harlem man to be foreman of a New York County grand jury[2] or the summoning of the first black women to jury duty in the Fifth Judicial District Court in New Jersey,[3] both of which occurred in 1941—but to blacks they were evidence of some advance in their status, some reason for optimism, some hope that perhaps times *were* getting better.

But with the good news invariably came the bad news, and more often than not it outweighed the good: reports of lynchings in the South, increasing incidents at army camps, discriminatory hiring practices, Jim Crow treatment aboard trains and buses. To be a black then was to experience a constant flux of emotions.

A sampling of the news stories that filled black publications reads almost like a checklist of grievances. A national society of barbershop quartets banned four blacks who won the New York City championship from competing in country-wide finals in St. Louis in the summer of 1941 because many of its members and chapters "are in the South, where the race question is rather a touchy subject."[4] In the same summer, the Missouri Supreme Court affirmed a lower court decision denying Lucille Bluford, managing editor of a black newspaper, the *Kansas City Call*, admission to the University of Missouri School of Journalism.[5] That fall, even mainstream white newspapers reported how blacks attending the first convention of the Illinois Congress of Industrial Organizations in Springfield were turned away from hotels and restaurants. "Delegates were chagrined," the *New York Times* said, "that these incidents occurred in a city which is associated so closely with the life of Abraham Lincoln and is the site of his tomb."[6]

Frequent letters and reports from military camps kept blacks continually aware of segregation in the armed services. An anonymous enlisted man complained to the NAACP's *Crisis* in 1940 that at his camp in the Northwest a black soldier was restricted to only one row of seats in the base theater and "is treated as if he isn't wanted" at the library and post exchange.[7] The following fall, the Socialist Workers Party's newspaper *Militant* reported that sixty members of the Ninety-fourth Engineer Battalion were marching along a highway near Camp Robinson, Arkansas, when they were forced to walk in a ditch in knee-high water by state troopers who told their white officer to "get those niggers off the highway."[8]

At times, the reports from military bases depicted an ugly and violent incident. In August 1941 the *Militant* told the story of Pvt. Ned Turman. He was sitting near the front of a bus in Fayetteville, North Carolina, when military policemen appeared. The MPs beat a companion soldier over the head with clubs. When Turman said the man needed medical attention, he was struck on the shoulder. Turman threw up his hands to ward off the blow—an "unpardonable" act in the South, where, the *Militant* article said, "crackers don't like Negroes to lift their hands to a white man, even in self-defense." Other MPs struck Turman, who broke away, pulled out a revolver and started shooting. He wounded two MPs, one of them fatally, before he was shot dead. That night, all five thousand black troops at nearby Fort Bragg were "rounded up, cursed, beaten, and driven by MPs armed with sawed-off shotguns out of the camp to another nine miles away."[9]

The Saturday after Japanese planes bombed Pearl Harbor, the New York weekly *Amsterdam News* carried column after column of articles related to America's entry into World War II and the response of patriotic Harlemites to the crisis. As usual, the plethora of articles was both positive and negative.[10]

On the positive side, there was the front-page story quoting Chief of Staff Gen. George C. Marshall as saying that an entire black division would be formed in the spring of 1942 at Fort Huachuca, Arizona. At the same time, Gen. Benjamin O. Davis, Sr., reported, after an inspection tour of eight army installations in the East and the South, that much of the unrest and dissatisfaction black recruits had first experienced seemed to have subsided.

Congressman Arthur W. Mitchell of Chicago, who had won his fight for equal treatment aboard trains, told the House of Representatives that "the Negro proposes to give and will give all he has, including his life, for the success of our effort to withstand Hitlerism." Mitchell vowed that fifteen million blacks were ready to make sacrifices to win the war.

The navy recruiting office in downtown Manhattan, another page one story read, was being swamped by young black men and boys eager to join up. An accompanying article, headlined "Suicide Squadron Being Organized by Harlemites," reported that a group of black doctors was joining together for the purpose of going anywhere in the world to face any danger in defending the country. "America is faced with bullets and bombs right now," its organizer was quoted as saying, "and there's no discrimination when it comes to that."

A front-page editorial declared: "America is at war. This is no time for superficial distinctions based upon skin-color. This is no time for subversive race prejudice. We will show those Japs and Nazis that as one nation indivisible, we fight the battle for democracy. We fight to win!"

There was, however, a flip side to the stories. In the same article announcing the formation of an all-black division, a colonel attached to the Adjutant General's office felt constrained to explain, as the reporter put it, that the army would, however, remain segregated. "The army is not a sociological laboratory," the officer said. "It operates on the broad principles evolved through years relating to all persons in the service."

The story about the navy recruitment office quoted a naval officer as saying, "We have an unlimited quota for enlistment of colored men," and then adding, "but they are being enlisted only in the Messman branch at this time."

The headlines of numerous other stories throughout the newspaper drummed home the problems and difficulties blacks continued to face:

"Police Terror in Harlem"—a front-page account of incidents involving blacks and policemen included the fatal shooting of an unarmed man during an alleged burglary, and the arrest and beating of a teachers' union official who was picketing in front of the mayor's home.

"Admiral Byrd Bitterly Assails Discrimination in Defense Employment"—the noted Antarctic explorer warned, in a radio broadcast over NBC, that discrimination in war industries was "the negation of the American tradition of liberty and equality."

"Senator Glass Asked to Include Ban on Bias"—the National Negro Congress announced that it would try to seek the support of the chairman of the Appropriations Committee, a Virginian, to include an antidiscrimination amendment in a defense bill.

"Draughtsman Is Refused Post"—a black engineering draftsman who had applied for a job at the Boeing Aircraft Company in Seattle was rejected because, the company said, it "has no place for Negro workers."

"Railroad Moves to Replace Pickup Drivers by Whites"—the merged Louisiana and Arkansas Railway-Kansas City Southern Railway Company threatened to cancel its contract with a New Orleans trucking firm unless black drivers were replaced by whites within thirty days.

The caption under a photograph of a Harlem milliner and the secretary to the Theresa Hotel's manager described how the two women had literally held onto their seats when confronted by conductors and police officials who tried to make them move into a "jim-crow coach" while traveling to Charleston, South Carolina.

Another photograph pictured a couple whose two-year-old daughter died in St. John's Hospital in Brooklyn three hours after the child had been left there to have her tonsils removed. The local chapter of the NAACP was looking into the case.

"Gene Wallops Jim Crowism"—Band leader Gene Krupa cancelled a southern tour because he was told that his featured trumpet player, Roy Eldridge, would have to be replaced by a white musician. The story noted that Artie Shaw had earlier refused to have his band fill thirty dates in the South when he learned that lead trumpeter and vocalist, "Hot Lips" Paige, would have to be left behind. An accompanying article noted that Charlie Barnet—the "white Ellington"—had Harlem favorite Cootie Williams sit in with his brass section on a recent radio program.

The *Amsterdam News*'s "guest editorial" that week was a reprint of an editorial from the *Baltimore Sun* that quoted Georgia Gov. Eugene Talmadge's reaction to the conviction of six men who were charged with twenty-three instances of flogging blacks, one of whom died. "Good people," said Talmadge, "can get mixed up in things like that." The *Sun*'s editors declared: "That may be true in Georgia and Germany but if so it is an indication that Georgia's civilization is only skin-deep."

By J. Edgar Hoover's standards, the *Amsterdam News* was "comparatively conservative" and one of only seven black newspapers about which the Federal Bureau of Investigation, which he headed, did not complain. There were 155 black weeklies in 1940 and a number of them—the *Amsterdam News*, the *Baltimore Afro-American*, the *Chicago Defender*, the *Norfolk (Virginia) Journal and Guide*, and the *Pittsburgh Courier*—appeared in every section of the country.[11] They accounted for nearly half of the circulation of more than 1.6 million readers that the black press enjoyed.[12] Unlike white papers, the major financial support of black newspapers came from circulation, their readers, rather than from advertisements taken by businesses and stores. As a result, as Walter White observed, they "of necessity remained more responsive" to their readers' wishes.[13]

Ever since 1919, when the FBI was born as the General Intelligence Division of the Justice Department and Hoover was named as its first director, he had waged a campaign to attack the black press. He tried to indict as subversive numerous black newspapers such as the *Militant* as well as journals such as the *Crisis*. To his mind, the preponderance of negative articles and editorials—whether stories dealing with instances of discrimination or editorials criticizing government policies—was proof that the black press was not just troublesome or radical, but un-American. He believed that the press between the two world wars had played into communist hands, or had been outright supporters of communism. Even after the Soviet Union became an ally in World War II, Hoover raised the menace of communist influence and infiltration.

As early as 1940, growing criticism of racial injustices and discrimination in the armed services prompted Hoover to send FBI agents to visit the offices of the country's largest black newspaper, the *Courier*. The Pittsburgh paper had been carrying a series of articles dealing with the attempts of blacks to vote in the South. The agents complained to several writers that the articles were "holding America up to ridicule."[14]

The truth was that black newspaper reporters could be as irresponsible as their white colleagues. Stories frequently went unchecked, and too often no attempt was made to give both sides of a story. The black version of an incident was the only one related. Blacks were rarely pictured as instigating confrontations when the police, military authorities, or whites were involved; instead, they were depicted as innocent bystanders, or the target and victims of white hate no matter what the circumstances might be. Walter White realized that too many of the black publications "insufficiently corroborated stories, and sometimes printed rumor for truth," using "flamboyant headlines."[15]

Some observers went further than White, criticizing the interpretation of news in the black press as being slanted. Virginius Dabney, the respected liberal editor of the *Richmond Times-Dispatch*, held black publications responsible for virtually all the friction that existed between whites and blacks.[16] However, other white journalists defended the black press, in the realization that it reported news that the white press either ignored or to which it devoted little space. In a lengthy article published in his magazine, Thomas Sancton, managing editor of the *New Republic*, declared:

> When a nineteen-year-old gets a Ph.D. from Chicago, they are proud of him and want the details; when the body of a Negro soldier, hands tied, is found hanging from a tree at Fort Benning, they are enraged; when the first Negro captain of an American freighter takes her through the submarines, they want to know; when a radio show reveals a Negro in the character of a self-respecting human being, they want to thank the director; when the President's valet

goes into the navy they want a bigger story than The New York Times or The Richmond Times-Dispatch can give them; when young Lt. Maria August, RN, of Atlanta, arrives in North Africa with thirty white nurses, they want to know; when William Thaddeus Coleman, brilliant Harvard law student, goes into the army they want to read about it. All these things affect them in their personal feelings as Negroes, and make them furious or proud. Why? Because they are a Jim-Crowed minority who, brought here long ago against their wishes, have never been allowed to feel that they were just the same as other Americans.

Sancton acknowledged that the "fundamental weakness of the Negro press is its strong tendency to overcompensate." But the reason for that, he said, was that the white press slighted reports of black achievements. Nevertheless, he continued:

Negro writers, over and over, in all possible variations, with a variety of tones and shadings, with none of the ambiguous and deceitful language by which hard facts are softened in the white press, tell the Negro exactly what the white man is doing to him. It is not a bad thing for a white man to see how he looks through Negro eyes, and it is even better for him to try to understand why it is so.[17]

Roy Wilkins happened to arrive in Washington on Sunday, December 7, 1941, to find the capital in shock over the Japanese attack on Pearl Harbor. He had gone there as a representative of the *Crisis* to attend a conference of twenty black editors and newspapermen, scheduled for the next day, on how black manpower could be best used if America got involved in the war. Wilkins, for one, was concerned because for the past two years "everything that had been done in the way of national defense indicated that Negroes would be subjected to the shabby treatment they had received during World War I."[18]

The meeting went off as scheduled, Wilkins said, with the War Department wanting "us to buy the idea that a little cheerleading was all it would take to keep black men in fighting trim." When "more timid editors" said segregation was a factor that "worked against the effective use of black leaders," the government officials said nothing could be done about it. Together with the editor of the *Chicago Whip* and a representative of the Negro Associated Press, Wilkins argued that "morale would be rotten" as long as segregation existed—"it was as deadly as nerve gas. Jim Crow had to go."[19] Wilkins despaired:

> Here we were about to fight a war against racial bigotry and barbarism, to depend heavily on nations of color elsewhere, yet, the War Department proposed to shame our own black soldiers. Once drafted, they were to wait months for induction, ostensibly because the government had not had enough time to build Jim Crow facilities for them. At training camps they would find themselves set apart from their white comrades-in-arms. There would be separate buses for them, separate counters for cigarettes and candy, separate movie theaters on base, and a Jim Crow roost in the theaters in town.[20]

Hoover's campaign against black newspapers continued unabated after Pearl Harbor, fueled in part by fears that existed well into 1942 over whether the United States could win the war. In a matter of months after Pearl Harbor, as Japanese forces swept through the Pacific, the Philippines fell. In Europe, German troops were on the offensive in North Africa and Russia. The outlook on both fronts was bleak. However, unswerved by anxieties about the progress of the war, the black press never silenced its criticisms. Hoover believed it was feeding German and Japanese propaganda, to the detriment of the nation's commitment.

There was some justification for Hoover's concern. During World War I, the Germans made attempts to win over blacks by telling them that in Germany they were equal to whites and that, if Germany won, blacks the world over would be equal to all whites.[21] Nazi propaganda was now preying on white and black fears—white fears that blacks would rape their womenfolk or, given guns, would turn on their white leaders, and black fears that white domination would be assured by an Allied victory. Roi Ottley, who had worked for the *Amsterdam News* and was later a war correspondent, quoted Hitler as saying, "Negroes must be definitely third-class people to allow the whites to lynch them, beat them, segregate them, without rising against their oppressors!"[22]

The Japanese took an altogether different tack, one that gained some acceptance in the black community. The Japanese, Ottley noted, were trying to persuade the "darker millions of the world that Japan is fighting a war to liberate oppressed colored peoples."[23] He quoted an *Afro-American* reporter as telling the president's wife that he had attended meetings "where Japanese victories were slyly praised and American defeats at Bataan and Corregidor brought amused and knowing snickers."[24] Ottley noted that there was "little active anti-Japanese feeling prevalent in the Negro community . . . no letters-to-the-editor condemning Japanese treachery and few editorials castigating the Japanese foe."[25]

Ottley's assessment was supported by two events that took place in Harlem—a meeting of seventy black leaders representing eighteen black organizations held a month after the Japanese attack on Pearl Harbor, and an astonishing survey taken in Harlem three months later. Blacks at the meeting, which had been called by the NAACP and the National Urban League, adopted, with only six delegates dissenting, a resolution drafted by William H. Hastie that declared that American blacks were not "wholeheartedly, unselfishly, all-out in support of the present war effort."[26]

Such a statement was not a surprise, at least not to blacks. Many viewed as hypocritical the Four Freedoms that Roosevelt had enunciated in his annual message to Congress in January 1941. Harlem resident Ellen Tarry said blacks were angry: "Wherever there was a gathering of Negroes there was bound to be hostile talk, which they considered righteous indignation."[27] Roy Wilkins declared:

> Negroes did not need us at the N.A.A.C.P. to tell them that it sounded pretty foolish to be against park benches marked JUDE in Berlin, but to be *for* park benches marked COLORED in Tallahassee, Florida. It was grim, not foolish, to have a young black man in uniform get an orientation in the morning on wiping out Nazi bigotry and that same evening be told he could buy a soft drink only in the 'colored' post exchange.[28]

The survey made in the spring of 1942 reinforced the statements of black leaders. Members of the Office of Facts and Figures—forerunner of the Office of War Information—interviewed 1,008 blacks and 501 whites in New York City in the spring of 1942. The results of its report, *The Negro Looks at the War: Attitudes of New York Negroes Toward Discrimination Against Negroes,* were shocking. In general, predictably, the whites interviewed overwhelmingly supported America's war aims. Nine out of ten of them believed that it was more important to beat Germany and Japan than to make democracy work at home. Almost two of every three whites thought that blacks had as good a chance as whites to get defense jobs, and the same ratio of whites held that blacks would be treated better if the United States won.[29]

The response of the blacks interviewed was strikingly different. Some of the blacks had been questioned by white interviewers, some by black interviewers. Invariably, those interviewed by whites tempered their answers, tending, the report said, "to take the middle ground or to answer 'Don't Know.'" Despite such hedging, the overall result was damning. One in seven blacks felt they were "worse off now" than before the war started. Almost half the blacks said America's prime concern should be making democracy work at home rather than defeating Germany or Japan. Two out of three thought a black's chances of getting defense work were not as good as a white's chances, and about one in two believed labor unions to be unfair. Similarly, about half the blacks thought the army was unfair, while about two-thirds labeled the navy as unfair.[30]

By and large, both blacks and whites expressed the opinion that America would eventually win the war, though blacks expected the war to last longer. But although both groups saw no advantage for blacks if Germany won the war, an alarming 18 percent of the blacks interviewed by blacks—nearly one in every five blacks in the survey—thought that they would be treated better than they were currently being treated if Japan won. Most of them, the report said, gave their reason as: "The Japanese are colored and would not discriminate against dark people."[31]

The authors of the report tried to determine the reason for the attitudes of the blacks who were questioned. They found that most blacks listened to the same radio stations and read the same newspapers that whites did, specifically the *New York Daily News*, which had an antiadministration bias. The authors concluded, however, that the real difference in attitudes was probably due to the influence of the black press. The overwhelming majority of blacks—more than eight out of ten—read some black newspaper, usually either the *Amsterdam News* or a more militant weekly that Adam Clayton Powell, Jr., had begun publishing in February 1942, the *People's Voice*.[32]

Lack of patriotism was not the issue. *Life* reported that there was "no place" in the country where civil defense was "a more burning topic than in Harlem." At least a quarter of its residents, the magazine said, were "doing some kind of war work." About fifteen thousand of them were enrolled as air-raid wardens, and thousands of women were "learning first aid, knitting sweaters, serving in canteens, studying internal-combustion engines."[33] But there was a downside, too. *Nation* magazine noted that the people of Harlem "have asked the question, 'What will the war bring us?' The answer as most of them see it, is 'Nothing.' They still want the United States to win but only casually. They are for the United Nations as a matter of form but their hearts aren't in it."[34] Playwright Loften Mitchell said, "Irritated black people argued that when colored Ethiopia was attacked, Uncle Sam hadn't raced to her defense, but when white Europe was in trouble, Uncle was right there."[35]

Another poll taken five months later by the *Pittsburgh Courier* underscored the fact that the results of the government survey were not an aberration but were widely and universally echoed. Asked whether blacks should "soft-pedal" their demands for "complete freedom and citizenship," more than 80 percent of the respondents answered in the negative. Similarly, when asked whether they had been "convinced" that statements by "national leaders" about "freedom and equality for all peoples" included American blacks, the response was just as impressively negative.[36]

A number of persons, congressmen and government officials, believed Japanese sympathizers were taking advantage of any wedge between blacks and whites. John E. Rankin of Mississippi thought "Japanese fifth columnists" were "behind this drive to try to stir up trouble between the whites and Negroes here in Washington by trying to force Negroes into hotels, restaurants, picture shows, and other public places." Speaking in the House of Representatives, Rankin declared, "The white people of the South who have always been the Negroes' best friends . . . will have no trouble with the colored race if these fifth columnists and the flannel-mouthed agitators throughout the country will let them alone."[37]

Hoover fully appreciated that blacks were responding to Japanese propaganda even before the study of black attitudes in Harlem. He sought an indictment under the Espionage Act against the *Afro-American* chain of five East Coast papers when, shortly after Pearl Harbor, they printed a story that contained the comments of Richmond, Virginia, blacks about what they felt Japan's attitude would be toward blacks if it won the war. "The colored races as a whole would benefit," said one of them. "This would be the first step in the darker races coming back into their own."[38]

Hoover only had one success. In December 1942 four Harlem residents who were members of the Ethopian Pacific Movement, a pro-Japanese organization, were indicted. They were the first blacks to be convicted in the nearly 150 years since the Alien and Sedition Acts had been enacted.[39]

Hoover continued to try to control the black press at every turn. He was incensed when the Oklahoma City *Black Dispatch* complained about black soldiers riding in trains for twenty-hours without being fed. When they did eat, the paper reported, it was in "dirty, filthy, Jim Crow" kitchens in the rear of white restaurants.[40] Critical stories like that prompted Hooever to try to get Postmaster General Frank Walter to cancel the second-class mailing privileges of black newspapers. But Walter refused to take any retaliatory measures. However, at Hoover's request, Attorney General Francis Biddle, who ordinarily was sympathetic to blacks, asked the editors of several leading black newspapers to a conference in Washington. When they showed up, issues of numerous papers—among them the *Courier*, the *Afro-American* and the Chicago *Defender*—were laid out on a table. Each contained stories about clashes between black soldiers and whites in April 1942 at Fort Dix, New Jersey, and Tuskegee, Alabama, that left three people dead and others injured. Such articles, Biddle said, were a disservice to the war effort, and if they were not discontinued he was "going to shut them all up" for being seditious.[41]

Biddle never did carry out his threat. Indeed, in a speech in Philadelphia on February 12, 1943, he acknowledged that black newspapers "throughout the country, although they very properly protest, and passionately, against the wrongs done to members of their race, are loyal to their government and are all out for the war."[42]

But other government officials, including Hoover, kept up the pressure. Poet Archibald MacLeish, who left his post as Librarian of Congress to head the Office of War Information, asked black editors to lay off the racial issue at least for the duration of the war.[43] G-2—the Army Intelligence Section—suggested on more than one occasion that certain black papers and journals be banned from army posts; though no such official policy was ever adopted, some base commanders took it upon themselves to have black papers confiscated.[44] Army censors were successful in stifling news of racial problems at bases at home and abroad. The *Baltimore Afro-American* saw little point in having its war correspondents remain in Britain because, it charged, only "sweet stories" were being approved.[45]

At one point in the war, the president took Walter White aside after a White House conference to say that the Justice Department was being pressured to indict editors of the black newspapers for sedition and "interference with the war effort." Roosevelt had also been urged to deny newsprint to them. White told him that abolishing segregation in the armed forces and ending discrimination in war industries "would transform these papers from critics of the war effort into enthusiastic supporters."

White did, however, feel compelled to ask the editors of twenty-four of the largest black papers to meet with him at the NAACP's office in New York in late January 1943. White offered to have the NAACP's Washington bureau check out any story or statement issued by the government. As a result of the meeting, the Negro Newspaper Publishers Association was formed and adopted a code of ethics to curb sensationalism.[46] Nevertheless, that September, the FBI singled out forty-three black newspapers in a 714-page "Survey of Racial Conditions in the United States." All the papers had caused discontent, the report said, and thirteen of the forty-three had communists on their staffs.[47]

Although Hoover was never personally successful in obtaining an indictment against a single black newspaper or magazine, he still harassed its editors and reporters. Marvel Cooke, who worked for the *People's Voice*, recalls being approached on the street by two FBI agents who tried to question her about the newspaper. She brushed by them without saying a word.[48] St. Clair Bourne was similarly approached. The agents, he says, spent several hours with him, trying to get him to say that the *People's Voice* was under the control of communists. It was not, he persisted. Bourne thought the black community was certainly "fertile ground" for the communists, but that most people in Harlem rebelled against the idea of having to follow the party line.[49]

Meanwhile, although A. Philip Randolph had cancelled the protest rally in the nation's capital in the summer of 1941, he still kept alive the March on Washington movement. In an article in the black journal *Survey Graphic* after America became involved in the war, he declared that he had not found any blacks who wanted to see the Allies lose, but insisted that the war for democracy would not be won "if freedom and equality are not vouchsafed the peoples of color":

> That is why those familiar with the thinking of the American Negro have sensed his lack of enthusiasm, whether among the educated or the uneducated, rich or poor, professional or nonprofessional, religious or secular, rural or urban, north, south, east or west.
>
> That is why questions are being raised by Negroes in church, labor union and fraternal society; in poolroom, barbershop, schoolroom, hospital, hair-dressing parlor; on college campus, railroad, and bus. One can hear such questions asked as these: What have Negroes to fight for? What's the difference between Hitler and that 'cracker' Talmadge of Georgia? Why has a man got to be Jim-Crowed to die for democracy? If you haven't got democracy yourself, how can you carry it to somebody else? . . .
>
> Negroes in Uncle Sam's uniform are being put upon, mobbed, sometimes even shot down by civilian and military police, and on occasion lynched. Vested political interests in race prejudice are so deeply entrenched that to them winning the war against Hitler is secondary to preventing Negroes from winning democracy for themselves. This is worth many divisions to Hitler and Hirohito.[50]

It would be wrong to say that all blacks agreed with the positions of Randolph or White. There was dissent within the black community. Eddie W. Reevers, editor of the *Messenger* and a spokesman for conservative blacks, felt that William Hastie and others were inciting racial hatreds. Dr. William Pickens, who had once been director of branches for the NAACP, believed that blacks "could demand their full citizenship rights after Hitler and the Axis Powers had been defeated. Everything must be sacrificed in winning this war. Such sacrifices are not sacrifices at all."[51]

But their voices were in the minority. By and large, most black leaders and the greater part of the community they represented insisted, if not demanded, that changes be made *now*. What it came down to was that the black community and the Roosevelt Administration were fundamentally divided over priorities. They could agree about the need to win the war, but there their agreement parted. The president's first and foremost objective, winning the war, affected all his decisions about the armed services and war production. His second, though he never spoke explicitly in these terms, was to win elections—the congressional elections in the off-year of 1942 and later his own to a fourth term in 1944, goals that influenced his response to political exigencies. Blacks were for winning the war, but their second objective was the abolition of discrimination and segregation in all phases of American life. Early in the war, the *Pittsburgh Courier* coined the "Double V" slogan: Victory over the Axis and Victory over racial discrimination at home. Roosevelt's aims were informally known by a different "Double V" slogan: Victory over the Axis and Victory over domestic political opponents.

The divergency in those goals affected the relationship between blacks and whites throughout the war.

TEN

The Experience of War

I'm just a Negro soldier
Fighting for "Democracy,"
A thing I've often heard of
But very seldom see. . . .

They expect me to be loyal?
But in my heart I'm not
For how can a second-class citizen
Be a first-class patriot?

—Bill Horton[1]

In spite of reservations about the war, large numbers of blacks flocked to enlistment centers for a variety of reasons—patriotic fervor, to be sure, but some saw the chance for a paying job and others wanted to prove their manhood. At first, though, many were turned away. Although promised that the enrollment of blacks in the military services would be equivalent to their percentage of the population, the promise was never kept. First Army headquarters in New England sought to exclude blacks from the initial call-up by secretly ordering draft boards not to induct them, and in 1940 the War Department tried to get Connecticut's draft boards to fill quotas with whites only.[2]

In truth, there just were not enough separate facilities to accommodate all the blacks that wanted to serve. One young black who was faced with serving in a segregated unit refused to report to duty and took his case all the way to the U.S. Supreme Court. The court upheld the army's policy of racial quotas and segregation. It declared that "if Congress had intended to prohibit separate white and Negro quotas and calls we believe it would have expressed such intention more definitely than by the general prohibition against discrimination." "What we are doing, of course," Selective Service Director Lewis B. Hershey acknowledged, "is simply transferring discrimination from everyday life into the army."[3]

For most blacks who did serve, much of their life in the military was demoralizing. The experiences of men such as Foster Palmer, Jack Scarville, Walker Smith, and Dr. James Jones were typical in many ways.

For one thing, a black who enlisted had little choice about his posting, and little chance to see combat. Foster Palmer tried to join the elite Eighty-second Airborne Division only to be told that it was restricted to whites. Instead, Palmer ended up in Europe in an army labor battalion.[4]

Scarville, who enlisted in 1942, was more fortunate. He was assigned to a combat unit, the Ninety-second Division. The division trained at Fort Huachuca, an isolated camp built during the Indian Wars at the base of the Huachuca Mountains in southern Arizona, thirty-four miles from the nearest rail junction. Both the Ninety-second and the Ninety-third Divisions spent more than a year in training at Huachuca and at Camp Young in California, marking time because, the *Amsterdam News* declared, "somebody in the Army doesn't want Negro combat troops overseas."[5]

Scarville's company commander in the Ninety-second was a southerner who had been a gas station attendant before the war. The officer, he says, never called him "nigger," but he did refer to him as "boy," a term that Scarville, who grew up in Paterson, New Jersey, resented bitterly. He quotes his commander as saying, "Wait til I get your ass in combat. You ain't going to live."[6]

At one point, the army chaplain at Huachuca was Grant Reynolds, who subsequently resigned in protest over the blatant racism he encountered. Reynolds had served at a number of bases in Virginia, Massachusetts, Michigan, and California as well as Arizona. He immediately discovered at his first posting, Camp Lee, east of Petersburg, Virginia, "the South more vigorously engaged in fighting the Civil War than in training soldiers to resist Hitler."[7] Reynolds sarcastically charged that War Secretary Henry Stimson "must have been told that the Negro soldier is demoralized, that he does not want to fight—unless a second front is opened in Mississippi, Texas, Georgia, South Carolina, Louisiana, or just *anywhere* below the Mason and Dixon Line—that his heart is not in this war."[8] Black soldiers were convinced, he insisted, that "this is a war to maintain the white man's right to keep the colored man in social and economic bondage," that "this is a white man's war, 'lock, stock, and barrel.' "[9]

The problem was a complex one. At the start of mobilization, white southerners made up the majority of officers in the peacetime army, and the command of black troops was often the cause of embarrassment and social ostracism. If a white officer was a hard disciplinarian, blacks considered him prejudiced; if he stood up for his men, other whites called him a "nigger lover."

Complicating the situation was the fact that the preponderance of blacks who were drafted or enlisted were from the South. Three-quarters of the country's black population then lived in the South and half of them resided in backward, rural areas.[10] Their lack of education was a serious problem. Between 70 and 90 percent of the blacks who were recruited scored in the lowest test categories, compared to only 20 to 40 percent of white inductees.[11] Three out of every four blacks who failed the test were from the South or border states.[12] War Secretary Stimson acknowledged that the army "had adopted rigid requirements for literacy mainly to keep down the number of colored troops," but the policy had backfired, "preventing us from getting in some very good but illiterate [white recruits] from the southern mountain states."[13]

Walker Smith ran into the same difficulty that plagued army recruiters—undereducated southern blacks. Smith, who reached the rank of sergeant and was an instructor with a tank battalion known as the Black Panthers, was posted at various times at Camp Hood, Texas, and Camp McClellan outside of Anniston, Alabama. It was "pretty hard," he recalls, to teach some of the black recruits from the South because they were either completely uneducated or had dropped out of school. Many of them had to repeat basic training.

On the other hand, northern blacks, Smith says, presented a different problem. They especially resented the way they were treated. They were not accustomed to being called "nigger," or to the

Jim Crow restrictions on and off base. "They wouldn't let them eat in different places, wouldn't let them go to the bathroom in different places—stuff like that in surrounding towns like Waco or in Alabama."

Smith found the hostility of white civilians particularly disturbing. When going on leave to nearby Cold Spring, he and other black soldiers from Camp Hood, Texas, were often told by bus drivers that there was not enough room for them, even though the bus might be half empty. He and some friends were walking down the streets of the town one day, looking for a shoe repair store, when they were confronted by a gang of "white boys" who forced them off the sidewalk. "The officers—the captain or the major—would tell us when we went to town, 'Just be normal. Don't mess around, you won't get hurt, you won't get into fights. Be careful, because they would gang up on you.' You didn't fool around with white women."

Smith says some northern blacks resented the way they were treated so much that "they didn't want to qualify, didn't want to go overseas. Some of them just had it in them, 'What's the use to fight? What's the use to go through all this for nothing?' "

The northern blacks organized gangs akin to urban street gangs to protect themselves against whites. "You didn't fool with them," Smith, a West Virginian by birth, says. "We got the same food, had the same barracks, the same amount from the supplies, the same things, but they still going to find fault. Some of it might have been true, some not. You had to be careful all the time. You had to be on your p's and q's, black and white."[14]

Although there were numerous camps where blacks trained for service, more of those destined for combat served at Fort Huachuca than at any other base. It was known, Grant Reynolds said, as "the home of the Negro soldier." But the chaplain had another sobriquet for it: Fort Huachuca was the War Department's "Foreign Legion."[15] The post commander at the time Reynolds submitted his resignation was a "red-neck" from Tennessee, "an excellent example of a plantation boss."[16] He had issued a bulletin declaring that any white officer with the rank of first lieutenant was superior to any black officer who was a captain. Such white officers could swim in the base pool, but black officers, even though superior in rank, could not.[17] Children of black officers had to attend a "colored school" with the children of

Apache Indians.[18] Reynolds claimed that the electrified barbed wire fence that surrounded the black soldiers' barracks was constructed to protect the white women on the base.[19]

Arthur Tritsch, a white officer who commanded black troops, witnessed not only the hostility of other white officers but also the results of the army's failure to adequately train blacks for combat roles. In one way, Tritsch was not surprised by the way his fellow officers reacted. Although a Canadian by birth and raised in Brooklyn, he had attended the University of Alabama, so he was "used to the segregation" and the attitudes he encountered.

But Tritsch's commander was something else. Tritsch was assigned to the Second Cavalry Division at Fort Clark outside Del Rio in southern Texas, on the border with Mexico. The wife of its company commander had allegedly been raped by a black soldier at another post. "He swore he was going to kill them all," Tritsch remembers. The residents of Del Rio were so hostile to black soldiers that the men had to be trucked across the Rio Grande to Ciudad Acuna when they were on weekend leaves.

Tritsch's unit was an armored combat outfit, but the entire Second Cavalry, though ostensibly trained for combat, was broken up into service units when it reached North Africa in 1944. Instead of tanks, Tritsch's troops manned dump trucks and served as a labor battalion, which, Tritsch says, was just as well. "They were not qualified or properly trained. Many were qualified on paper but not *in persona*. A lot of officers didn't want to take them into combat. You had troops not as good as they could have been or should have been. We were looking at our own butts. They were putting us in an untenable position if we had to go to war."[20]

The labor battalion to which Foster Palmer was attached eventually wound up in France. Before being transferred there, it was stationed in the British Isles, where Palmer met troops of the very unit he had wanted to join, the Eighty-second Airborne. The encounter was unpleasant. "We had a certain type of air force boots. And the air force boys'd say, 'You're not supposed to wear these things, nigger.' And that's when a fight would begin."[21]

The presence of blacks in Great Britain—about 130,000 of them spent one time or another in the country—created a host of problems. Black troops who had gone abroad in World War I had served primarily in France; few were ever stationed in Britain. But that changed in World War II with the enormous buildup of American forces prior to the D-Day invasion of Europe in 1944. There were numerous confrontations between black and white American troops like the one Foster Palmer experienced—fifty-six incidents during one three-month period alone. Most of them—fights, assaults and riots—took place in pubs, at dances, and on railway stations in the southern half of Britain, where blacks were based in large numbers.[22]

The British government found itself adopting, endorsing, and enforcing American racial attitudes. It equivocated at first about the stationing of black troops. Few blacks lived in England, and there were no barriers, social or economic, against those who did. Moreover, Britain had abolished segregation in its own colonial forces, and many British citizens welcomed black GIs into their homes. The clashes between black GIs and white GIs, however, forced U.S. Army authorities to set up alternate leave days and, where possible, separate recreational zones. Local authorities and constables were often placed in the position of having to enforce the restrictions.

After initial efforts to try to persuade the United States not to send any black troops, the British government was assured that no more than 10 percent of the American forces stationed in the country would be black. A lengthy debate ensued in the British Cabinet. How should the government respond to their presence in England? What behavior was proper? What should it tell its citizens? The official rationale for the position the British government took was expressed by its secretary of war, James Grigg. It was his opinion, he said, that "coloured troops themselves probably expected to be treated in this country as in the United States, and a markedly different treatment might well cause political difficulties at the end of the war." Put in other words, the British, with an eye to the future, when peace would be restored, did not wish to offend their most important ally. To treat black soldiers differently than they were treated by their own army and at home would embarrass American authorities.[23]

The situation was compounded by the attitudes expressed by top American military officials. The commanding general of the European Theatre of Operations, Dwight D. Eisenhower, confided to a visiting Hollywood actress in August 1942 that he was worried about black troops because they were running off with English girls. He believed

in blacks having equal rights, but said those rights should be "modified when it concerned women and liquor."[24] When Eisenhower returned to Washington for fourteen months, his place was taken by
John Clifford Hodges Lee, a native of Kansas whose grandfather had
been a captain in the Confederate Army. Lee was doubtful that blacks
and whites were "equal in God's sight."[25] Col. Ewart Gladstone
Plank, a Missourian who was a deputy chief of staff in Britain, declared: "Colored soldiers are akin to well-meaning but irresponsible
children. . . . Generally they cannot be trusted to tell the truth, to
execute complicated orders, or act on their own initiative except in
certain individual cases."[26]

Jack Scarville finally got a chance to fight for his country when
the Ninety-second Division was sent overseas to Italy. It was the only
black division that ever saw extensive combat.

In an apparent effort to prepare the American public for the use
of black combat troops, Gen. Benjamin O. Davis joined the Ninety-
second in Italy to film a propaganda film entitled *Teamwork* and the
army hypocritically boasted of the vital role the Ninety-second was
playing along the so-called Gothic Line, although the division had
not yet taken up its position. In addition, to allay black criticism about
the army's policies, a phony battlefield promotion was staged in front
of war correspondents and photographers. Gen. Mark Clark, the
American commander in Italy, upgraded a black first lieutenant by
plucking the captain's bars from one of his staff and placing them on
the black's shoulders.[27]

The Ninety-second fared poorly. An army inquiry attributed its
spotty record—the mass frustration, mismanagement, and confusion
the division displayed—to segregation.[28] Scarville himself blames the
Ninety-second's performance on its white officers. They "weren't the
best," he says, and there was a great deal of hostility between them
and the black troops under them.

More frightening to Scarville was the fact that his unit, a rifle
company, was "never allowed live ammunition. Even if the enemy
was on top of the hill and we were under fire, they had to come and
pass out ammunition to us. They didn't trust us with live ammunition."[29]

Once in combat, the Ninety-second enjoyed some initial successes, largely against light resistance while making its way to the

foothills of the Apennines north of Rome. But once in the mountains, the division faltered. Some men ran, others hesitated, still others advanced sluggishly. One black officer said he was "heartsick" at the Ninety-second's performance, but, pointing to the aggressive fighting spirit some contingents showed, insisted that the division's performance was not a complete failure.[30]

Scarville was so upset at the way the Ninety-second was run that he "played crazy"—refusing to eat or vomiting when he did—in the hope of getting a Section Eight discharge, but an army psychiatrist saw through his ruse and threatened him with jail.[31]

A Section Eight discharge was known as a "blue" discharge, one without honor and that carried no veterans benefits. That Scarville sought one was unusual. However, out of the nearly forty-nine thousand Section Eight discharges issued during the war, nearly eleven thousand of them went to blacks, way out of proportion to their percentage in the service.[32] A prime reason, blacks felt, was the army's readiness to bring up on court-martial charges black GIs whose offenses were minor, including those who went AWOL for a day or two, or those who objected to being called "nigger."[33]

Unlike Jack Scarville, Foster Palmer was never trained in hand-to-hand combat, and, in fact, was issued only one bullet for his carbine, about which he quips, "I guess that was to kill yourself."[34] Toward the end of the war, when the Germans launched their final, last-ditch counterattack in the Battle of the Bulge, the army, in a major break with traditional policy, asked for volunteers from black service units to fight "shoulder to shoulder" with hard-pressed white GIs. More than four thousand blacks responded and underwent a six-week course in tactics and weapons. But when the soldiers went into combat they discovered that they were not going to fight in integrated units, as promised, but in blacks-only platoons that were made part of white divisions. Once in battle in the mixed outfits, though, they ate, slept, and used the same sanitary facilities as white soldiers, and they fought brilliantly. After the Battle of the Bulge was over, however, the blacks were returned to their segregated units.[35] Palmer, who had initially wanted to serve in the all-white Eighty-second Airborne, was not among those who volunteered. "I laughed. I wasn't going up there. I offered my services three years ago—now you want me? Hell, no."[36]

All during the war, blacks were especially angered by the way black servicemen were treated in comparison to German and Italian prisoners of war. Singer Lena Horne was so troubled that she caused a contretemps of sorts when she walked out on a performance for troops at Camp Robinson in Arkansas. Horne was touring for the USO and scheduled to put on two shows, one for white officers, the other for black GIs. Before the second performance, she looked out at the audience and was surprised to see a sea of white faces. Told that they were German prisoners of war, seated in the best seats in front of the black soldiers, Horne said, "Screw this!" and walked out of the auditorium, telling her black driver, "Take me to the NAACP!" She afterwards performed, at her own expense, only at black army bases.[37]

Horne performed in one of the few USO camp shows that were organized for the entertainment of black troops. By the middle of the war, only two of twenty-five such shows on the road were for blacks, and the black performers involved found that, while white performers were fed and provided with hotel rooms or sleeping accommodations while traveling, black performers did not enjoy similar provisions. They had to fend for themselves—find restaurants that would feed them and places to stay overnight, and sit up in day coaches. And instead of including black plays similar to the dramas that white troops saw, the shows for blacks, one participant said, were "patterned on the 'Shuffle Along' of twenty years ago." A reporter for the *Amsterdam News* wondered why black artists such as Duke Ellington, Cab Calloway, Fats Waller, and Ethel Waters had not been asked to go abroad to entertain black troops. "There have been no calls for Negro overseas units," answered the man who ran the operation for the War Department.[38]

Dr. James Jones, who had taken part in the boycott of the Child's restaurant on 125th Street in the 1930s, was also witness to the fact that enemy POWs were treated better than black soldiers. An oral surgeon, he served as an army public health officer in Belle Glade, Florida, where there were separate medical and hospital facilities for blacks and for whites. The latter included, to his vexation, German and Italian prisoners of war who received the same medical treatment as white American servicemen and in the same facilities.[39]

Dr. Jones's mentor during his internship at Freedman's College (later part of Howard University) in Washington had been Dr.

Charles Drew, the black physician who had developed the process of preserving plasma that made blood banks possible. Ironically, the Red Cross at first would not accept blood donations from blacks. The army and the navy had sent the Red Cross a secret memo saying the War Department was only interested in collecting blood from white donors. Even after the American Medical Association stated that there was no basis for discrimination between white and black blood, the Red Cross maintained its policy. It announced that "if a Negro soldier needed blood and did not wish to use the white blood which was stored in the bank, then live Negro blood would be provided."[40] Later, after William Hastie, the special assistant to Stimson that Roosevelt had appointed, demanded an explanation, the War Deparment modified its stand. Henceforth the Red Cross accepted black blood, but it ingenuously announced, "in deference to the wishes of those from whom the plasma is being provided the blood will be processed separately so that those receiving transfusions may be given plasma from blood of their own race."[41]

As stories filtered back about how blacks were being treated in the military, some civilians tried to resist being drafted. It may have seemed to them that they would not only be risking their lives in battles overseas, but that they might very well be risking them just by being in the service at bases where blacks and whites clashed. St. Clair Bourne, the managing editor of the *People's Voice*, recalls that there were many Harlemites who didn't want "to go to war and get killed."[42]

One of those who tried to get out of serving was Frank (Frankie) Manning, a dancer born in Jacksonville, Florida, who grew up in Harlem: "I may sound unpatriotic, but I didn't want to go in the Army, I really didn't. I wasn't for that. And I did everything I could to, you know, to try to get out of it."[43] But he passed the physical examination and was inducted. Once in the army, Manning feigned illness. "I didn't want to train. I didn't want to [do] nothin'. I just laid around. I told 'em I had to go [to] the hospital all the time, you know." Manning's attitude changed after he viewed films of Japanese martial practices—"judo, jujitsu, and all that kinda stuff like that"— and he and others in his unit were taken to hospitals where they saw men wounded in the fighting in the South Pacific, "all shot and banged up, and without legs and without arms, and all that kinda stuff." Manning decided "right then and there I better learn how to fight, 'cause they gonna ship me out to the war anyways, so I might as well learn." Manning participated in the invasions of New Guinea and the Philippines in one of the few units of the Ninety-third Division that finally saw combat, a mortar platoon that was made part of an all-white battalion.[44]

Perhaps the most flamboyant and imaginative draft resister was Malcolm Little (Malcolm X). Little, in his early days in Harlem in 1940, became embroiled in its underworld life. He worked as a runner for a marijuana cigarette dealer and was scared, he said, about only three things: "jail, a job, and the Army." In 1943, the New York draft board called him up to appear at its induction center in lower Manhattan. Convinced that black Army Intelligence spies were searching Harlem for draft dodgers, Little purposely began "noising around that I was frantic to join . . . the Japanese Army." Then, on the day he showed up for his physical, he went "costumed like an actor," dressed in a "wild" zoot suit and yellow knob-toe shoes. He "frizzled" his hair up into a "reddish bush of conk."

"Crazy-o, daddy-o," Little said as he reported in, "skipping and tipping." The other inductees stood around, dumbstruck, "with me running my mouth a mile a minute, talking nothing but slang. I was going to fight on all fronts; I was going to be a general, man."

As he had hoped, Little was singled out to see an army psychiatrist. He purposely hassled the doctor's receptionist, a young black woman—one of those "smug black 'firsts' "—who went into the office "to make clear, in advance, what she thought of me" before he was shown into the doctor's presence:

I kept jerking around, backward, as though somebody might be listening. I knew I was going to send him back to the books to figure what kind of a case I was.

Suddenly, I sprang up and peeped under both doors, the one I'd entered and another that probably was a closet. And then I bent and whispered fast in his ear. "Daddy-o, now you and me, we're from up North here, so don't you tell nobody . . . I want to get sent down South. Organize them nigger soldiers, you dig? Steal us some guns, and kill us crackers!"

That psychiatrist's blue pencil dropped, and his professional manner fell off in all directions. He stared at me as if I were a snake's egg hatching, fumbling for his red pencil.[45]

Declared 4-F—unfit for duty—Little was rejected and never bothered by the army again.

It would be wrong to imply that there was no progress whatsoever in the armed forces. Within less than a year after Pearl Harbor, the navy was training some blacks as gunner's mates, petty officers, quartermasters, and coxswains, albeit at segregated bases. A year later, the navy accepted thirteen blacks as officers and by the end of the war, when four million men were in the naval service, it had commissioned fifty-eight blacks as officers, though few saw combat. The Coast Guard consistently outdid the navy. Almost a year to the day of the first anniversary of Pearl Harbor a Dallas man became the first black to receive a pharmacist's mate rating in the Coast Guard.[46] By the war's end, the Coast Guard, comprised of only 240,000 men, had also commissioned seven hundred black officers. For the first time in history, the marines enlisted black recruits. Officer candidate schools in the army became integrated. The Army Air Corps established at Tuskegee the Ninety-ninth Pursuit Squadron, a totally black outfit commanded by Benjamin O. Davis, Jr. Over Dixiecrat opposition, in September 1942 Congress passed legislation suspending, for the duration of the war, poll-tax requirements for voting that affected black servicemen from eight southern states.[47]

Although black officers would constitute less than 2 percent of all officers in the military during the war,[48] by the end of 1944 there were more black officers than could be posted because the army continued to insist that only whites command black outfits. Moreover, no black could be ranked higher than the lowest ranked white; as a result, few black lieutenants were ever promoted,[49] and, outside of Benjamin O. Davis, Sr., none achieved the rank of general or, in the navy, flag rank.[50]

By the spring of 1943 more than half a million blacks were in the army. But only seventy-nine thousand of them were overseas, and most of them were service troops repeating the experience of their fathers in World War I. They unloaded ships, built roads, drove supply convoys. Many commanders did not want blacks in combat roles. Secretary of War Henry Stimson told Congressman Hamilton Fish, the white commander of black troops in World War I who had sponsored the draft-law amendment outlawing discrimination in the armed services, that blacks "have been unable to master efficiently the techniques of modern weapons." [51]

Perhaps, considering all the negative aspects of the black experience in the military, the abrupt, unexpected announcement that came from Washington a year after Pearl Harbor should not have come as such a shock.

Eleanor Roosevelt and Fiorello La Guardia confer over Civil Defense plans in 1941. The president's wife and the mayor shared liberal views. *Courtesy of The Bettman Archive.*

Walter White and his wife, Gladys.

Roy Wilkins.

Adam Clayton Powell, Jr., in 1944, shortly after his election to Congress.

A car owned by a white store proprietor burns out of control.

Shattered glass and what is left of mannequins cover the sidewalk
on 125th Street in front of three devastated stores.

Under police escort, rioters are taken to the Twenty-eighth Precinct
station house. Note how well-dressed they are.

A bleeding black man is hauled to the Twenty-eighth Precinct station house. The photo, taken by a *New York Times* photographer, won first prize at a Press Photographers Association exhibit.

A young looter lounges at the Twenty-eighth Precinct station house
atop merchandise pilfered from Harlem stores.

A shop that was spared, its facade covered with "Colored Store" signs.

The scene in front of the Twenty-eighth Precinct station house on West 123rd Street on the morning after the rioting broke out. The WNYC radio van was one of the sound trucks that La Guardia and community leaders used in touring the community. *Courtesy of the Schomburg Center for Research in Black Culture.*

Many blacks served as volunteers to restore order. Here, at the Twenty-eighth Precinct station house, a member of the Civilian Defense Auxiliary Police hands a nightstick to Bishop L. S. Jones of the Methodist Episcopal Church.

Truckloads of army MPs rushed to Harlem to clear all soldiers and sailors from the streets.

Police escort a man injured in the rioting.

ELEVEN

A Conditional Surrender

*We Negroes are often forced to the conclusion that white men are
very peculiar, so peculiar that amusement provoked by the ludi-
crous enables us to bear with some of our neighbors' whimsical
ways.*

—William H. Hastie[1]

William Hastie had always seen his role as different from that of
Emmett J. Scott, Newton Baker's assistant in the War Department
during World War I. He looked on Scott as a conservative, an adjuster
of racial ills rather than a voice for change and justice. Hastie was an
activist, eager to have the army reverse or at least alter its discriminatory patterns.

Hastie's role as special assistant to Secretary of War Henry Stimson, as outlined by Stimson, was to aid in the formulation and implementation of policies that would ensure equality and the most
effective utilization of blacks. He was also responsible for investigating complaints of mistreatments and was expected to offer sugges-
tions regarding army policies toward blacks. Stimson, however,
never mentioned a word about eliminating segregation or any discriminatory practices. Hastie, well aware of the War Department's
position—"The military would not be used as a sociological laboratory for effecting social change"[2]—had nevertheless accepted his
post in the hope of being able to "work effectively toward the integration of the Negro into the Army and to facilitate his placement, training and promotion."[3]

At first, Hastie devoted himself to studying how blacks were being utilized. By February 1941 he had written a memorandum on "The Integration of the Negro Soldier in the Army" that took issue with, among other things, War Department personnel projections that were made at the time of his appointment in October 1940. They showed that both the quartermaster and engineering corps—service rather than combat units—would have disproportionate representations of blacks.

Stimson agreed that most of Hastie's findings were well-founded, but the integration of blacks into the service, he wrote, represented "the hopeless side of the insoluble problem of the black race in this country."[4] The War Department was not about to change basic policy. This was not the time, the Army General Staff contended after the attack on Pearl Harbor, to "alienate the people from the Army and lower their morale," both of which "are vital to our national needs."[5] Chief of Staff Gen. George Marshall said that changes Hastie wanted to make toward integrating the army would be "tantamount to solving a social problem which has perplexed the American people throughout the history of this nation."[6]

On December 8, 1941, one day after the Japanese attack, Hastie took the occasion of a press conference held by Marshall to make known his disappointment with the army's intransigence. It was at this press conference that Marshall announced plans for an all-black division to be trained at Fort Huachuca. Both he and Col. Eugene Householder of the Adjutant General's Office claimed that steps were being taken to utilize the black soldier in the most efficient manner.

One unexpected obstacle Hastie encountered came in the form of the army's first black general, Benjamin Davis, Sr. Walter White later ran into the same roadblock. Davis tended to play down black complaints; he was what militant blacks called an Uncle Tom. The *New York Age* was shocked when Davis was quoted as saying that black soldiers "would be happier" if they knew that blood donations "came from their own people." The general, the Harlem weekly said, "is truly serving the Army rather than his race" and has "the gall and the intellectual and moral dishonesty to misrepresent" black soldiers and "to argue for the application of a Hitler method in the midst of a war to beat the pants off Hitler and his methods."[7] The Socialist Workers Party's *Militant* described Davis's job as "whitewashing Jim Crow conditions."[8] According to Virginia Murphy of Harlem, the general wore "dark glasses" that obscured his reaction to conditions.[9]

Murphy's nephew was sent to boot camp in Texas, where he struck a white sergeant who called him "nigger." The youth was court-martialed and put in jail. Davis answered Murphy's appeal for help by going to Texas, but he found the army had handled the case properly. "He came down not to see," she says. "We knew he wouldn't find any evidence." Her nephew was finally released through the intercession of Adam Clayton Powell, Jr.[10]

Davis, responsible in the Inspector General's Office for investigating the conditions encountered by black soldiers, concluded after eight surveys taken between October 1941 and September 1943 that the morale of black troops was excellent and that the attitudes in base camps and their surrounding communities were superior.[11]

Hastie ran into Davis's opposition when he asked to meet with Marshall and the army's inspector general in 1941 about having post commanders banned from using racial epithets. Davis thought the ban would be unwise "as I recalled the ill effect that resulted by the use of such an order in the early days in the Philippines." Surprisingly, Stimson sided with Hastie and, for the first time in American military history, an official order went into effect in mid-February 1941, forbidding all commanders "to injure those under their authority by tyrannical or capricious conduct or by abusive language."[12]

The order, however, was frequently ignored. A soldier stationed in South Dakota complained, "It is not a strange thing to hear a Lieutenant or Major use the word N——R."[13] A major at Camp McCoy in Wisconsin said, "On the post and off we are subjected to being called names, by both officers and enlisted men. . . . There is an inner tension going among the men. . . . Hell might break loose any minute."[14]

As for Davis's findings about morale and attitudes, other blacks told Hastie that service clubs and church services were off-limits. A group at Jackson Air Base in Mississippi reported that civilian police had threatened to kill several soldiers, that black soldiers were not allowed to walk in town, and that a lieutenant said "all Negroes need to be beaten to death."[15] A black at Camp Claiborne in central Louisiana said that because two white women had allegedly been raped by blacks at the camp, the woods around it were "swarming with Louisiana boogies armed with rifles and shot guns even the little kids have 22 cal. rifles and B&B guns filled with anxiety to shoot a negro soldier."[16] A private from the North was told by a train conductor in Claiborne that he was "a nigger, a god-damn nigger. You are down below the Mason-Dixon Line and you are all nigger boys down here." [17]

In November 1942, Hastie and Thurgood Marshall joined in submitting to the National Lawyers' Guild a report on the civilian violence that blacks in uniform suffered. It declared:

> [It] is a recurrent phenomenon. It continues unabated. It may well be the greatest factor now operating to make 13 million Negroes bitter and resentful and to undermine the fighting spirit of three-quarters of a million Negroes in arms. . . . To address a Negro soldier as "nigger" is such a commonplace in the average southern community that little is said about it. But the mounting rage of the soldier himself is far from commonplace. He may not express his feelings when he must wait until all the white passengers are accommodated before he can get transportation. He may even hold his tongue when he is forced to get out of the bus in which he is seated in order to make room for white passengers. But it is of such stuff that bitterness and hatred are made. In such a climate resentments grow until they burst forth in violent and unreasonable reprisal. [18]

Hastie also attacked the Inspector General's Office for what he thought was its failure to solve the numerous acts of violence directed at blacks: homicides at Fort Benning, Georgia; a shooting attack on black barracks at Fort Jackson, South Carolina; slayings at Fort Bragg, North Carolina; an attack on black soldiers by civilian police in Bastrop, Louisiana. But even after Stimson publicly expressed the War Department's concern about the incidents, the assaults continued.

To try to alleviate the situation, the War Department in May 1942 decided that, wherever feasible, northern blacks would be stationed in the North and southern blacks in the South. "We are suffering from the persistent legacy of the original crimes of slavery," Stimson observed in his diary. [19]

Besides the ban Hastie proposed on racial epithets, two other recommendations he made were put into effect by the War Department. One was that the department's news organ, *Army Talk*, carry articles about eliminating racial prejudices, the other that the department issue position papers to commanding officers aimed at improving relations between officers and black personnel. However, the distribution of a pamphlet entitled "Races of Mankind," which exposed the myth of white supremacy, was squelched by a Kentucky congressman who was chairman of the House Military Appropriations Committee. He threatened to cut off funds—in the midst of the war—if the War Department did not cancel its order for fifty-five thousand copies.[20]

Hastie's unhappiness with War Department policies came to a head over the Ninety-ninth Pursuit Squadron. He was so angry about the way the squadron was handled that he wrote a lengthy monograph, entitled "On Clipped Wings," that traced the history of the unit and described in detail the nature of the training that the nation's first black military pilots received.

Hastie charged that the department misled the public when it announced, about the time of his appointment in October 1940, that blacks were being trained as pilots, mechanics, and technical specialists. For one thing, the only training then was in civilian flying that was offered at a few black colleges and at one private company. Those trained had no military status and no promise of any.

It was not until March 1941 that the Army Air Corps began accepting applications for the Ninety-ninth, and actual instruction did not begin until several months later, at Tuskegee Institute, Alabama. Almost immediately Hastie questioned the type of combat aviation for which the young black cadets were being trained—the most difficult of all, pursuit flying. That could have been taken as a compliment, but Hastie was skeptical. He wondered why the cadets were not being trained as bomber or reconnaissance pilots. Was the white establishment purposively making it impossible for blacks to succeed by putting them in the most strenuous of air-combat roles? If so, Hastie wrote, the "idea was not conceived maliciously. It was bred of ignorance of the Negro and the acceptance of that stereotype which pictures the Negro as a lazy, inefficient individual without enterprise or initiative or very much intelligence."[21]

Hastie found the idea of a separate training base at Tuskegee "indefensible." Even in flight training, segregation was enforced. Black pilots could not fly from or to fields where white units were stationed. Hastie said he was sure of one thing if a black flier went into combat abroad: "He will not just fly out of a Jim-Crow base with his own Negro unit and fly back again." And if black and white pilots were to fly in combat together, "the best plan is to build mutual understanding and self-respect by training them together." The worst plan, he said, "is to keep them apart until they are forced together under the stress of circumstances in combat."[22]

In spite of the handicap, or perhaps because of it, during the first year of training, four out of ten black cadets received their wings, as compared to the average of six out of ten white trainees who qualified.[23]

Hastie was critical of Tuskegee Institute for working "hand in glove" with the air force to "establish, intrench and extend a Jim Crow air training program." The school, he said, showed a "cynical disregard for the larger interests of the Negro and of the nation."[24] Moreover, he noted that the recently appointed white commander at Tuskegee—which is located "in the heart of one of the most prejudiced areas of the south"—catered "to local prejudice at every turn." The commander disarmed black MPs assigned to patrol duty in town, and was only concerned with covering up an incident in which policemen in Montgomery beat up a black nurse from Tuskegee who tried to get onto a bus with white passengers.[25]

Hastie found himself the only one complaining publicly about Tuskegee. The black press supported him, recognizing the validity of his charges, but newspapers suppressed their protest because, according to a staff correspondent for the *Pittsburgh Courier*, "although the Tuskegee school is a jim-crow school and the press and the Negro leadership are unalterably against jim-crow in principle no matter how it is sugar-coated, they wanted their boys above all to make good airmen for Uncle Sam."[26]

Among other critical observations in "On Clipped Wings," Hastie reeled off the names of several black pilots who had been rejected by the Air Command. One had flown a fighter plane in the Spanish Civil War, another regularly flew to Canada American-made planes bound for England. In addition, Hastie could not understand why two black mathematics teachers were told there was no need for meteorologists after the War Department had announced the air force's "urgent need" for more than one thousand of them.[27] "Weather may be black, or it may be fair," he commented caustically, "but the skin of the man who makes the weather calculation has to match the skin of the flier who uses the information."[28]

The greatest difficulty the air force faced, Hastie noted, was the problem of ground crews. It believed that whites could not be trusted to service planes for black pilots. The air force reasoned, he said, that "all sorts of sabotage might occur." But Hastie had a different suspicion: "I for one could not help suspecting that underlying this rationalization was an unwillingness of the Air Command to put Negro flying officers in a position of authority over white enlisted technicians."[29]

Hastie was able to win a temporary victory regarding ground crews. Nearly three hundred blacks, enough to service a single squadron, were sent to Chanute Field in Illinois for training as mechanics in an unsegregated atmosphere. Even though the program was successful, however, the Air Command discontinued it.[30]

Frustrated at every turn, exasperated by the way the War Department treated virtually every reform or modification he recommended, William Hastie resigned as of January 31, 1943, after twenty-seven months as Stimson's special assistant. He issued a statement saying that "reactionary policies and discriminatory practices of the Army Air Forces in matters affecting Negroes were the immediate cause of my resignation."[31]

Blacks were quick to sympathize with Hastie's decision to quit the War Department. The *Washington Afro-American* thought his resignation was "quite proper."[32] In a gesture of its support, the NAACP that March awarded him its prestigious Spingarn Medal, lauding Hastie for his "every act and particularly his protest against racial bigotry in an army fighting for the preservation of the democratic processes." Its citation read, "Men of lesser character and of greater selfishness would have closed their eyes to prejudice in order to maintain themselves in a remunerative position."[33]

Walter White believed Hastie's resigning would prove a "severe jolt to Washington complacency."[34] But it didn't. Before Hastie resigned, Henry Stimson confided to his diary what he and many others in the Roosevelt Administration felt but did not say outloud: Stimson was "profoundly" disappointed with Hastie's attitude. He felt Hastie was "not realistic and I am afraid his usefulness is limited."[35]

TWELVE

❧

Images

. . . In time, for though the sun is setting on
A song-lit race of slaves, it has not set . . .

—Jean Toomer[1]

The stereotype of the black about which William Hastie complained —that of "the Negro as a lazy, inefficient individual without enterprise or initiative or very much intelligence"—was reinforced by the most influential mass medium of the time, the motion picture. A powerful visual means of communication, movies had superseded newspapers and radio in reflecting as well as setting the social standards of the time. Hollywood produced more than five hundred films each year, and Americans ordinarily attended a movie twice a week. Movie stars were celebrities; magazines were devoted to them. The images they projected on the screen created or buttressed attitudes about American culture that were frequently accepted by the public as the norm. When it came to blacks, that image was negative in the extreme.

At a writers' congress held in Los Angeles in the middle of the war, Walter White repeated an anecdote he had heard. Seems that a "distinguished" black poet, White said, was invited to talk at "one of our great universities." At dinner, the six-year-old daughter of the school's president asked him, "Will you teach me how to shoot dice?" The poet was startled by the request. He pointed out that craps was not one of his talents, and asked the girl why she had asked him to learn it. She innocently and promptly replied: "In the movies, all Negroes shoot dice!"[2]

120

Screenwriter Dalton Trumbo said Hollywood made "tarts of the Negro's daughters, crap shooters of his sons, obsequious Uncle Toms of his fathers, superstitious and grotesque crones of his mothers, strutting peacocks of his successful men, psalm-singing mountebanks of his priests, and Barnum and Bailey side-shows of his religion."[3]

The blacks whom whites ordinarily saw in movies—Stepin Fetchit, Ethel Waters, Hattie McDaniel, Butterfly McQueen, Eddie (Rochester) Anderson—played the roles of servants; in Fetchit's case, the quintessent example of lassitude. Baritone Paul Robeson, despondent over playing a sharecropper in a sequence of *Tales of Manhattan*, said he would never do another movie unless some other way was found to portray blacks besides the usual "plantation hallelujah shouters." Robeson said he had tried to get the script of *Tales* changed, but that "in the end it turned out to be the same old thing —the Negro solving his problem by singing his way to glory. This is very offensive to my people. It makes the Negro child-like and innocent and is in the old plantation tradition. But Hollywood says you can't make the Negro in any other role because it won't be box office in the South. The South wants us Negroes in the old style."[4]

Other blacks echoed Robeson's feeling. "We would like to feel proud rather than embarrassed," an anonymous reader wrote the *Amsterdam News*. "In several pictures I noticed our girls playing parts that are more ignorant than comical. Domestic service workers no longer look like Aunt Jemima. They are no different from anyone else." The reader, a woman, said she was the only black attending a theater that showed a movie in which a black girl played "one of these Aunt Jemima roles." The audience, she said, "just sighed and it was most embarrassing. I would like to see Negroes in parts which do not make people continue to think us fools."[5]

Loren Miller, a young California attorney, was appalled by the reaction of fellow blacks to an MGM film, *Trader Horn*. Writing in the *Crisis*, Miller noted how one scene depicted the "beautiful" blonde heroine in the clutches of "savage" Africans until saved at the last minute. "The audience," wrote Miller, "burst into wild applause when the rescue scene flashed on the screen. I looked around. Those who were applauding were ordinary Negro working people and middle class folk." The effect, Miller thought, was insidious. The white man is pictured "as the overlord," while blacks are portrayed as "either buffoons or ubiquitous Uncle Toms." Newsreels, he said, "poke fun at Negro revivals or baptisms and avoid such 'dangerous' subjects as the Scottsboro case." Miller said that it was "easy enough to see that the movies but reflect the traditional American outlook on the Negro question."[6]

"Somewhere," wrote W. E. B. Du Bois's wife, Shirley Graham, "there may be Negroes like the ones depicted in *Green Pastures, Porgy and Bess* or *Cabin in the Sky*—just as somewhere there are probably whites like those shown in *Tobacco Road*. But I assure you that the acknowledged leaders of thirteen million American Negroes are neither as long suffering as 'De Lawd' nor as naive as 'Little Joe' nor do they wear Ethel Waters' wide smile."[7]

Films such as *Cabin in the Sky* and *Stormy Weather* appalled Walter White. He thought that the latter film had Lena Horne doing "vulgar things" that producers would not ask a white actress to do.[8]

One onerous animated short from Warner Brothers, booked for the spring of 1943 at the Apollo Theater, roused such protest from Harlem blacks that its showing was cancelled. Entitled *Coal Black and the Seven Dwarfs*, it depicted a black woman as a "blackmarketeer" standing over a large bag of hoarded sugar. The seven dwarfs were seven black soldiers.[9]

The other side of the coin was the total absence of black characters in a movie. Cpl. J. H. Becton, who was stationed at Fort Huachuca, complained that a film he saw on base, *This Is America*, pictured "not a single one of 'my people' on the screen." Becton wondered why the armed forces didn't release all its black troops and fight its own war, "for if 'America' is for 'whites' only, we, the 'negroes[,]' have nothing to fight for."[10]

The deception suggested in the movie *Bataan*, which was released in 1943, was more galling. By then, the stereotypical army unit in movies symbolized America's ethnic and geographical diversity and ordinarily included, for example, a Kansas farm boy, a Brooklyn Jew, and an Irish youth from Boston, but no black, of course. In *Bataan*, however, there was also a black soldier in the platoon, even though the army was segregated and no blacks whatsoever served in an integrated combat unit.

The Office of War Information encouraged filmmakers to depict such integrated combat units. The OWI, a consolidation of several propaganda agencies that was created in 1942, was staffed by white liberals such as CBS radio commentator Elmer Davis, Pulitzer Prize playwright Robert Sherwood, Librarian of Congress Archibald Mac-Leish, and Gardner Cowles, Jr., the founder of *Look* magazine and a key backer of Republican Wendell Willkie. At the time, polls showed that 92 percent of the public favored continued racial segregation.[11]

The poll may have influenced its tolerant, freethinking staff. Deputy Director George A. Barnes said the OWI's policy regarding blacks was "in effect a direct and powerful Negro propaganda effort as distinct from a crusade for Negro rights."[12] The OWI emphasized in a manual prepared for the movie industry that the war was a "people's war, not a national, class or race war."[13] A pamphlet it published in mid-1942, "Negroes and the War"—the agency's first effort to appeal directly to blacks—implied a "fight or else" threat and was sharply criticized by all factions. Southerners called its depiction of black progress since 1933 subversive. Republicans saw the pamphlet as an electioneering device. For their part, blacks were put off by the pressure to "fight or else" and by its representation of America as a symbol of progress and hope.[14]

Philleo Nash, an anthropologist who served as the OWI's chief troubleshooter on racial matters, said the agency cooperated with "the less extravagant" black leaders, but equally strong was its desire to alleviate tensions—to "keep the lid on" because racial tensions were already building dangerously in 1942. The agency, he said, hoped to "lower hostility on the part of whites and reduce militance on the part of blacks."[15]

The OWI did not have formal censorship powers, but all studios except Paramount submitted scripts to it for review, and most of its recommendations were followed, primarily because the government controlled whether a movie could be distributed outside the United States market. Once in a while, the OWI's influence worked to the benefit of blacks. A prime example was the agency's role in MGM's *The Man on America's Conscience*, which was filmed in 1942. The original script was sympathetic to the southern point of view, with former slave owners returning after the Civil War to their plantations and allying themselves with the Union. Thaddeus Stevens of Pennsylvania, a champion of freedmen, was portrayed evilly as cajoling President Andrew Johnson into drunkenness. Walter White, for one, was troubled because the film glorified Johnson, a president who had opposed the vote for blacks. When the movie, retitled *Tennessee Johnson*, was released, however, material that blacks felt was offensive was toned down.[16]

The OWI all but abandoned its efforts to change Hollywood's portrayal of blacks in the spring of 1943 after the agency became the target of attacks in Congress because of its position on race relations. Spurred by conservatives and southern racists, Congress cut the budget of the OWI's Domestic Branch to less than a tenth of a its former size, thus, in effect, terminating its operations.[17]

A later Columbia University survey of wartime films found that of one hundred black appearances, seventy-five perpetuated stereotypes, thirteen were neutral, and only twelve positive. The survey said there was some evidence that blacks were simply being "written out" of movies, because membership in a black actors' union dropped in half during the war.[18]

Before its office in Hollywood lost its funding, the OWI's Bureau of Motion Pictures acknowledged that movies such as *Cabin in the Sky* and *Stormy Weather* presented blacks as "simple, ignorant, superstitious folk, incapable of anything but the most menial labor."[19] It released an analysis of black roles in films that reached movie theaters in late 1942 and early 1943, concluding that "in general, Negroes are presented as basically different from other people, as taking no relevant part in the life of the nation, as offering nothing, contributing nothing, expecting nothing." Blacks appeared in 23 percent of the films released during the period studied, the OWI bureau reported, and in 82 percent of them they were shown as "clearly inferior."[20]

What were blacks to think? At the same time that movies were promoting patriotism and the need for national unity, they were also sustaining the distorted views held by so many whites. The image of blacks that Hollywood projected reinforced the bias of bigots and affected white attitudes throughout the war. Blacks resented it.

THIRTEEN

Advances and Retreats

Day dawned, and soon the mixed crowds came to view
The ghastly body swaying in the sun. . . .
And little lads, lynchers that were to be,
Danced round the dreadful thing in fiendish glee.

—Claude McKay[1]

Four days after the Japanese attack on Pearl Harbor, Japan's allies, Germany and Italy, declared war on the United States. All of a sudden, America was at war at opposite ends of the world.

Americans, stunned by the Japanese attack, quickly galvanized into action. The first year of the war, 1942, was marked by both advances and retreats, and victory seemed as far off as the distant battlefronts. Japanese offensives led to the fall of Bataan and Corregidor in the Philippines, the surrender of Singapore, a severe setback for the United States Navy at the Battle of the Java Sea, and the fall of the Netherlands East Indies. But Americans struck back, bombing Tokyo, frustrating the Japanese advance on Australia at the Battle of Coral Sea, defeating the Japanese navy at Midway, taking the offensive with U.S. Marine landings on Guadalcanal.

On the other side of the world, however, the balance of the war with Germany shifted dramatically. The British Eighth Army opened an offensive in Libya. A few months later under the command of Dwight D. Eisenhower, combined United States and British forces launched a major offensive in North Africa—Operation Torch—with landings at Casablanca, Oran, and Algiers. On the Continent, British commandos raided St. Nazaire and Dieppe in France and a thousand

125

British bombers carried out raids on Cologne, Essen, Bremen, and the Ruhr. The first independent American bombing attack was carried out by flying fortresses of the Eighth Air Force on the rail yards of Rouen. In Russia, however, the battle seesawed back and forth with the change in climate. In the heavy snows of winter, Soviet forces regained some Russian cities that had fallen to the Germans. As the snow thawed and summer came, the Germans gained the upper hand again. Then, another winter, and another Soviet counteroffensive.

At home, the black struggle for equal treatment and equal opportunity also swung back and forth, the advances raising expectations, the retreats escalating frustrations.

Some good came of William Hastie's criticisms. The commanding officer at Tuskegee Air Base whom he found so offensive was replaced. Blacks continued to be trained separately, but, among other changes, recreational facilities were integrated, the officers' club was opened to blacks, flight surgeons were trained in integrated facilities, blacks were trained as heavy-bomber pilots, and another unit, the 332nd Fighter Group, was created. Pamphlets dealing with the concept of equal opportunity were distributed to servicemen and civilians. A movie about black achievements, *The Negro Soldier*, was produced and shown to all soldiers as well as in movie theaters around the country except in the South until an NAACP suit in federal court forced its showing there, as well.[2]

There were advances on the civilian side as well, all the result of the increasing shortage of manpower created by the war. As early as March 1942, a full two years after the nation's rearmament began, blacks represented only 2.5 to 3 percent of all workers in war production. In the next two years, their employment in defense industries almost tripled, and the total number of black workers increased by a third, from 4.4 million to 5.9 million.[3] At the same time, the income of blacks was catching up with white income; it rose dramatically, from about 40 percent of white incomes to about 60 percent.[4] By 1944, the average black worker was making $37.77 a week or about $1,976 annually—about the same as the average female worker. The average white worker was making nearly $50 a week, or $2,600 yearly.[5]

One survey showed that the percentage of black workers in 113 plants in Delaware, New Jersey, and Pennsylvania rose from 4 percent to 7 percent. Another study said nonwhite employment in industries other than shipbuilding in the Los Angeles area—which would have included Mexican-American as well as black workers—jumped almost fourfold while the total labor supply only grew by 50 percent.[6]

Lester Granger of the National Urban League reported that once America entered the war the number of black shipbuilding workers, both skilled and unskilled, doubled within a year's time, and that two companies were taking extraordinary steps to enlist black labor, seemingly without arousing any white backlash: The Sun Shipbuilding Company of Chester, Pennsylvania, had announced it would open a new shipyard manned entirely by black workers of all skills, and Higgins Industries of New Orleans, which made landing craft, was planning an all-black assembly line.

Granger also found that Curtiss-Wright plants had taken on more than three thousand blacks and that blacks were being employed by companies such as Glenn L. Martin, North American Aviation, Consolidated, Brewster, Bell Aircraft, and Lockheed Vega.[7] Black gains, said the president of Tuskegee Institute, F. D. Patterson, "have given new impetus and hope to the educational and training efforts of Negro youth."[8]

Doris Saunders, who was then living on West 142nd Street in Harlem, was one of the fortunate few who was able to find a defense job in New York City. The city did not have the manufacturing resources of other areas of the state or the country, but a factory in the West Forties rewired and repaired shrapnel-riddled instrument panels and sometimes the chassis of B-29 bombers that were damaged in bombing runs over Europe. Saunders was a solderer. Two sisters were able to find defense-related work, too.[9]

Yet the black experience was like a treadmill. Every step forward seemed to go nowhere. Two years after rearmament began, a survey found that, despite increased employment, four-fifths of all black workers still remained at unskilled jobs.[10] What did that mean for the future? Willard S. Townsend, a leading black union official, cautioned: "The Negro worker is definitely worried. He is worried about today. He is worried about tomorrow. He is restless. He remembers only too well the stirring slogans of the last war. He remembers too well the broken promises. He is more grim today in his determination to enjoy some of the freedoms so glibly mouthed."[11]

Despite the generally heartening employment news, Lester

Granger was still critical of the federal Board of Education, saying that it was ineffectual in training blacks for war production work, particularly in the South. He quoted the board's own figures for eighteen southern and border states: blacks made up 22 percent of their population but only 4 percent of all trainees. In addition, Granger reported, out of more than forty-six hundred training courses being held in southern states, a fraction, only 4 percent, were open to blacks. In Florida, where blacks comprised 27 percent of the population, less than 1 percent were being trained. Two months after Pearl Harbor, in Texas, where they constituted more than 14 percent of the population, blacks numbered less than 2 percent of the nearly 12,500 individuals admitted to training courses.[12]

The *Militant* even questioned official statistics that showed sizeable increases in black defense jobs. It cited a War Manpower Commission study that it charged the Office of War Information tried to bury. The study revealed, the socialist newspaper said, that the employment of blacks in war industry actually rose only 1.5 percent in the twelve months after July 1942, a "tiny" increase that "comes in the face of the most severe labor shortage in the history of the country."[13]

Labor shortages provoked an immense migration north and to areas where defense industries were clustered. It was a repeat of the migration that occurred during World War I but was much vaster in scope. The lure of work attracted not only an estimated four hundred thousand blacks from the rural South, but also a comparable number of southern whites.[14] They flocked to industrial cities like Detroit, where the materials of war were produced, or to seaports like Baltimore, where enormous quantities of war goods were shipped overseas. Crowded and squeezed into a few neighborhoods, they competed directly for jobs and housing.

The first full year of the war, 1942, was filled with stories of clashes between civilians, white and black, sparked by overcrowding. Most times, whites were responsible for instigating the incidents, and more often than not, police forces took the side of whites no matter who the instigators were.

In Baltimore, where 175,000 blacks were forced to live in three square miles of what the *Militant* called "chiefly slum territory," two thousand blacks assembled for a protest march on the state capitol in

Annapolis to demand that the Maryland governor end the beatings and killings of blacks by Baltimore police.[15]

Continued job discrimination led to mass rallies that drew thousands upon thousands of blacks in Chicago, in St. Louis, and at Madison Square Garden in New York.[16] Blacks also protested the choice of Mrs. Oveta Culp Hobby, the wife of the former governor of Texas, to be director of the WACS. They believed her southern background might bespeak a discriminatory attitude about accepting black women in the women's corps. The National Negro Council urged Secretary of War Henry Stimson to name, instead, Mary McLeod Bethune, who had become an official of the National Youth Administration.[17]

The unrest affected the Deep South as well. Southern whites complained that blacks were getting too uppity. In August 1942, Col. Lindley W. Camp of the Georgia State Guard put the state militia on alert because of—in his words—"suspected subversive influences" who were trying to cause race trouble in the state. Camp, who said that the "same condition" existed in Alabama, South Carolina, and other southern states, reported that there had been "an unusual number of assault cases and attempts to assault white ladies," and that communities "have reported efforts on the part of Negro men and women to demand certain privileges which are not granted in Georgia and which never will be."[18]

That October, the *New York Times* reported, there were three lynchings of blacks within one week in Mississippi.[19]

Even more common was violence involving black servicemen. Black soldiers were killed in incidents in El Paso, Texas; Mobile, Alabama; and Columbia, South Carolina. A riot broke out in the black section of Alexandria, Louisiana, when a white MP reportedly started to beat a black soldier who had not paid for a movie ticket.[20] Military police fatally wounded two black privates and wounded five others at Fort Dix, New Jersey. Tuskegee police officers attacked and injured several blacks, and at Camp Lee, Virginia, a white guard shot and killed a black private who stepped out onto a balcony of the prison barracks.

Blacks found three incidents involving soldiers and civilian law-enforcement authorities particularly onerous. In one, Raymond Carr, a black MP, was killed by a Louisiana state policeman when Carr refused to leave his post guarding a military site. The state trooper was suspended for one day.

Another involved Sgt. Thomas B. Foster of the Ninety-second Engineers Battalion. Foster questioned the method used by white MPs in arresting a drunken black soldier in Little Rock, Arkansas, and was struck down. A Little Rock police office then shot him five times, killing him, as he lay dazed on the sidewalk. The Justice Department took up the case but eventually abandoned the prosecution of the policeman because it said there was no prospect of conviction.

In the third incident, Pvt. Charles J. Reco was ordered off a bus in Beaumont, Texas, after he took a seat in the "whites only" section. As soon as he left the bus, a city police officer hit him with a nightstick and forced him into the back seat of a police car. During the trip to the station house, the officer allegedly shot him twice, once in the shoulder and once in the arm.[21]

Soon after Sergeant Foster's death, in March 1942, Adam Clayton Powell, Jr., wrote a blistering editorial in the *People's Voice* entitled "Mr. President, Just What Is It We Are Fighting For?" Powell charged that "more Negro men have been killed and beaten, so far this year, than in any similar period of this century." He said the "cold-blooded, premeditated murder" of Foster "will go down in history as one of the most wanton murders of all time." Powell laid the blame for the

> mounting tide of racial hatred, of civilians vs. soldiers . . . squarely at your feet. . . . You alone have the power to deal with this correctly and you must do it and do it promptly, with firmness and exactness. If not, then this nation will rapidly move toward a national race riot. Such a pogrom will . . . spill the blood of Negro people on the streets of America.[22]

But violence against blacks, both servicemen and civilians, stepped up. Reco had been shot in July. That same month, black newspapers carried a string of other stories dealing with beatings and shootings. White MPs and civilian police beat up a private and his mother when he tried to use the telephone in the white waiting room of a Houston rail station. New Orleans police beat up a draftee and his mother when the youth stepped out of line to say goodbye to her.

A company guard in Birmingham, Alabama, beat up, then shot to death a black miner who protested a pay deduction made by the company clerk.

Mary McLeod Bethune was an enthusiastic supporter of the war program, but even she, she said, was finding cause for "concern." Writing in the *People's Voice*, Mrs. Bethune declared that she had been "asking questions, making inquiries, looking people in the eye ":

> Soldiers in uniform denied food for 22 hours because no restaurant would serve them—a government worker beaten over the head because he attempted to enter a cafeteria that a guard felt should be reserved exclusively for white workers—unarmed soldiers shot on little or no provocation by civil and military police—one group of draftees being examined and inoculated in the boiler room, while other draftees are, at the same time, examined and inoculated in the immaculately clean and white clinic rooms of the induction center—
>
> All the victims Negroes—none of the perpetrators of these insults and crimes punished![23]

On Christmas Day 1942, more than one hundred members of the Fellowship of Southern Churchmen, meeting in Black Mountain, North Carolina, issued a statement urging complete social, political, and economic emancipation for blacks:

> We who deny and defy the boastful claim of racial superiority by the dictators must stop asserting this claim by word or by deed amongst ourselves. . . .
>
> The defense of the liberties of this nation is seriously hampered so long as the Negro is not given a just and equitable share in the defense of the freedoms for which we now struggle.[24]

But as the war ground on and thousands of Americans were being killed and wounded abroad, the war at home also continued without respite. The year 1943 was no better than 1942 had been. In fact, it was worse.

FOURTEEN

Violence on the Home Front

We were not made eternally to weep.

—Countee Cullen[1]

At a time when national unity was a prime concern of the federal government, the legacy of decades of prejudice grew in intensity, both in civilian life and in the armed services. Tensions between blacks and whites escalated, fueling explosive confrontations. All winter and spring of 1943, racial provocations turned into clashes in city streets, at defense plants, on military bases.

The year 1943 began, on January 2, with the news that a Cleveland judge had thrown out a suit brought against two local war plants charged with refusing to employ black women because of their "color." A number of women had taken training courses as machine-shop operators, attracted by the companies' advertisements for help. But when they completed the training and were even commended, they were told that there were no jobs available. The judge said that nothing could be done legally about the situation, thus confirming, as the *Militant* observed, "the oft-made charge that Executive Order 8802 is completely toothless and ineffective."[2]

A few days later, Walter White took the occasion of the annual meeting of the NAACP in Manhattan to argue that the Allies could not win "unless there is drastic readjustment of racial attitudes."[3] The issue White brought up was a critical one. Could the nation win a tough war, fought on two fronts, when there was so much racial divisiveness and escalating violence on the home front?

Eleanor Roosevelt stated publicly that there could be no real peace if the race problem were not remedied. Taking the occasion of a lecture-concert at the Golden Gate Ballroom in Harlem, she affirmed that "now" was the time for Americans to begin to correct the evils of racial prejudice.

Mrs. Roosevelt's speech elicited a lengthy editorial of praise in the *Amsterdam News*. She belonged, it said, to a small group of "honest, courageous persons" such as Pearl Buck. The "Bilbos, Rankins, Dixons," the newspaper continued, "would rather see the U.S. lose the war than to see the Negro citizens get their rightful civil, economic, educational, political and other deserts. They have already said as much." The newspaper said that "would-be white liberals" of the ilk of Virginius Dabney, editor of the *Richmond Times-Dispatch*, "contend that dire results will take place in this country if the Negro citizens don't pipe down about their rights," and that "now is not the time" to demand their rights. Such liberals, the newspaper stated, "quite often cause more damage to racial amity and progress" than the "group of bigots."[4]

Mrs. Roosevelt's words and influence did little to abate entrenched racial attitudes, particularly in the South. Southerners like Gov. Chauncey Sparks of Alabama continued to extol the virtues of segregation. In a candid speech that was quoted nationwide, Sparks told a Founder's Day audience at Tuskegee Institute that "absolute segregation" and "independent development" should govern the conduct of the white and black races in the South. "Talking plain," as he put it, to his black audience, Sparks declared that "the two races are distinct. They occupy spheres in life that began in different origins, have continued in diverging channels and should remain separate, as they have always been since the Creation." The governor said that "no influences from outside should or can change these fundamental safety principles," and that "outside agitation" could "never be helpful." Sparks added that the two races could work out their problems if not interfered with by "the demagogues among the whites" and "the social climbers among the Negroes."[5]

Sparks's predecessor, Frank Dixon, had gone even further, warning that Alabama would secede rather than grant equal treatment to black citizens.[6]

As the months went by, the inequities—and the incidents—continued. Bus companies in New Jersey[7] and Washington[8] refused to hire black drivers. The navy reiterated its ban on black women being allowed to enlist in the WAVES and SPARS.[9]

Typically, that winter, when a severe storm clogged city streets leading to a military installation in Seattle, black troops were brought from Camp Lewis, sixty miles away, to help remove the snow. The NAACP protested, pointing out that no white troops were ordered to shovel snow. It was just one more instance, the NAACP felt, of a consistent pattern of treating black soldiers as laborers.[10]

The black leadership continued to keep up its pressure on Washington to put some teeth into Executive Order 8802. A. Philip Randolph's March on Washington Movement sent a telegram to President Roosevelt, saying the order would be nothing more than "the proverbial scrap of paper" unless he prodded the FEPC to order railroads to end their discrimination.[11]

Such protests were often met with silence, or, in one case, a court-martial. An army chaplain, Luther M. Fuller, got into a dispute with Truman K. Gibson, who had replaced William H. Hastie at the War Department. Fuller complained that abuses were common against black servicemen being transported to posts in the South Pacific aboard navy ships. Gibson said Fuller's charges were untrue. In response, the chaplain enumerated what he had witnessed: an officer cursing, kicking, and threatening to throw overboard a black soldier; another soldier dying because a surgeon refused him medical attention; and other black GIs fed bread and jam "and seldom anything else unless given them by the ship crew." Fuller said a riot was narrowly averted when blacks came to his assistance after the regimental adjutant ordered him off an island.[12] For his candidness, the outspoken chaplain was subsequently ordered to face court-martial proceedings.[13]

Something must have finally gotten through on some level because in May the War Department tried a public-relations ploy to win the support of black publications by sponsoring a press junket to an undisclosed post. Fifteen newspaper reporters and editors were invited to observe firsthand the maneuvers of the Ninety-third Division. Gen. Benjamin Davis was their official host on the B-24 Liberator bomber that flew them to "somewhere in Louisiana." The one-star insignia of Davis's rank was prominently displayed in the window of the plane's cockpit, but the attention of Roy Wilkins,

who was on the trip, was drawn to the white members of the crew—
"fine, clean-cut young Americans." He reported to the *Amsterdam News* that he could not understand why black youths were not being trained as yet to fly the bombers as well: "Negroes judge the sincerity of our stated war aims by the degree to which they are permitted to participate in the war. It is not—and never has been—a question of supporting the enemy. It has been a question of how much we are to be permitted to fight for our own country."[14]

The newspaper's managing editor, Dan Burley, who was also on the junket, wrote that while both black and white troops grumbled about food, promotions, and accommodations, only blacks had no means of transportation to recreational facilities available in a "God-forsaken hole called Leesville" about thirty-five miles away from camp "over winding tortuous roads." The only bar in Leesville open to black soldiers on passes was a "hell-hole of a place, comparative to the size of a telephone booth," where prices were "sky high" for everything. There was no movie house or dance hall they could attend, no library where they could go to read. "They, these black soldiers," Burley said, "are told on the one hand that they are free, that they are citizens of the United States. They are told they are fighting for justice and democracy, but find their effort dissipated in a miasma of rank, old Southern prejudice which hampers their efficiency and hinders their growth in the principles of Americanism." There is, Burley went on,

> a stolid look of resignation to their fate as "second rate Americans" on the faces of the black boys I have seen from Louisiana, Texas, Alabama and certain other southern states. And there is a deep resentment, a dangerous, smouldering hatred that can be discerned in the eyes and faces of the Negro soldiers from the North—from Chicago, New York, Detroit, Cleveland, Boston and Philadelphia [—]that augurs ill for those or for the situations which press them too far.[15]

As the year wore on, the catalog of incidents took an ugly and violent turn. Burley's report appeared in the same issue of the *Amsterdam News* that featured a page one story about the arrest and beating in Columbus, Georgia, of a black lieutenant from Fort Benning. According to the Negro Associated Press story, the cashier of the Royal Theater, a white woman, told the lieutenant and his wife that "Nigger" tickets were sold at a different window. No sooner had they moved off than ushers and a Columbus policeman stopped the lieutenant and detained him for the way he "spoke to that white woman." Both he and his wife were taken to the city police station. There, fourteen policemen began berating the officer, knocking him down several times. His wife was struck when she bent over to help him.[16]

Some 160 miles away on the eastern coast of Georgia, a soldier based at Camp Stewart, outside of Savannah, wrote the *New York Age* that "practically everywhere you may go, you find so much segregation here, until you are left with the feeling that slavery time has started all over again." The soldier, who was anonymous, wondered why "so many" blacks returned from weekend leaves with bandages "all over their heads."[17]

Camp Stewart, one of the largest training centers in the country, was a constant trouble spot. In the words of one Harlem army veteran, it was a "concentration camp." New York's own 369th Coast Artillery, which was based at Pearl Harbor at the time of the Japanese attack, transferred to Camp Stewart in the spring of 1943 to act as cadres in the training of other blacks as antiaircraft personnel. The 212 members of the 369th had passed through Harlem on leave before heading South and were feted by local black organizations at parties and at a special service at the Abyssinian Baptist Church, whose assistant pastor was the former chaplain of the 369th.[18] Once the men reached Georgia, however, the treatment they received changed dramatically. The men of the 369th were kept standing in the rain for several hours before being billeted in a garage with a leaking roof.[19]

Families, friends, the NAACP, the National Negro Congress, and black newspapers were soon deluged with hundreds of letters about the "deplorable conditions" that the men suffered daily. The regiment's black officers had been transferred, replaced by white officers; the contingent as a whole was "completely isolated from the rest of the camp" and its rations were scanty—"after a full day's work, a cold cut sandwich which was called supper."[20] When on leave in Savannah, Walter White reported, "a long succession of indignities were heaped upon these men to 'teach these northern Negroes their place.'"[21]

On the night of June 9, black troops at Camp Stewart rioted over the report that young black women were being molested. Where or when the molestations occurred was not clear. The army said the report was based on "false and malicious rumors." It never identified the black troops involved, so it is not known whether members of the 369th participated. In the riot, a white MP from Georgia was killed and four others were wounded. No blacks were injured.[22]

Similar outbursts took place in Duck Hill, near Grenada in northern Mississippi, and at the Shenango Personnel Replacement Depot near Greenville, Pennsylvania, south of Erie. Black soldiers from nearby Camp McCain shot up Duck Hill, peppering the town with bullets for twelve minutes. Army officials refused to comment about the incident. The incident at Shenango, a fight between black and white soldiers, started at the post exchange. The depot commander separated the two groups, but the blacks reportedly returned armed with rifles and ammunition and started firing on the whites. Military policemen returned the fire, killing one black soldier and wounding seven others.[23]

As devastating as the violence at military bases was to morale, in some ways violence in civilian life was even more damaging to the war effort. In cities as diverse as Newark, New Jersey; Mobile, Alabama; Los Angeles, California; Chester, Pennsylvania; and Beaumont, Texas, the violence often brought an abrupt halt to defense manufacturing. All work shut down when whites protested the hiring or promoting of blacks, when blacks were placed in production departments or made plant guards, or when white workers demanded separate toilet facilities.

In Newark, a series of street fights between blacks and whites lasted for three days in two city wards swollen by wartime population. During the fighting, a fifteen-year-old black youth was shot in the back and died. Local authorities said friction between the two races had developed as they vied for work and argued over seniority rights and job upgrading.[24]

A few weeks before the riot at Camp Stewart, black workers were attacked at the Addsco shipyard in Mobile, a city of shipyards that had attracted tens of thousands of workers and swelled the population by 60 percent. White welders armed with bars, clubs, and bricks assailed black welders who had been upgraded and assigned to work in the same areas as the whites. The fighting spread to other parts of the shipyard. Before it was over, eleven blacks were in the hospital. Peace was restored and work resumed a week later after the company announced that the black welders would be assigned to a separate work area.[25]

Such unrest in urban centers of war production became so commonplace that in the three-month period starting in March 1943 alone, at least 101,955 man-days of work were lost—all, the U.S. Labor Department reported, the result of racial bigotry.[26]

As the civilian violence mushroomed, white officials found an easy scapegoat: juvenile delinquents. It was a simplistic and conventional explanation for the increases in violence and crime that communities were experiencing, and diverted attention from the root causes of so much of what was occurring.

Crimes committed by youths did increase substantially during the war. Dislocations produced a major social upheaval, with more than 27 million Americans on the move at one time or another. The moves were especially difficult for teenagers, who frequently found themselves in alien neighborhoods, or living next to areas populated by a different ethnic or racial group. In addition, the manpower shortage created a demand for workers of all ages. More than a million boys and girls between the ages of fourteen and nineteen left school in the war years. A number of boys lied about how old they were and enlisted in the military, but most were lured by the chance to earn money on manpower-starved farms and in businesses and factories. By May 1943, about 1.8 million boys and girls under the age of eighteen were working on farms or in factories. One Lockheed plant alone employed fifteen hundred boys as riveters and electricians or on assembly lines and in metal-fabrication shops.[27]

While most crime rates declined overall because of the drain of young males who entered the armed forces, juvenile delinquency rates soared. Suddenly, many teenagers found themselves with ready cash to spend. With their fathers away at war and their mothers busy working in war plants, many youngsters were on their own, unsupervised, and engaged in stealing cars and robbing people. Those who had jobs often spent their money on liquor and partying, a lethal combination that sometimes ended in a murder.

Crime figures in the first full year of the war alone were so "alarming" that J. Edgar Hoover called on law-enforcement agencies to mount a "counter-offensive" before there was "a breakdown on our home front." Hoover told graduating agents at the FBI Academy, "Something has happened to our moral fibers when the nation's youths under voting age accounted for 15 per cent of all murders, 35 per cent of all robberies, 58 per cent of all car thefts and 50 per cent of all burglaries."[28]

In 1942, youths aged nineteen predominated in the number of arrests recorded by the FBI on the basis of filings from 318 of the nation's larger cities. In 1943, the predominant age fell to seventeen for males, eighteen for females. The arrests of boys under eighteen rose by almost 24 percent in the second half of 1943 alone; the arrest of girls under twenty-one—then the voting and legal age—rose nearly 48 percent.[29] In all, 112,281 males and females under voting age were arrested in 1943—approximately one in every five arrests throughout the nation.[30]

The juvenile crime statistics should not have surprised authorities. Juvenile delinquency rates had risen during World War I not only in the United States but also in England, France, and Germany, among other nations. The pattern was being repeated in World War II. The French spoke of "blousons noirs" or black-jacketed juvenile delinquents, the Germans of "halbstarke" or half-mature youths. In Australia, delinquent boys were known as "bodgies" and girls as "widbies." Among Italians, delinquents were called "vitelloni" or fat calves.[31]

Many of the youths who got into trouble in the United States wore distinctive apparel—the zoot suit. It became identified with what authorities called hoodlumism and what sociologists termed a posturing, flaunting subcultural gesture of challenge to authority.[32] The style first became popular when the photograph of a black bus-boy in Gainesville, Georgia, dressed in a custom-made zoot suit, appeared in *Men's Apparel* in February 1940. The suit was apparently inspired by the long coat and peg trousers worn by Clark Gable in several scenes in the movie *Gone with the Wind*. Also known as a "killer diller," the fashion spread rapidly to Mississippi, Alabama, and Louisiana and then leapfrogged to Harlem, where it became *de rigeur* for black teenagers and young men.[33] The suit consisted of a long, loosely cut jacket that had wide, padded shoulders and reached to midthigh, and pants known as "drapes" or "reat pleats" that ballooned out below the waist and around the legs but were cut tight around the ankles. Customarily worn with the outfit was a wide-brimmed hat with a feather, a long watch chain, a T-shirt or a sport shirt with long collar points that was buttoned but without a tie, and thick shoes.

The zoot suit soon became a symbol of juvenile crime. Malcolm Little had deliberately worn one when he was called up for induction in the army. He had also purposely spoken in the jargon associated with "hip" zoot-suiters.

The flamboyant suit and all that it represented became the focal point of a major race riot during the war that pitted white soldiers, sailors, and civilians against zoot-suited youths.

The prime targets were Mexican-American youths known as *pachucos* who lived in the Skid Row area of Los Angeles. Like blacks, they had long suffered discrimination in California in public places such as swimming pools, restaurants, and schools. They were the children of working-class immigrants, alienated by customs, beliefs, and language different than their parents. The situation became especially aggravated in Los Angeles, which had mushroomed in size since 1940 and doubled in population before the war was over. Drawn by the lure of work in war plants, a large influx of blacks had also moved into the city to join the quarter of a million Mexican-Americans,[34] and many of their teenage children joined *pachuco* gangs.

Hostility against *pachucos* had been building up for some time, encouraged in part by anti-Mexican remarks made by officials. The animosity was fed by the false impression that Mexican-American youths were crime-prone. Actually, available statistics showed that delinquency had increased less among them than among other ethnic groups.[35] Yet local authorities ignored the facts and continued to play on the bias against Mexican-Americans. One, a captain in the sheriff's office, told a grand jury that Mexicans were predisposed "biologically" toward criminal behavior.[36] And newspapers made such a point of playing up the crimes committed by them that at one point the Office of War Information sent a representative to Los Angeles to reason with the publishers. As a result, the press dropped the word

"Mexican" when identifying in their stories youths arrested for crimes. But they substituted for it "zoot suit."[37] A zoot suit youth became the synonym for a Mexican youth.

The *pachucos* roved Los Angeles in organized bands that gathered after dark and allegedly engaged in thievery, petty crimes, and sometimes knifings. Their presence was anathema to servicemen who were enraged by what they perceived as the youths' lack of patriotism and their attitudes in general about the war. The polarization between *pachuco* gangs and predominantly white servicemen resulted in a number of minor confrontations—that is, until the night of June 3. That night, members of one *pachuco* club were asked to a meeting at a police substation in Los Angeles to discuss how to keep peace in the neighborhood. At the conclusion of the meeting, squad cars dropped off the members at a corner where most of them lived. No sooner were the police out of sight then whites, among them soldiers and sailors, attacked the youths, apparently in retaliation for earlier assaults on them.

The violence continued unabated for four more days. On one day alone, a crowd of nearly four hundred sailors roamed an amusement zone called the Pike in Long Beach south of Los Angeles in search of *pachucos*, who, in turn, stoned a streetcar filled with sailors bound for the harbor.[38] That Sunday and the next morning, Monday, June 7, newspapers in Los Angeles contained unconfirmed reports that an armed mob of five hundred zoot-suiters were planning to avenge friends that night. Spurred by the rumors, a mob of more than a thousand whites went on a rampage. They burst into every movie house along a twelve-block stretch of Main Street in downtown Los Angeles, dragging Mexican-Americans and blacks from their seats and into the street, where they were beaten and kicked. The whites then raced through the Mexican section on the city's east side, attacking youths indiscriminately in theaters and bars whether or not they were wearing a zoot suit.

More than sixty zoot-suiters were arrested during the almost week-long rioting. But no servicemen or white civilians were taken into custody. They were acting in self-defense, so official reasoning went. As Los Angeles authorities toted up the casualties—scores of injured—the City Council voted to make the wearing of a zoot suit a misdemeanor. At the same time, acting in response to rumors at military bases that servicemen were planning to form vigilante groups, both the army and the navy declared Los Angeles out of bounds to all servicemen. State Sen. Jack Tenney, whose committee had been investigating communist and fascist movements in California, suggested that the zoot-suiters might have been manipulated by subversive elements.[39]

Community leaders in Los Angeles dismissed the idea that the street battles were a symptom of racial discrimination. Instead, they insisted that the rioting represented a serious statewide problem of juvenile delinquency.[40] Their reaction was typical of other cities throughout the United States. Yet the most telling statistic of the FBI's annual report for 1943, buried at the end of lengthy tabulations, indicated something more profound. Of the grand total of 490,764 persons of all ages arrested during 1943, 125,339—or one in every four persons—were blacks. That was double their proportion of the nation's population.[41] No one—that is, no white local, state, or federal official—ever raised a question about why blacks were so over-represented. And few officials heeded the warning signs of the continuing violence and production disruptions.

In the same week as the Zoot Suit Riots, a particularly nasty race riot, this one involving adults, broke out in Beaumont, Texas. The outburst was precipitated by the alleged rape of a young white woman, the mother of three children, by a black man. Whites roamed the streets of Beaumont's black section, attacking residents without regard to age or sex. Martial law was finally declared, but before order was restored, one person had been killed and about a dozen others injured.

On the same day that rioting occurred in Beaumont, two other racial incidents occurred. In one, a black awaiting trial for the murder of a white man in Marianna, a town in western Florida, was taken from jail by a white mob and beaten to death.

The other incident took place in Chester, Pennsylvania, at the Sun Shipbuilding and Dry Dock Company, which had fulfilled its promise to set up a separate black work force. The first ship built entirely by blacks was launched in early May.[42] But little more than a month later, on June 16, blacks and whites clashed when a black security guard ordered workers back to work after lunch. Outside the cafeteria, the guard exchanged words with a white worker, then slapped him in the face. In the melee that ensued, five black workers were shot.[43]

A similar racial clash occurred later at the plant of the American Steel Foundries Company in East Chicago, Indiana. This time, a white foreman accused a black laborer of malingering, then slapped him in the face and fired him. In protest, hundreds of blacks barricaded the doors of the plant, shutting down all production.[44]

That spring, one riot stood out from all the others, a classic example of the traumas evoked by the war. It occurred against a background of ferment: a history of labor disputes that pitted blacks against whites, overcrowding and rivalry for housing created by the sudden influx of hundreds of thousands of migrants from the South, the persistent prejudice encouraged by racist groups and individuals, and the yearning of blacks for equal treatment. As one observer put it, "A blind man could see it coming."[45]

The riot took place in the nation's fourth largest city, the very heart of America's industrial empire, where 35 percent of its vital ordnance material was manufactured—Detroit.[46]

FIFTEEN

A State of Siege

The white man is a tiger at my throat,
Drinking my blood as my life ebbs away . . .

—Claude McKay[1]

Michigan received more defense contracts than any other state with the exception of New York, which had almost three times the population. Most of those contracts went to plants in the four-county Detroit area.[2]

Since rearmament had begun in 1940, the city's population had swelled by between two hundred and three hundred thousand. By June 1943, Detroit was home to nearly two million people, one in ten of whom were black. The newcomers included fifty thousand blacks.[3] The rest were whites—"hill-billies," Michigan residents called them[4] —from states such as Kentucky, Tennessee, and West Virginia, as well as the Deep South.[5] So many came that thousands of white workers were forced to sleep in boxcars, tents, church pews, and jails. Lucky ones were in ubiquitous trailer camps, others slept in shifts in overcrowded apartments.[6] The two hundred thousand blacks who lived in the city were squeezed into a neighborhood where twenty years earlier only a quarter of that number had lived.[7]

The blacks had some political clout and enjoyed a variety of well-paying jobs. Michigan's labor commissioner in the mid-40s was black, as was a state senator. The FEPC had successfully prodded a number of factories to open their employment ranks. Detroit's transit system employed about a thousand blacks in a variety of capacities—as motormen, bus drivers, and conductors, among other jobs. One of the

144

major auto manufacturers in the city, Ford, had a reputation for hiring blacks for its assembly lines, though the company evidently employed them as a cheap countermeasure to a whites-only AFL local. The blacks at first were anti-unionists, but when the joint United Auto Workers-Congress of Industrial Organizations was set up in the mid-1930s and welcomed them, many joined it. One local, UAW's No. 600 at Ford's River Rouge plant, the largest union local in the world, counted eighteen thousand blacks among its ninety thousand members.[8] On the other hand, blacks were underrepresented on Detroit's police force—only forty of its thirty-six hundred officers were blacks[9]—and the police had a reputation among blacks for being both racist and brutal.

Little new housing was built to accommodate any of the migrants, in great part because of the interference of local real estate developers. A special assistant to Attorney General Francis Biddle called housing conditions for blacks especially "deplorable."[10] They were met by open resistance when they tried to move into predominantly white areas that were filled with immigrants from Europe or second-generation Americans.

Only one new federal housing project was built for blacks—a two-hundred-unit development named after the Civil War heroine Sojourner Truth—but the first twenty-four families who tried to move into it in late February 1942 were greeted by a burning cross and hundreds of whites carrying picket signs and armed with knives, guns, rifles, and clubs. Police made no attempt to search or disarm the demonstrators.[11] As the black families, supported by friends, tried to cross the picket line, fighting broke out. It was not until two months later that, as eight hundred state troops stood by with fixed bayonets, the families were able to move into the project.[12] Afterwards, federal investigators reported that "unless strong and quick intervention by some high official, preferably the President, is taken at once, hell is going to be let loose in every Northern city where large numbers of immigrants and Negroes are in competition."[13]

Nothing was done to alleviate matters either on the federal or the state level. Federal funds for public improvements directly related to war production never met local needs, state spending on health education actually declined, and virtually no additional housing was built. At one point in 1943, the vacancy rate in the four-county area was a mere 0.5 percent, and there were seven responses for every housing advertisement.[14]

The heightened tensions proved fertile ground for the Ku Klux Klan. Its members and other racists proclaimed white supremacy from soapboxes all over Detroit, and sympathizers worked in every plant. "Basically," a black leader said, "the trouble goes back to the Civil War when the immigrant whites saw in the freed slaves a threat to their economic security, slim as that was."[15]

Abetting and inciting the racists were vicious radio commentators such as Father Charles Coughlin, one-time Louisiana preacher Gerald L. K. Smith, and Frank Norris, a Texas minister, all of whom built up sizeable followings in the city. An observer described their Sunday broadcasts over local radio stations as "a babble of racism, fundamentalism, ignorance and guile. They stank of an anti-democratic ferment going on below the city's surface. No city, North or South, could match this hellish Sunday symphony."[16]

One Sunday afternoon in April 1943, the NAACP's branch in Detroit responded to the blatant racism. It brought together black fraternal groups with black and white members of the UAW to sponsor a demonstration in downtown Cadillac Square against a list of complaints. The complaints included continuing job discrimination in local war plants and the refusal of many city restaurants to serve blacks. The Detroit branch subsequently played host to an emergency war conference of the more than six hundred branches of the NAACP to discuss "The Status of the Negro in the War For Freedom." The call for the conference went out, the NAACP announced, because "sectional, religious, class and racial prejudices" were multiplying "alarmingly":

> Jim Crow rides high in the armed forces. Negro women continue to be barred from the WAVE, SPARS, and the Women's Marine Corps Reserve. American soldiers die for want of nursing while Negro nurses, eager to serve, are turned down except for a small quota accepted for service only in jim-crow Army units. The Red Cross pleads for blood donations but continues to segregate Negro blood plasma in violation of every law of science.
>
> Jobs in war industries are still barred to Negroes despite the dire necessity created by the manpower shortage. . . . [the FEPC]

has been reduced to virtually complete impotence. Legislation to freeze labor already enacted will fix Negroes—particularly the nine million in Southern states—in their present menial and poorly paid jobs for the duration without hope or prospect of upgrading.[17]

The attempt to upgrade blacks on the job caused work stoppages and walkouts in Detroit at the U.S. Rubber Company, Vickers, and the Hudson Motor Car Company. Still another was prompted by the promotion of eight blacks, all janitors and all UAW members, to machine jobs once operated by whites in each of four main buildings at the Hudson Naval Ordnance Arsenal. Three thousand workers on the plant's morning shift immediately quit work,[18] effectively shutting down more than half of the plant's production.[19]

In June 1943, at about the time of the Zoot Suit Riots in Los Angeles, the promotion of three blacks at the Packard Motor Company, which manufactured Rolls-Royce engines for bombers and marine engines for torpedo boats, led to a wildcat strike by twenty-five thousand workers. A local UAW-CIO president charged that members of the KKK had fomented the strike.[20] The U.S. Labor Department singled out Packard officials, saying they had incited the workers to halt work.[21] Walter White, who visited the scene of the strike, said that both before and during the walkout, the company's personnel manager and general foreman openly urged the strikers to hold out against the hiring or promotion of blacks.[22] He overheard one striker saying, "I'd rather see Hitler and Hirohito win the war than work beside a nigger on the assembly line."[23] White's colleague, Roy Wilkins, said the walkout "stoked racial tempers around Detroit to the kindling point."[24]

Detroit exploded on the "steaming hot" evening of June 20. The humid weather had attracted thousands of families to the city's Belle Isle Park on the Detroit River. Two cars collided on the crowded bridge that connected the island to downtown Detroit. One driver was white, the other black. The two got into a fistfight. Their quarrel did not last long, but it set off a conflicting set of ugly rumors. Blacks heard variously that white sailors had thrown a black woman and her baby from the bridge into the river or that the sailors had thrown mother and child into a lake on Belle Isle. Whites heard that blacks had raped white sailors and were rioting at the park.[25] Another rumor circulated that a black had killed a white girl on the island.

As Detroit police stood by, a white mob invaded a movie theater on Woodward Avenue, dragging out blacks and beating them. Others stoned cars, stopped streetcars, and pulled out blacks and beat them. Shots could be heard throughout the city, but especially in peripheral areas where white and black neighborhoods converged or overlapped. Fires broke out everywhere.

Early the next morning, Walter White was awakened in his apartment in Harlem by a phone call from the president of the NAACP branch in Detroit, who told him what was happening and that the city was still in turmoil. Within a few hours, White was in an airplane, heading for Detroit. As he drove from the airport to the city he saw fleeting glimpses of mobs roaming streets, searching for blacks. By then, virtually all Detroit, he said, was a battlefield.

White had no luck with local officials. Detroit's mayor, Edward J. Jeffries, obfuscated. He claimed afterwards that blacks started the rioting. "The white people were slow getting started," the mayor callously declared, "but when they did get started they sure made up for lost time."[26]

White next turned to Michigan governor Harry S. Kelly, urging him to request federal troops, but the governor hesitated, so White personally got on the telephone to call the War Department in Washington.[27] At his urging and on Roosevelt's orders, six thousand troops finally reached the city at nightfall, a curfew was set up, and order restored. By then, after thirty hours of rioting, thirty-four people were dead; twenty-five of them were blacks, seventeen of whom were shot and killed by Detroit police.[28] Every one of the sixteen victims killed on the first day of the riot was black.[29] No white person who died was killed by a policeman. More than six hundred people were injured.[30] Seventy-three of the most seriously injured blacks included twelve wounded by police and thirty-six who had been beaten by whites.[31]

Thurgood Marshall, who had rushed to Detroit to join White, was shocked by the police brutality. "Much of the blood spilled," he said, "is on the hands of the Detroit police department." Writing in the NAACP magazine *Crisis,* in an article entitled "The Gestapo in Detroit (1943)," Marshall charged that "the police ran true to form":

The trouble reached riot proportions because the police once again enforced the law with an unequal hand. They used "persuasion" rather than firm action with White rioters, while against Negroes they used the ultimate in force: night sticks, revolvers, riot guns, submachine guns, and deer guns. . . .

The entire record, both of the riot killings and of previous disturbances reads like the story of the Nazi Gestapo. . . .

In no case did police do more than try to "reason" with these [white] mobs. . . . The police did not draw their revolvers or riot guns, and never used any force to disperse these mobs. . . . As a result of this, the mobs got larger and bolder and even attacked Negroes on the pavement of the City Hall.[32]

No policeman or police official was ever punished or reprimanded, a fact that troubled both Marshall and White, who published an extensive report on the riot.

More troubling to blacks was the attitude of the president. The Detroit riot, the Labor Department reported, cost a million man-hours of work at critical defense plants.[33] It was the worst setback in the production of war materials caused by any labor dispute in the country.[34] Put all together, the disruption of production in Detroit and other cities vexed Roosevelt. He wrote a New York congressman that "the recent outbreaks of violence in widely scattered parts of the country endanger our national unity and comfort our enemies."[35]

Additional anxieties were raised by the threat of more racial clashes throughout the country. The March on Washington Movement was threatening to hold a massive demonstration in Chicago.[36] News stories from Indianapolis spoke of the increasing frequency of interracial pressures.[37] A startling report from Baltimore—where some fifty-eight thousand people lived in each square mile of its black sections under "sanitary conditions which are conceded to be a virtual mockery of this great capital of medical science"—said black assaults on policemen, a crime once unheard of, were increasing. Blacks were continuing to pour into Baltimore at the rate of two thousand a month, seeking work in defense factories. Crime and "dissension" in the city, a *New York Times* correspondent wrote, were said to be mounting among blacks "in direct ratio to their deprivation, and agitation is finding a fertile field in unrest and irritation."[38]

Meanwhile, German and Japanese propagandists were having a

field day over the street clashes between blacks and whites in Detroit. A German radio station broadcasting in English from Europe said "a wave of sabotage" was sweeping across America because the war was not popular. Tokyo claimed that the "entire American economy is about to fall apart," and that "wartime America is teeming with labor unrest and lack of war enthusiasm." Both Axis countries stressed the race question. Nazi propagandists sarcastically described to South Americans "the fight between whites and Negroes in the country of equality." Tokyo told the conquered Chinese that the Detroit riot proved the existence of race prejudice in the United States.[39]

Roosevelt's prime concern, however, remained winning the war, and to do that, he felt he needed the continued support of the southern bloc in Congress. Mrs. Roosevelt penned him numerous memos, warning of the desperate living conditions in boomtowns throughout the nation. "Detroit should never have happened," she wrote a friend, "but when Congress behaves as it does why should others be calmer?" A friend of hers told the president that the race problem "can literally wreck our national endeavor"—the matter had become "a national menace."[40] One of his administrative aides, Jonathan Worth Daniels, a North Carolinian liberal who had been editor of the *Raleigh News and Observer*, wrote an analysis that declared that the Detroit rioting had to be seen "as a climax in what almost amounts to an epidemic of racial tensions in the United States." He said that nothing "could be more effective" in assuaging tensions than a presidential statement.[41]

Walter White and other black leaders agreed, as did white liberals. They all wanted Roosevelt to address the nation on one of his famous fireside chats. Mary McLeod Bethune, for one, thought that the only solution was a "straight forward statement and program of action from the President."[42] A plea in the *New Republic* took to task "the little group of yes-men and intriguers" who were Roosevelt's immediate advisers:

What have they been telling Mr. Roosevelt for months and years about the race crisis?

Okay, Boss. Okay, okay, okay. It's all okay, Boss. Everything will blow over. . . .

Long ago, a year ago at least, when riot rumors and hysteria had already swept the South; when cities . . . [were] plunged into

the first, inevitable race riots; when Ku Klux Klan oratory was lighting the fuses of Mobile and Beaumont and Detroit (and others yet
to come); the President should have come to this nation and talked
to us. . . .

Why, in these months when the period of open race war hung
upon the air, hasn't Mr. Roosevelt come to us with one of his greatest speeches, speaking to us as Americans, speaking to us as the
great mongrel nation; immigrants (and descendants of immigrants)
all of us; none of us the master race, none of us independent of the
other; why hasn't he come to us and talked to us in the simple and
genuine language that Lincoln might have used, why hasn't he
come waking memories of the old American dream, of live and let
live, of a land where all men are endowed with inalienable rights,
of a country where all are created equal? We are a people often cruel
and cynical; but a great moment does not fail to move us.

Why does not the President come to us NOW with such a
speech? He must! The race situation is not okay, Mr. Roosevelt,
whatever the subtle men whisper. There will be other riots in
America. Only a strong federal policy may prevent them. . . .

As a nation we sat with vacant eyes and waited for Pearl Harbor. For two years we sat and watched the Detroit riot in the making. How many other riots will we wait upon before acting? . . .[43]

Roosevelt mulled over the idea of addressing the nation, worried
that there were "no signs that this ugly situation will wear itself out."
At one point, he asked his press secretary, Steve Early, "Don't you
think it is about time for me to issue a statement about racial riots?"[44]
In the end, however, the president decided against making a public
address, convinced, his wife said, that "he must not irritate the
southern leaders as he feels he needs their votes for essential war
bills." The nation, Mrs. Roosevelt acknowledged ruefully, was "sadly
in the need of leadership" with regard to race relations.[45]

The alternatives that some administration officials presented to
solve the racial unrest dismayed black leaders. Attorney General
Francis Biddle suggested two of them: that the migration of blacks
from the South be halted "into communities which cannot absorb
them, either on account of their physical limitations or cultural background," and that an interdepartmental committee be set up within
the government to handle race relations.

Blacks were upset by both ideas. John Chamberlain, an economic and political specialist, said, "Only a severe case of emotional shell-shock could have pushed Attorney General Biddle into suggesting that Negroes be chained to their place of abode, for the world as if they were serfs on medieval manors, or slaves on the Roman *latifundia*." [46] Walter White told the president that a "superboard" or "Negro bureau" would divert attention from and confuse the discussion of real problems.

Administrative aide Jonathan Daniels agreed with White, though for a different reason. He thought a national committee would only serve as "another pressure point for the numerous agitators." He doubted that a special committee could effectively reduce racial disturbances. [47]

Contributing to Roosevelt's greatest worry, the war, at this time was his poor health, though the public was kept in the dark about his true condition. He had little time for much except issues directly connected to the fighting. There certainly was no time for dealing with civil rights issues on a long-range basis. Even day-to-day race problems were perceived as a nuisance. Malcolm S. MacLean, the FEPC's second chairman, believed that one of his duties was "to keep the heat off the 'Boss.' " [48]

Perhaps no city watched the events in Detroit with more concern than New York. Photographs in newspapers showed blacks lying dead or wounded in Detroit's streets and others begging for mercy from white mobs or running from whites armed with pipes and beer bottles. Other pictures depicted blacks, and only blacks, lined up, hands above their heads in surrender. One photo showed a black man being struck by a white rioter while being held by two policemen; still others pictured cars and other property owned by blacks being burned. [49]

How would Harlemites react to the violence? Would Detroit trigger a riot in Harlem, too? What could be done to prevent one?

The answer to those questions came, in different ways, from three men: New York Mayor Fiorello La Guardia, NAACP executive secretary Walter White, and the pastor of the Abyssinian Baptist Church and New York's first black city councilman, Adam Clayton Powell, Jr.

SIXTEEN

Leaders

. . . What, from the slums
Where they have hemmed you, . . .
What reaches them
Making them ill at ease, fearful?

—Sterling Brown[1]

The three men—La Guardia, White, and Powell—shared the same concerns. All of them believed in equality for blacks. But each of them had different priorities, and a different way of achieving his goals.

The two blacks—White and Powell—were so light-skinned that they could be taken for white; in fact, both men had passed as Caucasians at one time or another. Although they both championed black causes, they disagreed over methods and neither man counted the other as a friend. White, however, was a close friend of La Guardia's, though they sometimes did not see eye to eye.

Powell, the youngest of the three men, was the most militant. Only thirty-four years old in 1943, he was already a major driving force in Harlem affairs as the pastor of the Abyssinian Baptist Church, which, like other black churches throughout the nation, was a breeding ground for mass-protest movements. His status was underscored by his being the lone black on the City Council.

Powell cut a handsome figure and was easily taken for white: six-foot-three, with wavy black hair, an aquiline nose, blue eyes,[2] and so light-skinned that he once complained that as a youngster he would be picked on and beaten by both Irish and black boys. "I'm neither fish nor fowl," he told his first wife.[3]

Powell had inherited his light skin from his grandparents, all of whom were mulattos. Those on his father's side were a Virginia planter of German extraction who was killed during the Civil War and a Negro-Indian woman named Sally.

Powell had a reputation for being a rake—women called him "Mr. Jesus."[4] And where some saw him as a defiant battler against injustice, others saw him as an opportunistic, arrogant, irresponsible show-off and demagogue. Powell was, in writer Roi Ottley's words, "aggressive, articulate, unpredictable—no more contradictory character exists in Negro life . . . an incredible combination of showman, black parson, and Tammany Hall . . . at once a salvationist and a politician, an economic messiah and a super-opportunist, an important mass leader and a light-hearted playboy."[5]

Powell was also a spellbinding orator, a "master of mob psychology—he could manipulate a crowd," according to St. Clair Bourne, who was managing editor of Powell's *People's Voice*. Bourne recalls attending a rally in Harlem where Powell extemporaneously made a "fiery speech" that ended with a play on Abraham Lincoln's Gettysburg Address that Powell made up on the spur of the moment and then used as a stock phrase on other occasions: "peace and democracy *for* the people, Christians and Jews; *of* the people, black and white; and *by* the people, Catholic and Protestant."[6]

Powell's commitment to black causes began in the mid-1920s, when he was a student at Colgate University in upstate New York. He had been passing for white without even hinting at his ancestry. The college had assumed that he was a Caucasian and assigned him to room with a white. The few other blacks at the school were otherwise housed separately. Powell never disabused anyone about his family, but when he tried to join a white fraternity a background check disclosed his race. Both white students and the other blacks were incensed at Powell's duplicity. He never again tried to mask his black ancestry.

Powell was, if nothing else, open about his feelings. Though spoiled and sheltered as a youth, he was fully cognizant of the ghetto life around him and the sense of deprivation and despair that blacks experienced. He personified, an NAACP official said, "the conflict between what whites think a Negro ought to act like and a Negro who intends to act as he wishes."[7] Powell rejected an invitation from the White House to participate in a campaign against infantile paralysis connected to the celebration of the birthday of Roosevelt, who was a polio victim. He would have supported it, and gotten his church to do so, too, he said, "if it were not for the rigid practice of discrimination against crippled Negro children and youths now being practiced at Warm Springs, Georgia," where the president often went to enjoy the salutary waters.[8]

Powell inherited the stewardship of the influential Abyssinian Baptist Church from his father, Adam Clayton Powell, Sr. While the younger Powell was still a teenager, the congregation, founded in 1808, followed the exodus of blacks from mid-Manhattan to Harlem, moving in 1923 from Fortieth Street and Eighth Avenue to a new, imposing Gothic and Tudor church on 138th Street. When his father retired in 1937, Adam Jr. became its senior minister. By then he had already become a leading figure in protest activities. "Harlem is sick and tired of promises," he declared in the midst of boycott against an electric company's refusal to hire blacks. "The hour has struck to march!"[9] When only twenty-two years old he led a demonstration at City Hall that brought about the reinstatement of five black doctors fired from Harlem Hospital. He engineered boycotts of stores on 125th Street; battled against rent hikes; led demonstrations against bus companies and public utilities; convinced a newspaper and magazine company to hire blacks instead of whites for its newsstands in Harlem; and persuaded local movie houses to take on blacks as motion-picture projectionists. When New York City revised its charter and abandoned the aldermen system of government in favor of a council based on proportional representation, Powell ran and received the third highest total of votes among the six members elected from Manhattan in 1941. His first significant act was to introduce a series of measures dealing with discrimination in several municipal agencies, including the city colleges, not one of whose 2,282 faculty positions was held by a full-time black professor.[10]

Powell was not the first black to represent the black community, but he filled a void in its representation in municipal government in the 1940s. Democrats had tried to attract the black vote at the turn of the century, when Harlem first became a beacon and new home. They saw to it that a black was named an assistant district attorney in 1905; but his position, and several others filled by blacks, were all appointive. It was not until 1917 that the first black was elected to the State Assembly, and he was a Republican. In the following years, nine other blacks were elected to the Assembly. Beginning in 1920, ten blacks served at one time or another as aldermen, starting with publisher and Harvard graduate George W. Harris, a Republican.[11] But none was ever as outspoken, or achieved the prominence, that Powell did.

As articulate in print as he was in speech, Powell began a column in the *Amsterdam News* a year after the Harlem riot of 1935. He called it "The Soap Box." He shifted the column to his own weekly, the *People's Voice*, which he started on the birthday of abolitionist Frederick Douglass in February 1942, two months after Pearl Harbor. *People's Voice* characterized itself as "a working class paper"; its editorial policy, in the midst of war-time America, called for "a just quota of jobs in all city, state and federal agencies."[12] The newspaper, which had offices on 125th Street, was, Powell said, the "Lenox Avenue edition" of the communist *Daily Worker.*[13] Slogans on either side of its front-page logo read "A Militant Paper" and "Serving All People."[14]

Powell's open militancy attracted the attention of FBI director J. Edgar Hoover, who believed there were "strong indications of Communist affiliations on the part of Powell."[15] Powell called himself "a radical and a fighter,"[16] and though, in fact, he had been influenced by communist doctrine, he considered the German-Russian nonaggression pact of 1939 "the most classic doublecross in history" and believed that democracy was "the only thing left in the world for the masses to depend on."[17] A political maverick, he did, however, receive the endorsement of the *Daily Worker* when he ran for the City Council in 1941 (and when he left it, he endorsed a communist to succeed him). And he had called attention to his patriotism when he wrote, in answer to a question on a draft form whether he was claiming deferment from the army as a conscientious objector: "I haven't fully made up my mind."[18]

In addition, the federal investigators who studied the attitudes of Harlem's blacks shortly after Pearl Harbor, and reported on their negative feelings about the United States, devoted a lengthy paragraph in their summary of the survey to Powell, whose position "in Harlem life," they said, "is unique":

He is a militant leader with about 14,000 ardent followers, and his supporters are ever increasing in number. So far Powell's politics have remained a mystery. He claims that he is merely trying to get Negroes their rights and to provide unity for the country in the time of war. He is certainly not fascist-minded, but he makes it his business to keep Negroes acquainted with the abuses against their race. He is probably perfectly sincere in feeling that only by the elimination of Negro discrimination can this country obtain the unity it needs. . . . He feels the Negro population will not support the war wholeheartedly unless they are so integrated as to share both the successes and the sacrifices. . . . [He] told a Lincoln University conference on The Status of the Negro in a Fighting Democracy: "The Negro people are not wholly sold on this war, even since Pearl Harbor."[19]

The federal investigators surmised that an "important influence" on Powell's political position was "his extremely light color." They believed that he was "constantly faced with the problem of keeping his followers convinced that he is wholly on the Negro's side and he has not 'made any concessions to his white blood'. Were Powell to temper his demands and soften his blows, it is said he might very well lose some of his followers."[20]

Acting on Hoover's orders, the FBI began what would be a twenty-eight-year compilation of information about Powell. A preliminary report filed by the agency's New York office said a "perusal" of the *People's Voice* ascertained "that it follows closely the Communist Party line." A fuller, thirty-page report the New York office submitted in February 1943 said that Powell's "nationalistic tendencies" were "communistic," that he had spoken before and was active as a member of "many of the alleged Communist front organizations." St. Clair Bourne recalls making a point of telling an FBI agent who questioned him that Powell was only one of many persons who spoke at rallies protesting discrimination.[21]

A biographer thought that the guiding issue of Powell's public life was pointed out by Gunnar Myrdal in his *An American Dilemma:* "the discrepancy between what Americans *believed* and how they *acted* in regard to the treatment of blacks in society."[22] Powell himself once declared that "the United States was preaching 'the century of the common man' and the 'Four Freedoms,' yet it was denying any of these freedoms at home, even in the nation's capital. America was talking about the creation of a new world while its conscience was filled with guilt.''[23]

Powell enjoyed a love-hate relationship with La Guardia. The two men made an odd couple, Mutt-and-Jeff in size—Powell towering over the five-foot-two, rotund La Guardia—and father-and-son in terms of age—Powell almost half La Guardia's sixty years. Moreover, where Powell could sway an audience with his stentorian tones, La Guardia's nasal twang turned into an irritating screech when he was excited. More fundamentally, Powell was an activist in racial matters, regarding the war as an opportunity for blacks to achieve equality. La Guardia, on the other hand, was a gradualist who believed that in time—through education, not laws—tolerance would lead to the end of discrimination.

La Guardia, like Powell, was not a stranger to prejudice. He was a fighter in his own right, a feisty curmudgeon who was a crusader for equality. He was also an independent, outwardly a Republican but inwardly a New Dealer who hoped to develop a new Progressive Party along the lines of Wisconsin liberal Robert La Follette.

The mayor had a special compassion for immigrants, minorities, and religious diversities. He was born in the Italian section of Greenwich Village in Manhattan to a father who was a lapsed Catholic and a mother who was Jewish. Reared an Episcopalian, he married, first, a Catholic—she and their daughter died of tuberculosis in 1921—and then, seven years later, a Lutheran who had been his secretary for fifteen years.

La Guardia's father was a military bandmaster, and he spent his childhood on army posts in the West. The family subsequently moved to Trieste and young Fiorello worked for the American consular service from the age of seventeen through age twenty-three. By the time he returned to New York in 1906, he was fluent in Italian, Yiddish, German, Hungarian, and Serbo-Croatian. He put himself through law school while working as an interpreter at Ellis Island, and, once a lawyer, took up the cause of immigrant groups. During World War I, he piloted a bomber on the front in Austria.

After a stint as a congressman from New York, La Guardia ran as an antiestablishment candidate for mayor in 1933. His victory and his reelections four and eight years later as a reform candidate on a fusion ticket were unprecedented. He was even mentioned at one point as a possible successor to Roosevelt if the president had not sought a third term.[24]

While Roosevelt relied on La Guardia as a go-between with blacks, he resisted the urgings of A. Philip Randolph and Walter White to offer La Guardia the chairmanship of the FEPC after the mayor's critical role in drafting the provisions of Executive Order 8802. La Guardia had gone on to adopt the antidiscrimination employment policy of the order as New York's official municipal policy.[25]

As World War II drew closer, La Guardia hoped that Roosevelt would appoint him secretary of war, but the president's advisers thought him too independent. Instead he was appointed to parttime positions on civil-defense boards, including the directorship of Civil Defense nationwide. (Mrs. Roosevelt was his assistant for a time.) He tried on numerous occasions to obtain a military assignment, but was never successful. At one point, he offered to serve as a brigadier general overseeing the governing of captured North African territories and later Italy, and even went so far as to have a uniform made for himself, which he never got to wear.[26]

The "Little Flower," as New Yorkers affectionately called him, was a glutton for work. By the time America entered World War II, he was traveling to Washington every week to spend two days in his federal posts, then rushing back to New York to handle municipal matters. His goal was to provide the city with an honest, nonpartisan administration, but critics thought he sided with unions in labor disputes. He was instrumental in settling many strikes in the city, and repeatedly cautioned the police against using clubs or pistols in dispersing groups of striking or unemployed workers.[27]

La Guardia was also courageous to a fault. He was not above stepping into a fight, as he did when two sailors started slugging each other one day near the waterfront in downtown Manhattan. The mayor, who was speeding to City Hall in his official car, stepped out of the car and through a crowd of onlookers and broke up the altercation. "All in a day's work," he remarked afterwards.[28]

That was not the first time, nor the last, that La Guardia threw caution to the wind. He had what amounted to a penchant for racing to trouble spots, often beating the police and firemen to the scene of disturbances and fires. Oddly enough, although a former bomber pilot, he could not drive a car. Instead, he was chauffeured about in a customized small coupe that was painted green and white to resemble a police radio car. Like a fire engine, the car had two oversized red emergency lights surmounting its headlights. Mounted on the roof was a red-lensed light that flashed the word "Mayor." His five-starred emblem was painted on the car sides. The green hood carried the letters "N.Y.C." in white and five white enameled stars—one star more, the *New York Times* noted, than a full general in the army. The car had a two-way radio telephone for La Guardia's use, and, in the glove compartment, a pistol should he need one.[29]

As egocentric as he was, La Guardia was self-effacing in other ways. For many years he occupied an unpretentious top-floor apartment on Fifth Avenue at 109th Street, a modest, six-story brick building in Italian Harlem. He lived there with his second wife, two adopted children, and the small son of a dead brother. For a long time he resisted moving into Gracie Mansion, a postcolonial home overlooking the East River at Eighty-eighth Street that had been restored by the Park Department and made into a museum.[30] After nine years in office, he finally agreed to make it the city's official mayoral residence and moved his family into it just before Memorial Day weekend in 1942.[31]

La Guardia was popular among blacks. He garnered black majorities in each of his three election campaigns, winning more than 70 percent of the black vote in Harlem when he ran for a third term in 1941.[32] He prided himself on the fact that during his administration blacks throughout the city had "been given hope." He pointed out that he had named blacks to numerous posts, including as heads of the tax and parole commissions. "You know and I know," he told a Baptist convention in Harlem, "that when I go to appoint some one I am only interested in what they have in their head and in their heart —the color of their skins does not bother me."[33]

There were those in the city who believed that blacks were doing well. "New York is not the awful example," The *Times* editorialized. "Harlem, with all its tragic shortcomings, signalizes a marked advance in Negro health, economic opportunity and general well-being."[34] La Guardia did not subscribe to such a simplistic view, but his own belief was grounded in a misconception that was just as unrealistic: that blacks were akin to every other minority. He believed —as so many other white liberals did—that blacks, like Italians, Jews, or the Irish, would overcome discrimination through self-improvement and by impressing everyone with their worth.

That approach to race relations was best illustrated two days before Pearl Harbor, on Friday night, December 5, 1941, in a telling exchange of philosophies at a meeting of the West Harlem Council of Social Agencies. Dr. E. Franklin Frazier, a Howard University sociologist, took a militant stand. He urged New York's blacks to refuse to pay gas, electric, and phone bills unless more blacks were hired by utility companies, and he suggested that they seek local ordinances to force contractors working for the city to deal only with trade unions that admitted black workers to their membership. "If the Negro is to get anything," Frazier declared, "he will get it by fighting for it now."

The response to Frazier's remarks came from Manhattan borough president Stanley M. Isaacs, who expressed the view that La Guardia held, a view that most blacks considered näive: "If you folks rely on power alone you will get nowhere because you haven't got the power. A plea that power is the only thing that counts is a confession of failure. I think you will do better by relying on the fundamental decency of the American people rather than the methods of Hitler."[35]

La Guardia's constituency, as he saw it, included all New Yorkers, not just blacks. As a result, his decisions encompassed the needs of groups and factions other than just blacks, and that often drew him into confrontations with black leaders such as Powell, and even sometimes with the less pugnacious Walter White.

La Guardia and White were so alike—bound together by the same principles of fighting injustice, similar in both compassion and even insensitivities, self-centered yet moralistic and humanitarian, stressing fair play and political reform—that a historian once described them as brothers under the skin.[36] Unlike Powell, White was not a militant. Rather, he favored negotiation, an approach with which a gradualist in race matters such as La Guardia could identify.

White was white, his hair blond, his eyes blue. His father, a mailman in Atlanta, was one-fourth black, his mother even less so, one-sixteenth black. But the family lived in the black section of the city, known as "Darktown," and White was emphatic about his black heritage:

> I am not white. There is nothing within my mind and heart which tempts me to think I am. Yet I realize acutely that the only characteristic which matters to either the white or the colored race—the appearance of whiteness—is mine. There is magic in a white skin; there is tragedy, loneliness, exile, in a black skin.[37]

When he was thirteen years old, in 1906, White was riding in a cart with his father to a mailbox at Peachtree and Houston Streets in downtown Atlanta when they witnessed a mob of whites, incensed by virulent antiblack gubernatorial campaign oratory, attack blacks on the street. Father and son were so light-skinned that they were spared. But they saw the mob attack a lame bootblack who tried to outrun it but failed, dying under an avalanche of clubs and fists. A white hearse driver lashing out at blacks with a horsewhip almost drove into them. Seeing an elderly woman being chased by another mob, White's father handed the reins to young Walter while he pulled the woman to safety into their cart. The next morning, a Sunday, White later wrote in his autobiography, "Like skulls on a cannibal's hut the hats and caps of victims of the mob of the night before had been hung on the iron hooks of telegraph poles."[38]

That night, a white mob carrying torches descended on Darktown, heading for the Whites' home, shouting, "That's where that nigger mail carrier lives! Let's burn it down! It's too nice for a nigger to live in!" White's mother and his young sisters sought shelter at the back of the house, while White and his father, both armed, crouched anxiously by the windows of the front parlor:

> In the flickering light the mob swayed, paused, and began to flow toward us. In that instant there opened up within me a great awareness; I knew then who I was. I was a Negro, a human being with an invisible pigmentation which marked me a person to be hunted, abused, discriminated against, kept in poverty and ignorance, in order that those whose skin was white would have readily at hand a proof of their superiority, a proof patent and inclusive, accessible

to the moron and the idiot as well as to the wise man and the genius.[39]

Fortunately for the Whites, friends in a nearby building started shooting at the mob and distracted it from their house. But from that moment on, Walter White was committed to a mission.

As a teenager, he had to attend the preparatory school of Atlanta University because Georgia did not permit blacks into the state's public high schools. He graduated from the university in 1916, and first became involved in protests when the Atlanta Board of Education announced its plan to drop the seventh grade from black elementary schools in order to finance the building of a new white high school.

White subsequently was a leader in establishing a branch of the NAACP in Atlanta, and became its secretary. The success of his school protest was brought to the attention of James Weldon Johnson, an NAACP field secretary. White was asked to join the national staff of the organization in New York in 1918. When Johnson, then secretary, took a leave of absence from the NAACP, White became acting secretary, and on Johnson's resignation in 1931, he was promoted to executive secretary, a post he would hold until his death in 1955.

Considered an effective lobbyist and the ablest black leader in America, White focused the NAACP's efforts on legal battles against all-white political primaries, poll taxes, and segregation in housing and education. But he was not without his critics. Sociable and courteous in public, he was considered by some members of his staff as tyrannical and ambitious. Early in the 1930s, he and W. E. B. Du Bois, a leading figure in the NAACP since its founding in 1909 and for many years the editor of *Crisis*, were pitted against one another. Du Bois, an advocate of racial separatism and self-sufficiency, used the NAACP's magazine to promote his ideas. White, a believer in full equality and integration, refused to accept such racial segregation as an answer to black aspirations. At one point, Du Bois accused White of not understanding black problems because he was not really dark-skinned. "He has more white companions and friends than colored," Du Bois charged. "He goes where he will in New York City and naturally meets no Color Line, for the simple and sufficient reason that he isn't 'colored.' "[40] Eventually in 1934, Du Bois, then in his mid-60s, felt compelled to resign from the association rather than recant his beliefs.

White had made a name for himself as an expert on lynching. Passing as a white reporter for newspapers such as the *New York Evening Post* and *Chicago Daily News*, he investigated more than forty lynchings and eight race riots in the South in the years after World War I, the brutality of which he publicized in magazine articles and a novel, *The Fire in the Flint*. So it was no surprise that when informed of the Detroit riot, White thought nothing of stepping into a volatile situation, and immediately left home to fly there. And it was no surprise that after finding out that he was there, La Guardia wired him, asking his friend to telephone him with a situation update.

Both men were worried. The year 1943 had not been a peaceful one for race relations in New York.

SEVENTEEN

Conflicts

If we must die, let it not be like hogs
  Hunted and penned in an inglorious spot, . . .
Like men we'll face the murderous, cowardly pack,
  Pressed to the wall, dying, but—fighting back!

—Claude McKay[1]

As incidents of racial violence escalated around the country, differences both of approach and of opinion between La Guardia and Powell, and even between La Guardia and White, surfaced over a variety of disparate issues, all with racial overtones. The antagonisms that they set off aggravated an already tense situation.

It seemed that every time something happened, the mayor and the clergyman clashed. When La Guardia spurned Powell's request for political appointments as a reward for his support, their rift turned from bitter to angry. Powell had backed La Guardia in the past, and upon election to the City Council he expected the mayor to reciprocate by filling five or six municipal posts with blacks who had helped him in his campaign in Harlem. But the mayor thought otherwise, believing that the patronage would "encourage a permanent headache."[2] Powell never got over being rejected.

Powell played the devil's advocate, turning the heat on La Guardia and rarely letting up. He chided the mayor for not doing enough to discourage the spread of an image of Harlem as a hotbed of crime. The city's daily newspapers were constantly fueling the fears of the white community by claiming that a crime wave was sweeping Harlem and that muggings and armed robberies might spread into white neighborhoods.

La Guardia may have been particularly sensitive to the issue because of a predawn burglary that occurred a month before Pearl Harbor in an apartment directly across the hall from his. The break-in occurred when the mayor was still living in Italian Harlem, before his move to Gracie Mansion. The burglary set off an extensive roundup of pickpockets and loiterers. More than three hundred police reinforcements combed the area north of Central Park and adjacent areas on foot and in radio cars. Newspapers characterized the incident as part of "a crime wave in Harlem," a description that upset black residents. "The so-called recent crime wave," Powell told parishioners in a sermon on the Sunday afterwards, "is neither a crime wave nor is it recent. In the past twenty-five years the population of Harlem has increased five-fold, yet facilities for recreation, education and health haven't even been doubled. Into this ghetto have been crowded people living in century-old tenements, making less money but paying higher rents and higher prices for foodstuffs than any other group in the city."[3]

Actually, the economic situation in Harlem was easing somewhat. In the decade before 1940, the city's total black population had risen to nearly half a million, at a rate five times that of the increase in its white population.[4] But after 1940 the black population decreased by an estimated twenty-five thousand individuals, most of whom were either in military service or had moved to find jobs in defense-plant boomtowns.[5] While Harlemites still made up nearly one-fourth of those receiving home relief, total numbers dropped in half by midwar as a result of increased employment.[6] Among other things, black women were now being admitted to Bellevue and other city hospitals for training as nurses, and for the first time the Third Avenue bus company was hiring blacks as drivers and conductors.[7]

The crime issue was a constant and recurring thorn and it was inevitable that the two men would eventually clash head-on. In the second week of May 1942, a mentally unbalanced thirty-year-old black man attacked two policemen with a knife. One of the police officers fatally wounded him. The dying man was rushed to Harlem Hospital and within a short time an angry crowd of seventy-five blacks gathered at the entrance to the hospital's emergency ward to protest the shooting. The situation was on the verge of turning ugly when fifteen radio cars and two trucks filled with policemen, a total of forty-six officers in all, arrived and restored order.

Blacks were irate that a police officer had shot an obviously disturbed man and called for an investigation. While the matter was still before a grand jury, Powell announced that he was sponsoring a rally at the Golden Gate Ballroom to protest the slaying. Fearing that the rally might turn violent, La Guardia sought to dissuade Powell, but the clergyman refused to budge. The mayor, Powell wrote in the *People's Voice*, "is one of the most pathetic figures on the current American scene."[8] His editorial, entitled "Mickey Mouse vs. Mayor La Guardia—The Winner, Mickey!" said that La Guardia could no longer count on black votes, that his career in politics was finished: "We are therefore ignored."[9]

Periodically, whenever a coincident number of crimes occurred in Harlem, the threat of a crime wave resurfaced. It did so again following a series of robberies in the summer of 1942. In spite of a statement from the Juvenile Welfare Council that Harlem was not a "crime area,"[10] fears of a crime wave did not go away and rose once again with full force in early 1943.

From a white person's standpoint, the year had begun on a portentous note. Three policemen were stabbed by black men in Harlem in separate attacks on New Year's Eve.[11] Eight days later, a doctor known as the "White Angel" because of his work in treating poor families without fee, was mugged and robbed by four young blacks as he entered a dimly lit tenement on 117th Street.[12] Not long afterwards, La Guardia told a graduating class of the Police Academy to "shoot first and be quick on the trigger" in encounters with armed criminals. He would "much rather," he said, "provide a grave for a vicious criminal in Potter's Field than pin a medal on a police officer's widow."[13]

That March the teenage son of a Lutheran pastor was accosted and stabbed by a gang of ten black youths on 147th Street while returning from a church meeting six blocks away. The attack provoked an aggressive response from the Police Department. A special motorcycle detachment was set up. Its sixty-four men worked on shifts throughout the night and early morning hours in an effort to cut down on the assaults.[14] Newspapers again proclaimed, "Crime wave in Harlem," and the public believed it. One foreign correspondent was quoted in the *New York Times* as reporting to his readers in England that the city was threatened by "a full-sized crime wave of really formidable proportions" and a thriving black market in "meat, petrol and tires."[15]

But the reality was quite different. Once the war began, major crimes throughout the city decreased. A citizens committee said that 1942, the first full year of the war, had the best record of crime prevention in the New York's history. The incidence of eight "standard" crimes such as murder, rape, and larceny showed that the city had much lower rates than the combined average for large cities.[16]

The reduction in crime rates was truly amazing. After all, because of the blackout, the city streets were dark every night. Although New York City was in little danger from an air raid, it was considered the "nerve center of the nation" and a "tempting target which might justify an enemy in taking great risks."[17] Street lights were dimmed, storefronts were dark, the glare of auto and truck headlights reduced to a slit of light by tape. It would seem an invitation to crime. Only Times Square and the Broadway theater district, the once "Great White Way," which was still a mecca for late-night movie-and-theatergoers, attracted a disturbing number of muggers after dark.[18]

The pattern of crime that emerged in New York echoed what the rest of America was experiencing: felony arrests were down, but arrests for juvenile delinquency had risen markedly. Figures made public by the Domestic Relations Court showed an increase of nearly 11 percent in delinquency cases and a nearly 12 percent rise in the number of neglected children. Nearly half of the boys and girls brought into court in Manhattan were black.[19] Still, the director of the Community Service Society said she was surprised that "there is not more crime and delinquency among Harlem Negroes."[20]

In an effort to put a damper on press sensationalism in reporting crimes, a city magistrate proposed enjoining "any newspaper or news agency from identifying a defendant according to race, creed or color, unless the identification is an essential part of the story or of the crime charged."[21] Powell also tried to dispel the notion that made the words "crime" and "black" synonymous. He introduced a resolution in the City Council demanding that local newspaper publishers omit from all news stories any words that described the race of a person involved in a crime.[22]

The crime issue was only one of many that provoked clashes between Powell and La Guardia. Powell was irate, as were other blacks, when New York leased buildings at city-run Hunter College to the navy to house women recruits for the WAVES and SPARS, neither of which accepted black women. The navy's rigidity may have particularly irked Powell because he had announced in the City Council earlier in the year that, as a result of his meetings with officers of the armed services, the navy had promised to open its ranks to black recruits.[23]

Powell later publicly challenged La Guardia at the cornerstone ceremony for a Harlem Hospital annex, attacking him for not doing more to eliminate discrimination in the municipal hospital system. Disregarding the mayor's rejoinder that any qualified black doctor could be appointed, Powell declared, "Whatever gains have been made by the Negro people in New York have been made either by direct action or the threat of direct action."[24]

Two other incidents in the spring of 1943 enraged not only Powell, but also every black in the city, including La Guardia's friend Walter White.

The first was the closing of the popular Savoy Ballroom on charges that it was a "base for vice." Known as the "Home of Happy Feet,"[25] the Savoy was the largest dance hall in Harlem; it occupied the second floor of a building that took up the entire block front on Lenox Avenue extending from 140th to 141st Street. An immense cut-glass chandelier and marble staircase graced its lobby. The orange and blue dance hall was so spacious that there were two bandstands and a revolving stage. Its dance floor alone was 50 feet wide and 250 feet long.[26]

The Savoy, which opened in 1926, was also known as "the shrine of syncopation addicts the country over,"[27] and the home for such noted musicians as Cab Calloway, Louis Armstrong, and Erskine Hawkins. Its owner and its manager, both white men, had gone to great lengths to insure that it was a "place for clean fun" for both blacks and whites, for the Savoy had always attracted a large white clientele.[28] The ballroom had a liquor license, but served only ginger ale. It had long since dismissed all its dance hostesses and raised the age of admission from sixteen, which the law allowed, to eighteen. Its dress code was enforced. "You was always dressed in your best," said Norma Miller, a professional dancer who frequented the Savoy.

"But men in those days always were. If they didn't have nothin' else, they had a shine on their shoes, and their suit was pressed. That was a *must.*"[29] The ballroom did not tolerate unruliness. "You could not do nothin' wrong in there or else you would be escorted out," Miller said.[30] "If you misbehave, Black or white, your behind would be outta there."[31]

Wednesday night at the Savoy was usually reserved for fraternal organizations. Thursday night was "kitchen mechanics" night for sleep-in maids who had the day off. Dance contests, held on Saturday nights, attracted celebrities. On the average, about one in five persons at the Savoy on any night was white, and dancing by mixed couples was commonplace[32]—and a sore point with authorities. To appease them, the Savoy had stopped advertising in white newspapers. It had also been told not to book any white bands any more, because, as Powell's *People's Voice* reported, "that too would encourage white people to come to hear them. Cute, eh?"[33]

The Savoy was notified in late March that its license would be revoked, pending a hearing. Both city and military authorities charged that 164 servicemen had contracted venereal disease in the past nine months as a result of meeting women there. Undercover detectives had, in fact, arrested three prostitutes, a pimp, and a Savoy employee who solicited them.

Walter White argued that prostitution was a fact of life at other public places, including the Waldorf-Astoria Hotel. He feared that the Savoy's closing would underscore the view of Harlem as "a cesspool of iniquity and crime,"[34] and called upon La Guardia to reverse the police action. An NAACP inquiry reported that police authorities had for some time looked with displeasure at the mixed dancing at the ballroom. But, as Malcolm Little put it, "no one dragged the white women in there."[35] A *People's Voice* exposé of eight downtown taxi-dance halls disclosed, it said, that in "these 'meat centers' . . . 'dancing' is used as an excuse for a degenerate form of fornication right on the floor."[36]

Despite objections from Powell, White, and other Harlem leaders, the doors of the Savoy were padlocked on April 21. The *New York Age* denounced its closing, noting that it would mean the loss of jobs for ninety employees and "deprive Harlemites of one of their main means of pleasure and relaxation."[37] In an article in the *Amsterdam*

News, Roy Wilkins declared, "Chiefs of police, commissioners, captains, lieutenants, and plain rookie cops get purple in the face at the very thought of Negroes and whites enjoying themselves socially together." He said "Butch" La Guardia "ought to get some of the bile out of his system and become once more the square-shooter we elected and loved in 1933."[38] Powell's *People's Voice* pointed out that "it is strangely coincident that no other similar recreation hall had been subjected to the exasperating surveillance and hounding that fell to the lot of the Savoy." Its closing, the newspaper continued, "is one piece in the jigsaw puzzle that was started back in 1939 in anticipation of the opening of the world's fair and when completed would have meant the complete blackout of Harlem as an entertainment spot for visitors."[39] Powell himself wrote an editorial in the *People's Voice* denouncing the closing as a "Step Backward in Race Relations." It was, he said, "the first step toward segregation. . . . Hitler has scored a jim-crow victory in New York."[40]

The other clash occurred over the announcement that a major apartment complex, Stuyvesant Town, was to be built on the East Side in lower Manhattan. The Metropolitan Life Insurance Company, which was sponsoring the $50 million project in exchange for a tax exemption, made it known that blacks would not be accepted as tenants. The *Amsterdam News,* in a three-column headline over a front-page story, quoted the company's president, Frederick M. Ecker, as saying, "Negroes and Whites Don't Mix."

The black community was already upset, the newspaper said, because Metropolitan Life had been "snubbing Negroes for many years," never hiring them except as porters and janitors, despite the fact that the number of blacks holding its life insurance policies "is estimated to be close to two million and the amount of money poured into the concern's coffers has run into billions." Now here was Ecker saying that "perhaps" blacks and whites would mix "in a hundred years, but they don't now. If we brought them into this development, it would be to the detriment of the city, too, because it would depress all the surrounding property."[41]

Embarrassed as he was by the exclusive nature of the project, La Guardia felt compelled to support it in order to acquire private backing for much-needed and costly city housing. He later said he would support legal efforts to overturn the antiblack restriction, but the harm was done. Black leaders had not even been informed of the plans beforehand and they reacted with outrage to the public announcement of the project. Their complaints, however, were immediately dismissed by the mayor. "There are those," La Guardia said, "who try to use this issue to manufacture a problem so as to give themselves a cause, an interest and perhaps even a livelihood."[42]

The stories that spring and summer of disturbances at army installations, of strikes in defense plants, and of the Zoot Suit Riots in Los Angeles and the race riot in Beaumont, Texas, exacerbated tensions within New York City. Then, in the first week of June, just across the Hudson River in Newark, New Jersey, there was the gang riot between white and black youths that lasted for three days.[43] But it was the violence two weeks later in Detroit, more than six hundred miles from New York, that was the most frightening of all.

La Guardia returned from his weekly sojourn in Washington on Tuesday, June 22, two days after the riot broke out in Detroit, and immediately urged Harlem residents to keep "cool."[44] He had Police Commissioner Lewis J. Valentine send two police officers—one white, the other black—to Detroit as observers. They stayed in the city four days, reporting back to Valentine daily.

Meanwhile, La Guardia looked with concern across the East River to Brooklyn, where two heavily black-populated neighborhoods, Bedford-Stuyvesant and Brownsville, mirrored the problems of Manhattan's Harlem. The former, a middle-class white residential section in the 1920s, was now known as "Little Harlem." More than forty-four hundred crimes were reported in the area in 1942,[45] and, like other sections of the city, its juvenile delinquency rate was on the rise. It had gone up 25 percent in the latter part of 1941,[46] and was approaching a 30 percent or more increase in 1943.[47] The police attributed the mushrooming rate of delinquency in part to "various social and economic transformations" and to the "blackouts and the dim-out" that "have been conducive to crimes which would not have been committed under other circumstances."[48] Recent disturbances a few miles away in Brownsville prompted La Guardia to ask Valentine, "For goodness sake, please watch this section very carefully."[49]

That Sunday, in his weekly radio broadcast, the mayor warned "snake agitators" bent on starting trouble to stay away from New York. He urged all New Yorkers not to let their emotions be swept away by rumor or hearsay:

How many times have I said in the last two years that I fear panic more than enemy bombs? How many times have I attempted to explain how easy it is to start panic or disorder? How many times have I stated that a rumor, skillfully spread, might cause great consternation among groups of our people? We know that is a technique of the Nazis. We know that it is a technique of the fascists, but unhappily I must say that that technique is sometimes employed right here in our country.[50]

As soon as White returned to New York, La Guardia called him and several other black leaders together at Gracie Mansion to hear the report of the two New York policemen who had gone to Detroit and "to devise means of preventing repetition in New York City of the mistakes which had been made."[51] As a result of the conference, held on Monday, June 28, Valentine devised a series of actions to be taken in the event of a disturbance in the city.

The mayor asked White specifically to make contact with every black leader in both Harlem and Brooklyn. White, in a letter that went out in the mail before the end of June, urged them "to see that our people so conduct themselves during the next critical weeks and months" so as not to give any "cause for racial friction."[52] He assured them that "unlike the spineless Mayor of Detroit, Mayor La Guardia is taking every precaution to avert trouble here. We need have no fear that the police here will act as they did in Detroit."[53]

La Guardia took a number of other steps in the hope of reducing tensions. In an effort to enlist New Yorkers against racial disorders, he named workers of the Civil Defense Corps "Good Will Deputies"[54] in the hope that they would help assuage any ill feelings. He appealed to clergymen to speak out against racism in their sermons.[55] He asked the Office of Price Administration to place the city under immediate rent control. He announced that two new housing projects would be built in Harlem once the war was over. The mayor also tried to persuade Roosevelt to see Walter White "at the earliest possible moment," pointing out that White was instrumental in bringing order to Detroit. White was urging at the time that federal troops not be withdrawn from the city. La Guardia sent White's report on the riot to the White House, but the president made no attempt to meet with the NAACP official.

At one point La Guardia thought about setting up a biracial committee on race relations, but by mid-July, after White had submitted a number of names of possible blacks to serve on it—including himself and Adam Clayton Powell, Jr.—the mayor dropped the idea. The Fourth of July holiday had passed without incident in New York. The climate of race relations in the city appeared to have simmered down.[56]

But Powell kept tensions alive by what he liked to call his "ruckus raising."[57] As St. Clair Bourne, his managing editor on the *People's Voice* says, "There is also a time for a little rashness, this impetuous anger, because sometimes you have to shout."[58]

Powell took the occasion of the Detroit riot to strike out first at one of his nemeses, the FBI: "If they had spent half the time they used on rounding up crackpot Negro nationalists in rounding up perverted Klu Kluxers, Christian Fronters, and Coughlinites, then there wouldn't be any riots in America today."[59]

Then Powell took on La Guardia. Despite his standing in the black community, Powell had not been asked to take part in the discussions at Gracie Mansion. Ignored, he charged in the City Council that La Guardia and Valentine had refused to discuss with him and a group of representative black and white citizens ways to prevent a recurrence of what happened in Detroit in New York. "If any riot breaks out here in New York," he warned, "the blood of innocent people, White and Negro, will rest upon the hands of Mayor Fiorello La Guardia and Police Commissioner Lewis Valentine."[60]

Next, Powell made public an inflammatory letter that he had received from the "Grand Kligrapp" of the state's Ku Klux Klan. The KKK leader assured Powell that the Klan "had nothing to do" with the riot in Detroit, blaming instead ultra-conservative groups such as America First, Guardians of America, and the Guardian League. Then, the Grand Kligrapp added:

> But if colored people continue to work in the same places whites do, riots are sure to come. The government should have 100 per cent negro factories, just as they have regiments and no one will complain. . . .
>
> What white people resent is mixing the races together. God never intended this to be so. . . .
>
> Ugly rumors have reached us that unless the colored folks stay by themselves, the Detroit affair will be like a tea party compared to what will happen here. We have 97,642 members in New York.[61]

Powell had waited nearly a month after it was sent to him to reproduce, on July 24, the klan leader's letter on the front page of the *People's Voice*. In a dissimulating explanation in his "Soap Box" column the following week, Powell said he had not allowed the letter to be published earlier because it "would have done a great deal of harm to race relations in New York." But his associates had urged him to make the letter public, and now that it had appeared, he had something to say in response. His words were just as inflammatory:

> In the first place you can't frighten us. . . .
>
> In the second place, whites and Negroes are going to mix and nothing can be done about it. . . . The handwriting is on the wall. . . .
>
> My recommendation is that we set aside a certain portion of the earth for people like klansmen. Come to think of it, there is such a portion now. In the East the Japanese islands and in the West, Hitler's fortress—Europe. . . .
>
> The great mistake that any Axis agitator can make is to try to start something in New York. There is a different kind of a Negro here.[62]

As in Detroit, all that kept an explosion from igniting in New York City was a spark. Ironically, Powell, whose emotionally charged actions, statements, and editorials contributed to the atmosphere of unrest in Harlem, was out of town when it occurred.[63]

EIGHTEEN

The People's Voices

I will not toy with it nor bend an inch.
Deep in the secret chambers of my heart
I muse my life-long hate, and without flinch
I bear it nobly as I live my part. . . .

—Claude McKay[1]

August 1, 1943. A bright, hot, sweltering day. A day to go to the beach, or take in the Yankee game against the Tigers at the Stadium, or maybe go to midtown Broadway to see a film and hear a band on stage at one of the big movie houses. Or maybe the kind of lazy day to just turn on a fan, sit back and read the Sunday paper. Your outlook on things depended, of course, on what newspaper you read.

Take the *New York Times*, for instance. News of the progress of the war crowds almost everything else off the front page. The fighting is going well on all fronts: in Europe, in North Africa, on Sicily, in Italy, in the Pacific. Thousands of American troops have arrived in Britain after an uneventful crossing of the Atlantic, as the buildup for the long-awaited invasion of France starts to move from the planning board to reality. For the first time, an end to the war, a successful end, is in sight.

I really didn't give a damn about the war. What country?

—Foster Palmer[2]

A survey by George Gallup says that if the presidential election were held now, instead of next year, and Wendell Willkie, who has just announced his candidacy, were the Republican nominee, Roosevelt would win by a slightly larger margin than he did in 1940.

> *This "glory war" was foisted on us by politicians.*
>
> —Jack Scarville

Race relations in New York City are the subject of only one article in the voluminous Sunday edition of the *Times*. In an article in the magazine section, Robert Moses, the city's Park Commissioner, admits, "We have, it is true, a Negro problem in New York." He says that "the infiltration" of blacks in "many areas previously white" has "caused a drop in values, deterioration of buildings, retirement of responsible owners and mortgage holders, substitution of undersirable landlords without a corresponding decrease in rents." Moses strikes out at the likes of Walter White and Adam Clayton Powell, Jr., who are pressing for black rights. There is, he says, "a conspiracy of silence to hide the facts, because they are unpleasant, and because it is easier for demagogues to shout for immediate social equality than to work for attainable objectives." He chides "Negro leaders who will accept nothing but complete social equality," blaming them for "the stories of unrest among our colored citizens."[3] Moses's remarks are revealing. He is the man chiefly responsible for getting the Metropolitan Life Company to underwrite the whites-only Stuyvesant Town housing project.

> *The one thing my mother realized was "Who the hell are they?"*
> *She realized that these people, why was it that they were able to*
> *live so much better, or to have money, or whatever you want to*
> *call it?*
>
> —Fred Mays

If you live up in Harlem, the news this weekend as usual takes on a different character. Flipping through the *New York Age*, or the *Amsterdam News*, or the *People's Voice* that Sunday, a black reader would have been jolted, as usual, by the positive and the negative. The positive includes some minor victories.

The sports pages of all three weeklies are highlighting the eleventh annual "dream game" pitting East against West of the Negro Baseball League at Comiskey Park in Chicago that afternoon. Satchell Paige will pitch for the West. A photograph in the *Age* depicts the black woman now operating the elevator at the 168th Street subway station. The number of city blacks holding war jobs has risen to twenty thousand, "a threefold increase over last year." A story about the regional office of the Fair Employment Practice Committee lauds it for "probably" being a "major factor in putting the state ahead of all others in the placement of Negro workers in non-agricultural jobs." The FEPC, another story says, is responsible for getting three black women jobs as government inspectors at the Curtiss-Wright plant in Buffalo. More than 120 blacks from New York State are reported training as seamen at the Naval Training Station in Great Lakes, Illinois. The U.S. Employment Service reports that as of March, nearly a million non-whites, representing 6.7 percent of the total labor force, were employed in war plants around the nation. Black construction workers throughout the country, according to still another article, have earned nearly $4 millon since the beginning of a public-works war program.

On the other hand, the *Age*'s correspondent in Brooklyn reports that the labor shortage that "government spokesmen and private industry are raving and ranting" about does not really exist. Blacks are being "brazenly discriminated against." The Bulova Watch Corporation, the correspondent says, has been advertising for women workers, but has told black applicants that "there are no openings now . . . come back within a month."

> *People were naturally angry. They couldn't get jobs.*
>
> —Doris Saunders

> *As my mother and my daddy said, you must be 199 percent good —not 100 percent, 199 percent—in order to show that you are black and worthy of your color.*
>
> —Evelyn Hunt O'Garro

The *People's Voice* is running the second in a series of articles about "the common destiny of the Negro and the Jew." The series promises to take up the history of the Jewish treatment in Germany and "show how it is the pattern and framework on which the persecution of Negroes rests."

The war takes a back seat in Harlem's weeklies. For example, of sixteen stories on the front page of this weekend's New York *Age*, only two deal directly with the fighting abroad.[4] One is a photo of heavyweight champion Sgt. Joe Louis, who is about to go on an exhibition tour of military posts overseas. The other recounts the awarding of the Soldier's Medal for "extraordinary heroism" to Pvt. Abrady Hicks of Arkansas for rescuing an unconscious pilot from his burning plane after it crash-landed on an American-held island in the South Pacific. There is also a small item saying that, following protests, signs indicating separate toilet facilities for blacks and whites at West Point have been removed.

Other stories from the military are a grim reminder of the continuing explosiveness of racial issues. Thurgood Marshall of the NAACP is to represent three black soldiers at Camp Maxey, Texas, who have been sentenced to death for allegedly raping a white woman.

Another story in the *Age* says that Marshall has presented to Manhattan's district attorney a number of cases of discrimination in the city. He believes it imperative that the inequities be corrected. Marshall, who spent two and a half weeks in Detroit defending blacks who were arrested, says that one of the causes of the riot there "was the weakness of law enforcement. Little effort was made to enforce laws benefitting and protecting Negroes and other minority groups."

Still another story says that, in response to an NAACP demand for an inquiry, the War Department is looking into the case of a black private shot by a bus driver in Washington for taking a seat in the whites-only section of his bus. The Capital Transit Company in Washington, yet another article says, has resisted hiring and training blacks as drivers because of "public resentment and non-cooperation from instructors." The FEPC is threatening to take the situation to the White House unless the bus company takes "affirmative action." At the same time, the FEPC reports that three hundred black workers at a West Coast shipyard fired from their jobs for refusing to pay dues to a blacks-only auxiliary of the Boilermakers Union have been reinstated.

We are a group that are like crabs in a barrel. They don't want you to get too far above.

—Dr. James Jones

A Morehouse College sociologist declares that blacks should take the initiative to bring about "real democracy" in America. He points out that blacks are already "living dangerously" in the South. A similar statement appears in a story from Los Angeles in the *Amsterdam News*. A newspaperman there is quoted as saying, "The intolerant system of the South is a far more dangerous foe to American domestic tranquility than that of the Axis nations is to the entire civilized world." A printer replies to a "question of the week" in the *People's Voice* whether blacks should support Roosevelt for a fourth term, "the Negro needs a President who is not dependent upon the South."

The *Amsterdam News* also carries a story from Beaufort, South Carolina, where the NAACP recently formed a branch, that reports that the city's weekly *Gazette* is carrying on its front page an advertisement showing a klansman astride a white horse and the caption, "Ku Klux Klan Rides Again—Work To Do." In Atlanta, Rev. Martin L. Harvey of Chicago, who has paid for a Pullman berth, is beaten by a train conductor for refusing to leave the observation car of the Dixie Flyer and "go back to the place" where he belonged, a coach for blacks.

The St. Paul, Minnesota, branch of the NAACP reports that blacks stationed at the Army Air Force Technical Training Command at Sioux Falls, South Dakota, are being called "nigger" and "boy" by superior officers, denied service in local restaurants and hotels, and are barred from USO centers. Reports from Camp Selby, near Hattiesburg, Mississippi, say that all black newspapers "published north of Mississippi" will be barred from the base. Soldiers on furlough from Camp Stewart, Georgia, say the *People's Voice* is already barred there. An ironic note is struck by a promotional photo in the *Amsterdam News* of the cast of the new MGM film at two Loew's theaters in Harlem. The movie, *Bataan*, unrealistically includes a black soldier as a member of an otherwise all-white army unit.

I felt the sting of prejudice all over the place. How can you be that loyal if you feel like this? For instance, my father—we were for

*the concept of this country, but it didn't live up to it. Many felt
we hadn't achieved democracy, real democracy here. And they
resented it.*

—Marvel Cooke

The lead editorial in the *Amsterdam News* charges that despite
constitutional provisions "in existence since the Civil War period,
they have been employed only twice in an attempt by the Federal
Government to convict lynchers." Lynchings would stop if the Justice
Department would prepare "iron-clad cases."

*I have never reached the point of killing anybody, but pretty god-
damn close to it.*

—Arnold de Mille

One of the *Age*'s editorials criticizes the navy, which has just
announced a plan to admit black women to the WAVES, but on a
segregated basis. Another editorial denounces the "association of
race" in crime stories, the "restriction of Negro participation in moving pictures to undignified roles," racial segregation in the armed
forces, and the blood bank policy of the army and the navy, which, it
says, is "undemocratic and a gratuitous insult to the tenth of the
nation." A third editorial relates the story of the national secretary of
the Workers Defense League, who has been asked to vacate his office
in a building in Washington because he twice took black guests to a
cafeteria in the building and because he had "too many Negroes" in
the office itself:

Too many Negroes.
     And this in America—the land of the FREE and the home of
the brave. . . .
     Too many Negroes. . . .
     Would not this phrase adequately describe the feelings of the
vicious mobs who stormed through the streets of Detroit, stalking
black men and women in blind, blood-thirsty rage a few weeks
back. . . .
     Apparently, not only is it a crime to be black but it is an equally

grave offense to associate with Negroes—at least beyond certain limits. . . .

Too many Negroes. . .

There must be "too many Negroes" united in the desire for their rights as citizens to be ignored. There must be "too many Negroes" aroused and ever alert to the dangers that threaten.

The enemy—and they are just as dangerous on the home front as the Nazis, Fascists and Japs are abroad—has drawn the battle lines. It is up to us to see to it that all their assaults are repelled.

They can't win—as long as we can maintain in our ranks, fighting shoulder to shoulder—"too many Negroes."

A two-column advertisement in the *Age* calls attention to a Negro Freedom Rally to be held Thursday night. Its slogan: "THIS MUST NOT HAPPEN AGAIN: Mobile-Beaumont-Los Angeles-Newark-Detroit."

As a black person you have to take a stand on how much you're going to let them put on you.

—Virginia D. Murphy

I had the feeling it was an excuse, an outlet . . . an outlet for the pent-up rage. Rage against the landlords who were going to dispossess them, rage against the guy who overcharged them, rage that was the norm—black rage. It was rage against a lot of things, although they were saying the war and white people. It was so much more.

—Evelyn Cunningham

The spark, if you want to call it that, that ignited it was general foment, a feeling of dissatisfaction—what do you want to call it? Anger? Frustration? I don't think I was ever at the point of picking up a stone and throwing it at people in frustration. I'm not built that way. But I could understand it. I didn't feel above it.

—St. Clair Bourne

NINETEEN

The Harlem Riot

If Margie Polite
Had of been white
She might not've cussed
Out the cop that night . . .
She started the riots!
Harlemites say
August 1st is
MARGIE'S DAY.

—Langston Hughes[1]

On the surface, it was a wonderful day in Harlem. A typical Sunday. Streets were jammed, and, despite the heat, men, women, and children wore their Sabbath best. "We didn't walk, we strolled," as one resident described Sunday in Harlem. "Everybody was dressed to the teeth. You would wear the finest you had, like chiffon dresses, white hats, new shoes, and everything matches, from your pocketbook on down. . . . Everybody was out there. They would say if you stood at the corner of 125th Street and Lenox Avenue, you would see every important person you ever knew."[2]

A white reporter for the New York newspaper *PM* heard music and laughter everywhere, saw block upon block of tenements and apartment houses filled with "intense life." Children played in the streets, their parents watching from sidewalks, stoops, and window-sills. Soldiers ambled along with dates on their arms, mothers wheeled baby carriages. Youths in their zoot suits "looked uncomfortably warm" in their "finery." As the sun began to lower in the sky, the picture "was reassuring."[3]

But the lightheartedness was veneer. "All through the war," Malcolm Little wrote, "the Harlem racial picture never was too bright." Little, who was walking down St. Nicholas Avenue as sunset approached, said that tension had "built to a pretty high pitch. Old-timers told me that Harlem had never been the same since the 1935 riot."

At about 7:30, Pvt. Robert Bandy and his mother, Florine Roberts, entered the seedy lobby of the Braddock Hotel. The seven-story hotel, on the southeast corner of 126th Street and Eighth Avenue, had seen better days. At one time in the 1920s, its bar was a favorite haunt for Harlem show-business celebrities. But the hotel had lost its luster, and was now such a notorious hangout for prostitutes and pimps that the army had asked that it be declared a "raided premise." In addition, a series of petty brawls had occurred in and just outside the hotel since mid-June, and the police had irked neighbors by barring racially mixed couples from the hotel, even entering their rooms to eject white persons. A policeman was always stationed in the Braddock's lobby.

Mrs. Roberts, a maid, had journeyed that weekend from Middletown, Connecticut, to be with her son and his fiancée. The three had breakfasted at the hotel, then gone to church and afterwards visited with friends. Mrs. Roberts had checked out of the hotel at about four o'clock and, together with Bandy and his girlfriend, gone to a movie and then a restaurant. Mother and son had returned to the Braddock to pick up her luggage, which she had left with the desk clerk.

Mrs. Roberts was a native of Alabama and Bandy, who was twenty-six years old, had been born in that state, though he now gave New Haven as his hometown. He was a member of the 730th Military Police Battalion, stationed across the Hudson River in Jersey City—a "good soldier," according to his superiors.

As Bandy, who was in uniform, and his mother approached the front desk, an argument was raging between Marjorie (Margie) Polite, a guest in her midthirties, and the police officer on duty in the lobby, a rookie patrolman named James Collins. The genesis of the dispute is unclear. One account says that Polite had checked into the hotel a bit earlier, was dissatisfied with her room because it did not have a shower-bath, had gone to the front desk to seek a refund, and was refused. Another story says that Polite became irate when she asked an elevator operator who had helped her to return a dollar tip she had given him. Inasmuch as Polite lived only about a block and a half away, on West 127th Street, both stories raise more questions than they answer. Another account, more credible, says Polite had left a raucous drinking party in one of the hotel's rooms, was drunk and boisterous and got into the dispute with Collins as she was leaving the hotel.

Polite was screaming at Collins when Bandy and his mother arrived. Among other profanities, she called the policeman a "motherfucker." Collins told her she was disturbing the peace and ordered her to stop, but she continued to yell, at one point appealing to other guests in the lobby to "protect me from this white man!" Collins tried to arrest her. As he seized hold of her, Bandy remonstrated with Collins, who told him to mind his own business and apparently brandished his nightstick.

Bandy started to grapple with Collins, to loosen his grip on Polite. His mother joined him. In the scuffle, Bandy grabbed the policeman's nightstick and struck Collins on the head, knocking him to the ground. Bandy started to bolt, but Collins, still lying on the ground, was able to pull his service revolver from its holster and fired at the retreating soldier, hitting him in the left shoulder.

The shot stopped Bandy, though the wound was not serious. Collins rose to his feet, took Bandy by the arm and, walking together, the two men headed out of the hotel and onto Eighth Avenue, headed for Sydenham Hospital a block away, on the north side of 125th Street, between Seventh and Eighth Avenues. It was clear from the fact that Bandy was able to walk to the hospital that his wound was slight.

A small crowd of people had witnessed the argument and shooting in the lobby. The sound of the shot had drawn a larger number of people to the front of the hotel. Seeing the gathering crowd, other passersby rushed to see what had happened. As each person joined the crowd, the story of the incident was exaggerated, blown up, distorted. A white policeman had shot a black soldier soon became a white policeman had shot and seriously wounded a black soldier in front of his mother—and he was dying.

A crowd of a thousand people soon formed outside the Twenty-eighth Precinct on West 123rd Street, where some people thought

Collins had taken Bandy, but both men were inside Sydenham Hospital, having their injuries treated. Outside the hospital, a crowd had swollen to three thousand people within an hour. In the darkness, as dusk turned into night along the dimly lit street, someone shouted out that the soldier was probably dead. Suddenly, a bottle crashed against the wall of the hospital. The noise of the shattering bottle was like a signal for chaos. In the blink of an eye, men, women, and teenagers began running up and down 125th Street, tossing anything they could find at store windows. And with them a new rumor spread through the streets: A white policeman had killed a black soldier.

The rumor of Bandy's death, said Walter White, "fell like a torch into dry summer grass." No one doubted that a white policeman had killed him. Hadn't cops shot black GIs in Louisiana, Arkansas, Texas? Wasn't that always the case when the white man had the upper hand? Was New York another Detroit? Another Beaumont? Suddenly, all the rage and frustration Harlemites felt—the bias and discrimination they encountered every day, the hurts and humiliations they had endured themselves or read about and shared with blacks all across the country—erupted. What did the white man ever do *for* the black man? What hadn't he done *to* the black man?

About half a block away, Evelyn Cunningham was working in the New York bureau office of the *Pittsburgh Courier*, opposite the Theresa Hotel at the corner of 125th Street and Seventh Avenue. The *Courier*, like Harlem's weeklies, went to press on Tuesdays, and Cunningham was working that Sunday night to meet her Monday deadline for copy. All of a sudden, she heard "a lot of noise." Looking out from the office's ground-floor windows, Cunningham saw "lots of people running up and down, screaming, anti-white, anti-war." Hearing that a white cop had killed a black GI did not surprise her. "When you say 'cop,' you are going to have a riot. Everybody's angry with cops, more than anybody else. I know from the time I was a kid, the cop was a bad guy—he'd push you around and stop you."

Cunningham's editor quickly put in a phone call to the *Courier*'s home office in Pittsburgh, to tell them what was happening. His superiors there did not believe him, so the editor took the phone to the door, held it out and said, "You hear it now?"

Much would be made later on about how the riot was the work of hoodlums and teenage delinquents. But the people Cunningham saw screaming and running through the streets were what she identified as both lower and middle class. The only difference was that "the middle-class people weren't screaming as much." Other observers confirmed Cunningham's assessment. While poor men, women, and children were in the majority—as they were, anyway, in Harlem—"better-dressed members of the middle class constituted the remainder." As the crowd grew, young men and boys predominated. In their wake came teenage girls and children.

Ordinarily, Cunningham and other *Courier* staffers would have left the office to cover the story, but a new sound echoed through the neighborhood and they were too scared to leave: gunfire. "That really frightened me," Cunningham remembers. "It was the first time I'd ever heard gunfire. It's not like nowadays. It was so uncommon to hear a gun shot then."

The shooting unnerved Evelyn Hunt O'Garro, too. A teenager then, O'Garro was chatting with friends on the front steps of her apartment house at 145th Street and Eighth Avenue, when she first heard people "running and hollering and breaking glass." She heard people shouting, "White man kill black soldier! Get the white man! Get the white man! He's to blame!" O'Garro's mother herded Evelyn and her three sisters together and took them upstairs to their fifth-floor apartment, where the girls watched from a window and a fire escape as rioters swept through the street below. "I was scared. Then we started hearing shooting—'pop!' 'pop!' It was horrifying and that's when my nerves really went."

It was like a nightmare come true for six-year-old Claude Brown, who lived nearby. Brown, who would grow up to be a noted writer, had been asleep when he heard loud noises and thought bombs were falling and "the Germans or the Japs had come." Brown ran into his parents' room. His mother and father were looking out of the front window of their apartment, at the corner of 145th and Eighth. He thought they were watching an air raid and asked where the sirens were and why the street lights, though dimmed, were still on. "This ain't no air raid," his father said, "just a whole lotta niggers gone fool." Told to get back to bed, Brown could not sleep. "The loud screams in the street and the crashing sound of falling plate-glass windows kept me awake for hours. While I listened to the noise, I imagined bombs falling and people running through the streets screaming."

The smashing of windows and vandalism swept through Harlem along with the rumor about Bandy's slaying—first on both sides of 125th Street, then up and down Seventh and Eighth Avenues. Within minutes, 125th Street was in shambles. Few store windows were still in place, and many of the stores were gutted. Torn apart limb-by-limb by the angry mobs, white mannequin look-alikes lay sprawled across glass-strewn sidewalks. Off in the distance, police and fire sirens pierced the night air against the constant rumble of rampaging mobs. Rioters broke so many street lamps that entire blocks were plunged into complete darkness. Novelist Ralph Ellison remembered the "distant fire trucks, shooting, and in the quiet intervals the steady filtering of shattered glass."

The sudden outburst did not surprise Virginia Delany Murphy. She had just seen *Stormy Weather* at the RKO Alhambra on Seventh Avenue and 126th Street and was leaving the theater as news of the trouble on 125th Street was shouted out. "If you wanted to get upset, you could find something happening almost daily . . . arguments with the police and the community. There was always something to fight about. There's something about putting on those blue coats and brass buttons—they thought they were God or something."

Roy Wilkins and his wife, Minnie, were heading home from downtown on a bus when, at Seventh Avenue and 116th Street, a brick came hurtling through the window. "Get down on the floor," the NAACP official yelled at his wife. A barrage of missiles struck the windows, one of them shattering a window and badly injuring a woman passenger. The bus driver accelerated and did not stop until he reached Sydenham Hospital.

Wilkins was not surprised that people believed the rumor that was spreading like wildfire through the streets. Black soldiers had been "shot down by civilian police in Alexandria, La., in Little Rock, Ark., in Baltimore, Md., in Beaumont, Texas, and in a half dozen other places . . . humiliated, manhandled, and beaten in countless instances," he later wrote. "The Harlem mob knew all this. It hated this. It could not reach the Arkansas cop who fired a full magazine of his revolver into the prone body of a Negro sergeant, or any of the others, so it tore up Harlem."

Just as Wilkins reached home, he got a call from Walter White, a neighbor in the prestigious Sugar Hill apartment house at 409 Edgecombe Avenue. White had gone to bed early that evening, exhausted after three speaking engagements in one day. He told his wife, Gladys, he did not want to be disturbed even if "President Roosevelt or Cleopatra called." White was asleep only a few minutes when the Whites' phone rang. Gladys answered it. A member of the NAACP staff informed her that there was a full-scale riot in central Harlem. Despite her husband's admonitions, she immediately roused White.

White was dressed in five minutes and about to leave when the phone rang again. This time it was La Guardia. The mayor was calling from City Hall. He was about to rush up to the Twenty-eighth Police Precinct and wanted White to join him there as quickly as possible. He was summoning every black leader he could to an emergency meeting.

White was no more surprised than anyone else about the eruption of violence. He thought of all the letters that friends and relatives had received from the men of the 369th Regiment at Camp Stewart, Georgia, telling of "gratuitous insults and beatings and humiliations suffered by men who had fought in the Pacific and had been returned home to train other fighters." He thought of the "countless stories of lynchings and mistreatment of Negro soldiers," of the war plants "begging for men and women workers" while "those with black skins were daily told contemptuously that they were not wanted." The men and women on the streets, he realized, came from old tenements where they were packed "like sardines." They came with memories fresh with news of riots in Beaumont and Detroit "and the gory tales of black men hunted like wild beasts and killed."

The phone now rang in the Wilkins' apartment. It was White, calling to say that La Guardia was asking for help and that he was going down to the Twenty-eighth Precinct to meet the mayor. Afraid for his colleague—"White was as white as La Guardia; how long either of them could last on the streets of Harlem was anyone's guess"—Wilkins grabbed his hat and coat and headed for the lobby of the building to intercept and accompany White. The two men were able to hail a cab. "As we rode down Seventh Avenue," White recalled, "we could hear the smashing of plate glass windows and the roar of the crowd, as far north as 135th Street. We saw Negroes attempting to get at white people in automobiles who, unaware of the riot, had driven into the heart of it." The two men finally made it to 123rd Street "through all the bricks and bottles." White credited "Roy's brown skin" for saving them both from attack.

La Guardia and Police Commissioner Lewis Valentine were at the police station when White and Wilkins arrived, already implementing some of the measures proposed at the conference the mayor had held at Gracie Mansion after the Detroit riot. La Guardia had ordered all available police officers into the Harlem area. Their orders were strict. Patrolmen would operate in groups of at least two, accompanied by superior officers. They were to use force only "when necesssary" and shoot only as "the last resort." The use of tear gas would also be as a last resort. Traffic was being diverted from the area of the disorders.

La Guardia had also requested army headquarters on Governor's Island in New York Harbor to send military policemen to get all soldiers and sailors out of the community. But only white MPs were coming, and White was worried that "the crowds had already reached such a peak of frenzy" that the mobs would attack them. At his suggestion, the mayor got in touch with army headquarters again and asked for an equal number of black MPs with instructions that they be assigned to work in mixed pairs with the white MPs.

It soon became clear that, although some white civilians were attacked, rioters were focusing their hostility on white-owned property and the police. Two young British seamen were beaten as they left a 125th Street movie house, and a white patron at the Apollo was knocked down as he emerged from that theater. A sixty-one-year-old passenger on a trolley car was hit in his right eye when three black men reached through an open window and struck him. Two other white men, one forty-one years old, the other nineteen, were stabbed by blacks. A sixty-two-year-old woman on a bus was cut when a bottle was thrown into the vehicle. But other than those incidents, rioters focused their anger on the police. Bricks, bottles, ashcans, and other missiles came raining down on patrolmen from the windows and roofs of buildings. Capt. Walter Harding, commanding officer of the Twenty-eighth Precinct, was one of the first police officers to be injured. A bottle flung from a roof struck him in the left eye. Valentine immediately ordered all policemen to wear their steel air-raid helmets, and firemen were told to wear theirs, too.

By then, looting had broken out. At first, the mobs that ran through the streets were interested only in destruction, expending their rage by breaking store fronts and tossing window displays onto the sidewalk. They turned over any peddlers' carts that stood in their way. But as the rioting continued unabated, many people—men and women, young and old, poor and well-off—started making off with armsful of merchandise. The office of the *Amsterdam News* on Seventh Avenue and most shops known to be black-owned or whose owners posted signs ("Colored Store") were spared—"not a thing was touched, not a box out of place," according to one reporter—but otherwise every store in Harlem became fair game.

Malcolm Little was on St. Nicholas Avenue when he saw "all of these Negroes hollering and running north from 125th Street." A friend, "Shorty" Henderson, a nephew of bandleader Fletcher Henderson, told him what had happened. Little saw blacks "smashing windows, and taking everything they could grab and carry—furniture, food, jewelry, clothes, whisky." Rioters were calling one of the looters "Left Feet" because "in a scramble in a women's shoe store, somehow he'd grabbed five shoes, all of them for left feet!"

Hoping to avert the destruction, Chinese who ran laundries put hastily lettered signs on their doors: "Me Colored Too." Little remembered how rioters went into convulsions of laughter when a Chinese restaurant owner stuck such a sign on his door. For together with the pent-up rage and frustration that the rioting symbolized, an almost carnival-like atmosphere permeated Harlem, especially where looting was going on. Some boys jocularly sported stolen dress coats, silk hats, and blond wigs. Other boys and men paraded in new suits, hats, and shoes. Women ransacking a clothing store stopped to judge the size of dresses. In one grocery, a teenage boy stood behind the counter passing out articles of food to people waiting patiently in line. Middle-class blacks who had stood by, watching the rioting, now took part in the looting, which became almost systematic.

The scene at the Twenty-eighth Precinct was anything but carnival-like. The station house, on the north side of 123rd Street between Seventh and Eighth Avenues, resembled an arsenal. The street outside was filled with police squad cars, trucks with searchlights, and emergency vehicles. Surrounding it and patroling the district were heavily armed police officers and soldiers, police auxiliaries, air-raid wardens, and civilian volunteers. The last included men and women, most of them black, who were armed with nightsticks and wore arm-bands for identification. A steady stream of police officers poured into the small station house. They reported for assignments in an airless basement squad room, which soon became so crowded that it was hard to breath. Five thousand police officers were rushing to Harlem from throughout the city. All police leaves and days off were cancelled. Foot and mounted patrolmen as well as detectives and motorcycle and radio-car officers from all five boroughs had been called to duty.

La Guardia hoped to avoid calling up the National Guard or ask-ing the army to intervene. Gov. Thomas E. Dewey happened to be staying at the Roosevelt Hotel in midtown Manhattan that Sunday night. He was keeping in close touch with the situation, but as yet had not received any request from the mayor to mobilize the Guard, or to call on the White House for army support. The army could not turn out unless Dewey applied for help on the ground that city authorities had lost control of the situation. It was the last thing La Guardia wanted. But at the mayor's request, Dewey alerted the commander of the National Guard and had him order eight thousand members to report immediately for drills in various armories in the metropolitan area, where they would be readily available for riot duty if needed. They were prepared to move into action within thirty minutes. The guardsmen included the blacks of the 369th Regiment Armory at 143rd Street and Fifth Avenue.

Hearing that a mob was approaching the New York Central Rail-road's elevated station at 125th Street and Park Avenue, the "ebul-lient Mayor" sprang into action. He bundled White into a small police car. Valentine wanted to assign a squad car to precede the two men and another police car to follow them, but La Guardia was in a hurry and refused to wait the few minutes it would have taken to arrange for his protection. "He had his Italian up," Roy Wilkins said.

White was worried that La Guardia might be the target of rioters. He had tried to persuade La Guardia to sit between him and the driver of the small police car. He did not want the mayor to sit beside the window, where he might be exposed to injury. "I was con-cerned," admitted White, "not only for his sake, but also because I knew and feared the terrible publicity all Negroes would receive if any harm befell a man so well-known and beloved." But La Guardia insisted on sitting next to the window, where he felt he could be more effective in calming the rioters. "They know my face better than yours," he told White, "so you sit in the middle."

By then, the streets were empty of any moving vehicles except for police cars and fire engines. The entire western section of Harlem, Negro Harlem, had been effectively sealed off. All traffic was being diverted from the area. No buses or trolleys, private cars or trucks were permitted between Fifth and Eighth Avenues and from 110th to 155th Streets.

The elder Powell, seventy-eight-year-old Adam Clayton, Sr., who had lived through the 1900 and 1935 disorders, thought the riot was "the hottest hell ever created in Harlem." White himself was reminded of stories of the French Revolution. As the police car carrying him and the mayor sped through Harlem, he saw "wild-eyed men and women whose poverty was pathetically obvious in their shabbiness" roaming the streets, "screaming imprecations." White thought of the stories he had read about the "starved hordes" who had "poured from the sewers and slums of Paris, shouting their hatred of oppression and oppressors."

White and La Guardia arrived at the 125th rail station to find that the report of a mob gathering there was false. But as they returned through Lenox Avenue, they spotted looters pillaging stores. "Regardless of personal danger, the Mayor shouted, 'Put that stuff down,' to a group of youthful vandals," White said. "Utterly startled, they dropped what they had in their hands and fled." Later, when they passed a crowd standing outside a building that was on fire, La Guardia jumped from the car and shouted at the people to go home.

La Guardia seemed impervious to danger and undaunted by the taunts greeting his appeals. Wilkins joined the mayor and White when they went out again to tour the community. La Guardia "rushed on bands of rioters, ordering them to cease and desist, and most were too startled by the sight of the red-faced mayor to do anything but obey. It was a miracle nothing happened to him." As it was, La Guardia was almost struck by a missile thrown at him. White finally suggested "a small tactical retreat." He convinced "the perspiring mayor" to send for sound trucks.

With the help of White and Wilkins, La Guardia was able to contact a number of other community leaders. The mayor had already enlisted Max Yergan, head of the National Negro Congress, and Ferdinand Smith, secretary of the National Maritime Union, whom he met while going through the district earlier. Now they contacted two other men, attorney Hope Stevens of the New York Urban League, and Rev. John H. Johnson, rector of St. Martin's Protestant Episcopal Church, who was a police chaplain. They tried to reach several other blacks, as well—the mayor's archcritic Adam Clayton Powell, Jr., as well as such well-known Harlem residents as boxer Joe Louis and band leaders Cab Calloway and Duke Ellington—but they were all out of town.

Once the sound trucks arrived at the Twenty-eighth Precinct, White, Wilkins, Yergan, Smith, Stevens, and Johnson took to the streets, trying to spread the word that Bandy was alive and well—he had been taken to Bellevue Hospital downtown—and exhorting the rioters to return to their homes in peace. Soon afterwards, though, Minnie Wilkins got a phone call at home from a woman who lived in Central Harlem. "Mrs. Wilkins, it's awful!," the woman said. "I recognize Mr. Wilkins's voice in a truck. He's begging everyone to go home—but they won't." Minnie Wilkins told the woman to calm down and take another look outside. The woman returned to the phone with a more reassuring report. The sound truck had disappeared up Seventh Avenue without hindrance. Out on the curb an old man sat, gorging himself on a gallon can of vanilla ice cream that he had plundered from a store.

At one point, White rode up Eighth Avenue, "where the crowds were densest and angriest," in a sound truck with Ferdinand Smith. "Over and over again, as the huge vehicle nosed its way through crowded streets," they repeated their plea:

> The rumor is false that a Negro soldier was killed at the Braddock Hotel tonight. He is only slightly wounded and is in no danger. Go to your homes! Don't form mobs or break the law! Don't destroy in one night the reputation as good citizens you have taken a lifetime to build! Go home—now!

During a first swing through the area, White and Smith were greeted with "raucous shouts of disbelief" and the "rat-tat-tat" of bricks and bottles hitting the roof of the sound truck. A frenzied man waved at them with a raised fist. By a third swing up Eighth Avenue, though, the man was silenced and finally joined in urging the crowds to go home.

But every appeal, whether from the mayor or the community leaders, went largely unheeded. All through the night, mobs continued to race through Harlem. La Guardia finally took to the radio at 1:05 A.M. to make the first of five radio broadcasts. He had to go downtown to make the appeal, which was heard on three major local stations and rebroadcast on a fourth:

> Now I am going to protect the lives and the property of this city and that means in every section of the city, and you who are listening to me now, if you will just go downstairs and call the members of your family and your friends and get them off the street.
>
> The quicker we do that the better it will be. I do not want this to develop into anything very serious. There may be some people who may like to see trouble, but we do not want trouble in our city and certainly the people of West Harlem know that they have no cause to complain and should cooperate with me at this time.

La Guardia repeatedly gave the details of the shooting and said that "small groups walking around more in the spirit of mischief than anything else broke some of the store windows." He warned that unless people got off the streets "we may have serious trouble."

The mayor's remarks were an understatement. The scene throughout the night at Harlem Hospital resembled a horror movie. Arnold de Mille was on duty with the hospital's U.S. Ambulance Corps unit. Its office was inside the 136th Street emergency entrance to the hospital, which was just off Lenox Avenue. De Mille, the advertising manager of the *New York Age* and a freelance writer for the *Chicago Defender*, had been turned down for service in the army and the merchant marine for physical reasons, but still wanted to help out. Though he could not drive a vehicle himself, he had organized the hospital's ambulance unit and ran it. There were some twenty-odd members, all uniformed volunteers, who worked eight-hour shifts. The unit had three ambulances, each of which could hold eight patients. "We could have used twenty-three ambulances that night," de Mille recalls.

Harlem Hospital was accustomed to emergency situations on Friday and Saturday nights, when many people spent their wages in saloons, but the night of the riot was on a totally different scale. "We heard a lot of noise from out in the street—screaming and yelling." Ordinarily de Mille ran the operation from a desk, but he had called in all his crew and was now himself riding out on calls alongside a driver:

> I was crazy enough to tell people to get the hell out of the street—get off the streets. The lights were out.
>
> We went to the scene where calls came from—this was at the beginning. After a while, I would say no more than twenty-thirty minutes, we didn't wait for calls to come because we saw what was happening out on the streets. We just just went out and picked up. We would fill up the ambulance, go to the hospital, leave them, go out on the street again.
>
> And the floor of the hospital—the attendants had to mop up the blood every two minutes because people kept streaming in as well as those we brought in.
>
> All I remember really was the flood of blood in the emergency area. I have never seen anything like it since. It kept me awake a few nights—dreaming about the blood, about seeing people, the way they looked when we picked them up out of the street. But the blood—a river of blood. I couldn't sleep for several nights.

One of de Mille's crew members was St. Clair Bourne, the managing editor of the *People's Voice*. He was directing the injured as they staggered into the emergency room lobby. Early on, a squad of eight white MPs appeared with a young "shavetail" second lieutenant—"one of those eager beavers," recalls Bourne—who marched into the hospital and said he was going to take charge. Bourne advised him against going out into the riot scene, but the officer ignored him. About a half hour later, the squad returned, carrying the lieutenant. He had been slashed with a knife.

Bourne remembers the blood, too. The medical gowns of the doctors and nurses were splattered with it. "It was the kind of thing that happens when you get into a situation where everybody is throwing inhibitions to the wind—fighting, throwing stones, whatever."

By midnight, all of Harlem Hospital's interns and students were on emergency duty, and visiting surgeons were keeping two operating rooms busy. A surgeon was also on duty at the Twenty-eighth Precinct to provide "instant first aid." The city's hospital commissioner had reserve teams on standby at Bellevue and two other city hospitals, all of which were stocked with additional supplies of blood, dressings, sutures, and sulfa drugs. Harlem Hospital was receiving the most victims, but Sydenham as well as two East Side hospitals, Knickerbocker and Joint Diseases, were also treating the injured. Most persons suffered cuts from flying glass or from climbing through shattered store fronts, but the wounds of more than fifty-five were so serious that they were admitted as patients.

One patient, a forty-year-old black man who had been shot by a policeman, was rushed to Harlem Hospital but was dead on arrival. The policeman had confronted the man as he was dragging a suitcase from a luggage shop on 125th Street. The man had allegedly drawn a knife when accosted.

By midnight, the police had cleared all people from devastated 125th Street between Seventh and Eighth Avenues, but the rioting had already spread like a ripple from the center of Harlem to Lenox Avenue on the east and to St. Nicholas Avenue on the west. Mobs reached as far north as 145th Street. Others headed south toward 110th Street in Spanish Harlem, on the fringe of Central Park.

La Guardia had ordered a curfew at 10:30 P.M. At the same time, all liquor stores in Harlem were closed. But neither measure cleared the streets. The wartime dimout was lifted so that the district could be brightly illuminated, but so many street lights had been broken that many areas were cast in shadows. Twenty policemen were stationed at the Braddock Hotel, which was shut down at 11 P.M. La Guardia now ordered all bars closed at 2 A.M., but that, the *Amsterdam News* said, only forced "revellers into the streets" and increased the rioting "by leaps and bounds."

Gunfire, sporadic at times, increased dramatically after midnight. Before long, on blocks as far apart as Eighth Avenue and Lenox Avenue, four blacks lay dying on the street, all but one shot by policemen, who said they were looters and had ignored orders to stop. One, a twenty-two-year-old, refused to divulge the contents of a bag he was carrying and was shot after he tossed it at an officer. Two other men were shot while pillaging a store on Seventh Avenue at 136th Street. A fourth was fatally wounded while looting a pork store on 127th Street and Lenox Avenue. A fifth black man who died was shot by a black bartender at a bar and grill on Eighth Avenue. The victim and another man had allegedly kicked in the bar's window.

At 12:37 A.M., in the midst of the increasing violence, four truckloads of black MPs escorted by motorcycle police arrived at the Twenty-eighth Precinct. The thirty-two military policemen in them were immediately dispatched to the streets to bring in soldiers on leave. In all, more than five hundred soldiers were rounded up.

It seemed as though no sooner did the police bring one block under control than rioting or looting broke out on another. By 3 A.M. one band of rioters reached the northern edge of Central Park at 110th Street. Returning to the Twenty-eighth Precinct from another of his tours, La Guardia, who had been jeered and booed at several places, was asked by a reporter how conditions were. The mayor pointed to several hundred patrolmen who were just then leaving the station house and heading for 110th Street. "There's your answer," he said glumly.

Within minutes of the mayor's remark, Valentine put all police in the city on eight-hour tours of duty, followed by eight hours on reserve and then another eight hours on duty. All members of the force above the rank of lieutenant who were on vacation were recalled. Firemen whose tours of duty had ended at midnight were already being held on duty for eight more hours.

For the most part, a *People's Voice* reporter insisted, the rioters and looters were "young hoodlums, night hawks and riff raff from the most distressed sections. They carried boxes of groceries, clothes from stores and cleaning shops, articles from pawn shops and radios. One man struggled with a whole calf from a meat market. Some carried boxes of liquor in bottles. One man even had a bag of wet wash."

Police were arresting the looters in droves. Soon, the Twenty-eighth Precinct's cell blocks and those at the Thirtieth Precinct on West 151st Street and at other station houses farther east and west were jammed to capacity. To handle the enormous number of looters, the huge National Guard armory at Park Avenue and Ninety-fourth Street was pressed into service as a temporary holding pen.

At 4 A.M. a rash of false fire alarms broke out. Fire engines hurtled through the streets, trying to avoid the shattered glass, their red lights flashing, sirens screeching. So many false alarms occurred that two firemen were finally stationed to guard each firebox in Harlem. Then the alarms turned out to be real. One group of blacks ran along Eighth Avenue, setting six fires in as many minutes.

When the sun rose a few minutes before six o'clock on Monday morning, rioting was still going on in isolated pockets. Looting was widespread.

His nightmare forgotten, young Claude Brown ran from his apartment house at dawn to catch up with two older friends, Danny and Butch Stinky:

> When I reached the stoop, I was knocked back into the hall by a big man carrying a ham under his coat. . . . Other men came running through the hall carrying cases of whiskey, sacks of flour, and cartons of cigarettes. . . . I was bowled over again. This time by a cop with a gun in his hand. He never stopped, but after he had gone a couple of yards into the hall, I heard him say, "Look out, kid."

When Brown finally got out of the building, he was not even sure it was his street. It was unrecognizable. Not one store had a window left in place. There was glass everywhere. He found his friends at home around the corner, eating what they had scavenged from neighborhood shops. One had his hand in a gallon jar of pickled pigs' ears, another was cooking bacon on the stove. Brown joined them when they set out again. They stopped in front of a pawnshop that had been set on fire. Firemen had torn down a sidewall to get at the blaze:

> So Butch and I just walked in where the wall used to be. Everything I picked up was broken or burned or both. My feet kept sinking into the wet furs that had been burned and drenched. The whole place smelled of smoke and was as dirty as a Harlem gutter on a rainy day. The cop out front yelled to us to get out of there. He only had to say it once.

Brown and the Stinky brothers next stopped at a seafood restaurant, where they were able to pilfer some shrimp and oysters. At a nearby grocery store, he stole two loaves of bread. A policeman spotted him as he was leaving the store. Brown ran all the way back to the Stinkys' home, dropping the oysters on the way.

Just about the same time, Walter White, with La Guardia again in a police car, saw "a toothless old woman" in a crowd in front of a grocery store clutching two dirty pillowcases in one hand and a teenage boy in the other. As soon as an opening in the crowd appeared, the woman, "with an agility surprising in one of her age and emaciated appearance, climbed through the broken glass into the store window." He could see her filling the pillowcases with canned goods and cereals that were scattered throughout the store. Back outside the store, the woman suddenly stopped and looked toward White and the mayor.

> Exultation, vengeance, the supreme satisfaction of having secured food for a few days, lighted her face, and then I looked at the sleepy-eyed child by her side. I felt nausea that an abundant society like America's could so degrade and starve a human being, and I was equally sickened to contemplate the kind of man the boy would become under such conditions.

White and La Guardia returned to the Twenty-eighth Precinct, where cables had been set up so that the mayor could broadcast from there. The rioting was now twelve hours old and the mood still incendiary. At the slightest provocation, a crowd would form and turn dangerous. A white proprietor who chanced into Harlem to check on his store had his car overturned and set on fire. The black smoke from its burning gasoline acted as a beacon for a crowd to form. A mob of three thousand people gathered at 145th Street and Eighth Avenue shortly after dawn. Urged by a black soldier to "let the cops have it," the mob stoned policemen who tried to disperse it. Later, four officers trying to arrest five blacks for looting were besieged for an hour by a crowd of seven hundred blacks until reinforcements arrived.

La Guardia, who had long since cancelled his usual Monday trip to Washington, went on the air from the Twenty-eighth Precinct at 7:30 A.M. to describe what had happened. He reiterated the details in another broadcast at 9:50 A.M., emphasizing—in an apparent effort to maintain order throughout the rest of the city—that the disorder was not a race riot, that whites had not been the sole or even prime target. But "shame," he said, "has come to our city and sorrow to the large number of fellow citizens . . . who live in Harlem." Traffic in Harlem would be restricted, he explained, and nonresidents denied entrance into the area. Pedestrians would not be allowed to assemble, looters would be arrested. "Law and order," he declared, "must and will be maintained in this city."

Later in the morning, with the worst finally over and the police fully in control of the streets, the mayor, White, Valentine, and the Reverend Johnson stood behind the booking desk as scores of prisoners were brought into the Twenty-eighth Precinct station house. Nearly six hundred blacks had been arrested, among them twelve servicemen. About one hundred of those arrested were women. Almost without exception, all were charged with suspicion of burglary. Most of them still carried in their arms the loot they had stolen. White, who had lived in Harlem for twenty-five years, said he had never seen "such concentrated despair as I witnessed that morning."

> Their anger spent, the men, women, and children were pathetic specimens of humanity as the consequences of their acts loomed before them. The loot which had been captured with them steadily mounted in the large lobby of the police station—clothing and household furnishings and food—particularly food."

Among those under arrest were Margie Polite and Private Bandy's mother, Mrs. Roberts. Both were charged with assault and were being held on $10,000 bail at the Women's House of Detention in Greenwich Village.[4]

Almost all Harlem was a scene of devastation—"a distressing sight in the glare of daylight," as White put it. Allen Worrell had watched "people carrying whatever they could" from his family's third-floor apartment the night before. Now the youngster stepped into the street. Glass was piled so high, he recalls, that it was "like snow. You had to watch where you walked." Some looters were still collecting goods in "ice wagons."

Fred Mays's parents had kept him at home during the riot, but teenage friends of his had taken part in the looting, getting "their goodies." "This was gravy, some action, something to do, you see," he says. "We could intellectualize this—black, white, and that sort of stuff—but in many ways it was that 'What did they have to lose?' "

The many Harlemites who had not engaged in looting were without food or milk. "We didn't have really nothing," remembers Evelyn Hunt O'Garro. "We had to live on each other's goodness, and those days we had a famine."

Walker Smith, on furlough from the army, arrived in Harlem to find that his wife's beauty parlor and a neighboring black-owned restaurant had been spared. Dr. James Jones had been home on furlough over the weekend, celebrating his twenty-ninth birthday, but he returned to duty in Washington shortly before the riot broke out. He rushed back Monday to see if his family was all right. The disturbance by then was "simmering down." He did not believe the rioters were anybody other than itinerant "lower levels." "You had a home," he says, "you had a church. You respected authority."

The worst damage was on Harlem's major arterial streets—125th, 135th, and 145th Streets, and Fifth, Lenox, Seventh, and Eighth Avenues. A *People's Voice* reporter described the main thoroughfares as looking as though "they had been rocked and fired by bombs." These same streets looked to a *Times* reporter

as if they had been swept by a hurricane or an invading army. Windows of many of the stores in the area had been smashed, stores were filled with wrecked fixtures, the sidewalks were covered with broken glass, and the gutters were piled with foodstuffs, canned goods, clothing, household furnishings and other articles that the looters had been unable to carry off.

"Sullen-looking Negroes," the *Times* reporter added, "were gathered here and there in small groups, muttering to themselves," but they were kept moving by police. "The police were everywhere."

Looters had left taverns, jewelry stores, restaurants, and haberdasheries wrecked. Four hundred stores had lost windows. Thirty of the forty liquor stores in Harlem had been broken into and cleaned out. Five thousand dollars worth of liquor alone was stolen from a store on 125th Street. Ten thousand dollars worth of wearing apparel was taken from Blumstein's windows down the street. Every suit in two clothing stores was lifted. Every bit of food and household goods was taken at a large market at 134th Street and Eighth Avenue, and some of the shelves as well. A cache found on the rooftop of a building on 129th Street included two hundred pounds of beef, seven typewriters, two guitars, a violin, and bed linen.

Pawnshops had been particularly hard hit. One, at Eighth Avenue and 127th Street, was completely wrecked and all the jewelry in display cases taken. The same was true at a pawnshop up Eighth at 135th Street, at a loan company a few blocks farther north, and at two other pawnshops near 145th Street. The looters were already out on the streets of Harlem, peddling to passersby the items they had stolen.

Arnold de Mille was finally able to leave Harlem Hospital at daylight. Harlem and other municipal hospitals had between them handled almost seven hundred patients. De Mille, on his way home to his room at the Hotel Theresa, where he lived, took a devious route:

> Windows smashed. Stuff spread all over the place, the streets. Empty stores—utterly empty. Ransacked. Looted. The things people didn't need were left on the shelves, if there was a shelf left.
>
> The pawn shop on 145th Street and Eighth Avenue—cleaned out. There was an A&P next door to it—cleaned out. On Seventh Avenue there might have been a half-dozen, if that many, grocery stores left untouched. There were a few laundries—Chinese laundries—I remember the signs. It's a fact. And they were untouched. . . .
>
> Stuff scattered, glass all over the place.

The father of James Baldwin, the writer, died on the Thursday before the riot, as Baldwin was to about to celebrate his nineteenth birthday. The funeral was held after the riot:

> [W]e drove my father to the graveyard through a wilderness of smashed plate glass. . . . As we drove . . . the spoils of injustice, anarchy, discontent, and hatred were all around us. It seemed to me that God himself had devised, to mark my father's end, the most sustained and brutally dissonant of codas. . . .
>
> I truly had not realized that Harlem had so many stores until I

saw them all smashed open; the first time the word *wealth* ever entered my mind in relation to Harlem was when I saw it scattered in the streets. But one's first, incongruous impression of plenty was countered immediately by an impression of waste. None of this was doing anybody any good. It would have been better to have left the plate glass as it had been and the goods lying in the stores.

It would have been better, but it would also have been intolerable, for Harlem had needed something to smash.

Jack Trotter, a columnist for the *People's Voice*, was in Chicago over the weekend to attend the Negro Baseball League's all-star game. After returning to New York by train, he took the subway from Pennsylvania Station up to Harlem. Stepping "out of the underground to see the devastation and damage that been wrought[,] with the community a virtual armed camp, there was an unexplainable empty feeling in the pit of our stomach."

"The most pathetic scene," the *People's Voice* reported, was the sight of William Wiener standing bewildered in what was left of his drugstore on Lenox Avenue. Wiener was one of the few white proprietors to return to Harlem that Monday. A pharmacist, he had worked there for twenty years. As his son rummaged through the debris, he said that he, like other shopkeepers, had no insurance. "I don't know what I'll do. I can't think. There is nothing left here to work with."

As the looting died down, only the sound of people crunching through the ubiquitous shattered bottles and store windows could be heard. There were no buses or trolleys. Few children were seen in the area's playgrounds. The army had declared all Harlem out of bounds. Even midtown in the Broadway theater district, zoot-suiters, usually numerous, were conspicuous by their absence. The streets were so quiet that Adam Clayton Powell, Jr., who had returned to the city, said it seemed like a holiday. Members of his political organization, the Peoples Committee, were distributing one hundred thousand leaflets, urging people to restore order and to bring all their complaints to the committee's headquarters at the Abyssinian Baptist Church.

There were still lingering reminders of what had occurred. A white waiter was arrested for receiving stolen goods. Nell Dodson, a *People's Voice* columnist, saw a small boy strutting along a street, wearing a woman's red hat pilfered from a millinery shop perched atop his head. A teenage boy, his arms loaded with lighting fixtures, was in the custody of two policemen, being taken to the Twenty-eighth Precinct. In the afternoon, Dodson and a few others from the newspaper went to have lunch at the Hotel Theresa's grille. It was the only restaurant in the area that was open. A "dog-tired" Roy Wilkins, who had been up all night, joined them.

On behalf of the *People's Voice,* Ferdinand Smith went with a photographer to the prison ward of Bellevue Hospital to interview Robert Bandy. The young soldier was sitting up in bed. He was going to be released to army authorities in a few days. He smiled for the camera but said, "I am somewhat nervous but do not feel so bad." Bandy told Smith, "I do not know how badly I am hurt, but the fact that I am able to sit up and shake your hand indicates that I am not too badly hurt." Smith asked whether Bandy had any message for the people of Harlem. "Yes," he replied, "tell them if I was out and in uniform, I would not agree to this rioting. In fact, they should cease rioting."

La Guardia, who had gone without sleep all night Sunday, finally took a break about midafternoon Monday. Both he and White returned to their homes for brief naps. The mayor's lasted an hour. He spent the rest of the day shuttling back and forth between City Hall and the Twenty-eighth Precinct in Harlem. After conferring with court, police, and military officials, he decided to keep Harlem shut off from the rest of the city. Fifteen hundred volunteers, mostly black, as well as MPs, air-raid wardens, City Patrol units, and the six thousand policemen still on duty secured the area. Police officers were stationed on street corners, in hallways, on rooftops, and in cars all over Harlem. The eight thousand National Guardsmen in regiment armories around the city remained on standby.

That night, the mayor and White toured Harlem once more. Its streets were brilliantly lit. Twenty-five men and ten trucks from the Department of Water, Sewage, Gas, and Electricity had crisscrossed the area, changing the twelve hundred bulbs that had been destroyed and increasing illumination in the area by more than 200 percent. The streets, White said, "were as quiet and empty as the financial district of lower Broadway on a Sunday morning." Afterwards, La Guardia made two final broadcasts, at 9:45 and 10:25 P.M. He reminded Harlemites of the 10:30 P.M. curfew, pleading with residents to get off the streets and go home. The riot was over, he reported, "the situation at this moment is definitely under control." He urged residents to return to work as usual Tuesday morning. Peace had been restored.

In the days that followed, life in Harlem slowly returned to some semblance of normality, though the scars of the rioting were evident. As early as Monday morning, the city's markets commissioner arranged to send three large truckloads of milk to Harlem. Personnel from the city departments of housing and buildings began boarding up windows; so many were damaged that ultimately nearly two hundred workers from the department of public works were called in to help. The task took three days. Meanwhile, more than twelve hundred sanitation workers and 250 garbage trucks scoured the streets. A police escort accompanied each work crew.

All through the night Tuesday, air-raid wardens and volunteers continued to assist the police in patrolling the heart of Harlem. City officials, edgy about the possibility of another outbreak of violence, had the patients in Harlem Hospital secretly evacuated to Bellevue Hospital that evening. Eight four-stretcher ambulances carried the patients downtown in convoys purposely routed through quiet areas, leaving Harlem Hospital's surgical wards ready for any possible emergency use.

Normal traffic in Harlem was finally allowed to resume on Wednesday, and many of the six thousand policemen were withdrawn. The curfew was lifted the next night.

At eight o'clock on Thursday morning, liquor stores, taverns, and bars, closed since Sunday night, resumed business. At the Braddock Hotel, where it had all begun four days earlier, the bar reopened, too, but the rest of the hotel remained closed down. Its owner was protesting the assignment of six patrolmen to duty at the hotel around the clock.

TWENTY

Recriminations

My hard luck started when I was born
Leas' so the old folks say.
Dat same hard luck been my bes' fren'
Up to dis very day. . . .
For I'm a Jonah, I'm a Jonah man. . . .

—Alexander Rogers[1]

Six blacks dead. Nearly seven hundred persons injured, including forty policemen. Some six hundred persons arrested. A total of 1,485 stores damaged and looted; 4,495 plate-glass windows smashed. Property damage estimated at $5 million.[2] In all, according to one count, thirty-two fires had been set.[3] (The Fire Department refused to divulge the number of fires, in an apparent attempt to minimize the extent of the riot.)

Yet the toll might have been much greater had the police not been under restraint orders and had the community not been sealed off. Compared to Detroit, where thirty-four persons had been killed, Harlem had gotten off relatively easy.

Jack Trotter of the *People's Voice*, who was away in Chicago at the time of the riot, was one of the few blacks who took the police to task. Of the six blacks killed, five were shot by patrolmen. Trotter declared: "There is something askew in a situation in which . . . not a single cop gets so much as a bullet wound, because the victims have no guns. There is no excuse for marauding hoodlums, I admit, but neither is there any excuse for itchy gun fingered cops."[4]

But Walter White and other black leaders complimented the po-

lice force and praised La Guardia, as well, for his handling of the
situation. Even Trotter's boss, Adam Clayton Powell, Jr., agreed that
the mayor had played a crucial role in keeping the riot from engulfing
the city in a racial war. In a signed appeal, he asked Harlem residents
to cooperate with the police and henceforth check out rumors before
they believed them. Powell, who in the same issue of the *People's
Voice* announced that he was launching a campaign to represent Harlem in Congress, urged: "LET'S GO HARLEM! LET'S RESTORE LAW AND
ORDER IMMEDIATELY!"[5]

"How different was Detroit!" said White. "There a weak Mayor
hid while Negroes were beaten on the steps of City Hall itself." White
credited La Guardia with being "in the thick of the trouble, often at
great personal risk." He said that Police Commissioner Valentine,
who had often been maligned by blacks, provided "an equally sharp
contrast" to Detroit's police chief. "Even more remarkable was the
attitude of the police themselves." Although thousands of patrolmen
had "poured" into the Twenty-eighth Precinct, White never "during
all those troubled hours" heard "one word about 'niggers,' as I had
heard so frequently in Detroit, nor was there any other manifestation
of racial animosity. They were simply concerned with restoring
order."[6] White was also "amazed and delighted" by the way both
the press and radio stations "handled the riot in the same sober
and realistic fashion."[7] Newspapers, white dailies and black weeklies
alike, also made it clear that the rioting was unlike Detroit. No gangs
of whites had hunted down blacks, and the police had not stood by
or aggravated the situation.

Despite such commendations, Arthur Garfield Hayes, chairman
of one of the investigatory subcommittees that had looked into the
1935 riot in Harlem, believed much more could be done:

> Above all, every officer stationed in Harlem should be instructed
> that the rights of Negroes, now flouted, are as much to be respected
> by the police as are those of more fortunate citizens who reside on
> Fifth or Park Avenues.
>
> Of course, conditions in Harlem, the wretched housing, unduly
> high rents, lack of recreation grounds, discrimination in industry
> against colored people, are largely responsible for an emotional situ-
> ation which might at any time cause a flare-up. But in addition to
> this is a lack of proper treatment of the people by the police.[8]

Most Harlem residents expressed remorse over the riot. The *People's Voice* ran Ferdinand Smith's interview with Bandy and the photograph of the smiling black soldier on the front page of its issue of August 7. But like a distress signal, its slogan—"Serving All People" —was run upside down, and an American flag and eagle next to its front-page logo was also turned upside down. An *Amsterdam News* correspondent blamed a "few irresponsible and misguided individuals" for destroying "in a single night" what law-abiding blacks had built up over the past ten years. "They are a disgrace to their race, a disgrace to the city and a disgrace and a shame to the nation of which they are citizens," he wrote. "New York is the fairest city in America to its *Negro* minority."⁹ Rev. John H. Johnson, who had joined La Guardia in helping to quell the disorders, said the riot was "another black eye" for Harlem. Rowdies and hoodlums, he said, "will never win one battle for us."¹⁰

Like Trotter, writer, poet, and playwright Langston Hughes was out of New York when the riot took place, a fact that he said he regretted. He wrote a friend that he was sorry he had missed it. Hughes seemed to be particularly tickled that upper-class blacks were embarrassed by the rioting. "I gather the mob was most uncouth— and Sugar Hill is shamed!" He told another, "The better class Negroes are all *mad* at the low class ones for the breaking and looting that went on." He said that letters he received "from the better colored people practically froth at the mouth. It seems their peace was disturbed even more than white folks." To still another friend, writer Carl Van Vechten, he wrote, "All the best colored people declare they have been set back Fifty Years. I don't know exactly from what."

Hughes said he believed that civil disturbances usually led to progress in race relations. But Van Vechten quickly disabused him of the idea. "I know WHY the riots," he wrote Hughes, "and so I can understand, and they MAY have done some good locally, but the effect on the general public is extremely bad." Chastised, Hughes said he was "sorry" in his soul: " 'NEW DAY A-COMIN' says Mr. Roi Ottley. NEW NIGHT would probably be better. (How sweetly optimistic is the cullud race!)"¹¹

One thing that many persons commented on was the absence of any anti-Semitic remarks during the rioting and looting. Jewish liberals had been instrumental in the founding and funding of the National Association for the Advancement of Colored People. Its prestigious Spingarn Medal was named for one of them, Arthur Spingarn, a founder of Harcourt, Brace and for twenty-six years president of the NAACP. But radical black nationalists like Marcus Garvey tended to hold Jews to blame for all the injustices that whites perpetrated against blacks. The hostility was most evident in northern ghettos like Harlem, where the whites that blacks encountered— the shopkeepers, rent collectors, teachers, and social workers—were more often than not Jewish. Most store owners on 125th Street in Harlem were. But, the *People's Voice* reported, no one heard any anti-Jewish outcries, or saw any posters or slogans decrying Jews. The Citizens' Committee on Harlem declared:

> Although most of the land is owned by white Christians—banks, insurance companies, estates and churches—the fact is that the landlord agents are, for the most part, Jews. It is they who have the unpleasant task of collecting rents, refusing repairs, keeping expenses down for the landlords, and even bringing about evictions. Similarly, the Jews predominate among the principals of the public schools in Harlem. On them is the onus of having to discipline children. The Jews are easy scapegoats for the suffering and frustration of the Negro people.[12]

Even before order was restored, everyone seemed to have an opinion of what had caused the riot. Ever mindful of the wartime threat of enemy fifth-columnists in America's midst, the *New York Times* editorialized that "sinister agitators" had deliberately spread "lies" to enflame Harlem's residents.[13] Judge Hubert T. Delany of the Domestic Relations Court, a black, blamed the press for instigating the riot.[14]

Police Commissioner Valentine disclosed that there had been rumors that organized gangs from certain Southern cities—presumably white supremists—had been sent to New York to cause trouble. They had been filtering into Harlem for some time. Valentine said he had detectives of the sabotage squad investigating.[15]

Park Commissioner Robert Moses, often criticized because of the lack of recreational facilities in Harlem, was quick to deny that the area was devoid of parks and playgrounds. No new parks had been established during his tenure, but, he pointed out, there were now twenty-nine playgrounds, twenty more than a decade ago. The cause of the disturbance lay elsewhere. "Those who shout for the millenium agitate, exaggerate grievances and make promises which cannot be kept," he said. They were "at bottom responsible for the kind of trouble illustrated by the recent Harlem riot."[16]

Almost all city and federal authorities and black leaders insisted that the Harlem riot was not a race riot. The mayor held "thoughtless hoodlums" to blame.[17] Similarly, FBI Director J. Edgar Hoover told a convention of police chiefs that outbreaks mushrooming throughout the nation were the result of teenage hoodlums.[18] The *Age* insisted it was "the hoodlums" who "fanned the flames of mob spirit" and "dragged into" a morass "the innocent thousands of their fellow Negroes."[19] W. E. B. Du Bois declared that "the black folk in this land have developed a dangerous criminal class."[20] Saying that he spoke for the "great mass" of Harlem blacks, A. Philip Randolph insisted that "we are definitely and unqualifiedly opposed to all forms of hoodlumism."[21]

But there were others who saw the riot as a symbol of unrighted wrongs. Lester Granger of the Urban League took the Roosevelt Administration to task for its "unforgivably timid" stance on race relations.[22] Marvel Cooke in the *People's Voice* described "the terrific explosion in Harlem" as "an almost exact replica of the 'Ides of March' of 1935." While Cooke also insisted that the "disaster" was not a race riot, she declared, "It was the violent and terrible expression of the community against unjustified discrimination in the armed forces at a time when national unity is virtually necessary for America's win-the-war program."[23] Roy Wilkins called the riot "the boiling over of pent-up resentment in the breasts of millions of American Negroes all over this country."[24] The socialist *Militant* agreed that "the events in Harlem and the tragedy in Detroit" were not alike, but "nevertheless, the underlying cause of the Harlem events was the same as the underlying cause of the Detroit events."[25] George Breitman in the *Militant* said the discussion of who was to blame for the Harlem riot "reminds us of many of the slave rebellions that took place a century or so ago."

We all know how cruelly the slaves were oppressed and exploited
—and that the arguments raised on behalf of the maintenance of
slavery sounded monotonously like the arguments raised on behalf
of the maintenance of Jim Crow today. . . .

We don't pretend that the Harlem outbreak was completely
identical with the slave revolts, but we do maintain that the same
spirit was in evidence. . . . The mass of Negroes today are ready to
fight and are desperately seeking the correct program.[26]

Author Roi Ottley worried about the "post-war racial convul-
sion" that might take place. "Delinquency," he said, "is a protest
and a rebellion against conditions under which parents live."[27] A
Washington correspondent for the *New York Times* wrote that behind
the riot was "an impatient, irresistible drive of the Negroes on the
one hand for a fuller realization of the equality which has long been
promised to them, but just as long denied. And on the other hand, a
stubborn, deepening, and in some places broadening, resistance of
the whites to that very aim."[28] Another *Times* reporter wrote: "The
Harlem problem is a racial one, rooted in the Negro's dissatisfaction
with his racial status not only in Harlem but all over the country . . .
a reflection of a nationwide attitude."[29] The idea that irresponsible
politicians—"Those who shout for the millenium"—were responsible for the riot was also in the mind of *Times* columnist Arthur Krock:

Ever since Negroes got the vote, and began to live in concentrations
in the Northeast and the Middle West that have given them a political balance of power, many politicians have sought their suffrage by
making promises they did not intend to, and were unable to, fulfill.
Instead of pledging themselves to help assure that Negroes should
receive, as rightfully they should, as good facilities in living, education, employment and recreation as the white majority, these politicians have pandered to those colored leaders—often demagogues
themselves—who demanded that all such facilities should be mixed
and shared. Since in most parts of the United States the majority is
unalterably opposed to this, Negroes have found the promises hol-
low, and this fact has been used to stir up resentment among them.[30]

The truth was that the rioters represented every social and economic class in Harlem. Of the 590 looters who were arrested—and
thousands more were not apprehended—only 129 were males be-

tween the ages of sixteen and twenty years old, legally delinquents. The remaining 353 males were all adults.[31] Moreover, the pinpointing of white-owned stores and the sparing of black-owned ones clearly demonstrated a racial overtone. But white officials, like La Guardia, did not want to underscore the racial aspect of the riot for fear it would fuel an already explosive situation. And black leaders did not want to prejudice any progress or advances they could obtain by calling the outbreak a black-white confrontation, especially with the war going on. Almost all the leaders deliberately hid their heads in the sand. They refused either to acknowledge what the riot meant or what had to be done to prevent a repetition. But not the *People's Voice*. Its message was a wake-up call—"PEOPLE WANT A NEW HARLEM":

> No More Jim-Crow in the Armed Forces.
> No More Second-Class Citizens.
> Equal Job Opportunities.
> No More Riots.
> Enforcement of Price Control.
> Unity for Victory at Home and Abroad.[32]

The *Amsterdam News* agreed. "Harlem has sung and danced when it should have been working and praying," the newspaper declared in an editorial:

In the late nineteen twenties and the very early thirties, novelists, poets, newspaper columnists and publishers combined to portray Harlem as Negro Heaven. . . .

Native Harlemites, who knew better, aided the conspiracy by pretending that they believed Harlem was heaven. . . .

Harlemites could explain away the "hot bed," wherein a land-lady rents a room to two lodgers, one sleeping by day and the other by night, with only enough time left in between to turn the sheet. Harlemites blamed it on the local congestion. Harlemites could explain away the diet of hot dogs and soda pop, or why milady never keeps much food in the icebox. They call it convenient. They insist it is easier to run to the store to buy a stick of butter four times a week than to buy a pound once a week. Harlemites explain away why they wore old clothes, no stockings, no hats, insisting that it's a fad or a new style. They call it big time to pay the rent by the week, instead of monthly as their leases require. Anything that doesn't sound big and look big can't touch them.

It's time now for Harlem to quit kidding itself. . . . Harlem never has lived up to its reputation. . . . Harlem is, and has been for years, in a bad way. It has refused to face facts. . . .

But it seems that the sham can no longer go on. . . .[33]

Reality was also underscored by the publication in 1944 of Gunnar Myrdal's two-volume study of black existence, *An American Dilemma*, and the preliminary findings of Kenneth Clark and his wife, Mamie Phipps, psychologists who were disturbed by "the degree" to which black children "suffered from self-rejection, with its truncating effect on their personalities, and the earliness of the corrosive awareness of color."[34] Myrdal was critical of the NAACP for not doing more to combat racism, especially with regard to education in the South. "The whole system of discrimination," he wrote, "is not only tremendously harmful to the Negroes, but it is flagrantly illegal, and can easily be so proven in the courts."[35] Southern states were spending twice as much to educate a white child as they were to educate a black youngster. Throughout the country, one-fourth of the entire black population was functionally illiterate.[36]

Still a believer that education and time would achieve racial harmony, La Guardia launched a radio series, *Unity at Home—Victory Abroad*, which ran for a little over a month.[37] The mayor and a writers' committee asked Langston Hughes to contribute material to help race relations. Hughes wrote two brief plays. One, *In the Service of My Country*, which dealt with blacks and whites working together to build the Alaska-Canada highway, was broadcast on the city's municipal radio station. But his second play, *Private Jim Crow*, about the day-to-day humiliations black soldiers faced, particulary in the South, was shelved.[38]

A number of steps were taken, chiefly at La Guardia's urging, to alleviate immediate problems in Harlem. Less than a week after the riot, the Office of Price Administration announced that it was opening an office in the basement of a branch library on 135th Street to look into the high food costs that were believed to have contributed to the outbreak. La Guardia announced his own plans to develop new housing in Harlem and other black neighborhoods in the city. A special committee, headed by Walter White and Algernon Black, leader of the Ethical Culture Society, was formed to help blacks obtain jobs and to keep the public conscious of black issues. The Board of Education in cooperation with a local charity foundation started a two-year education program in three Harlem schools in an effort to provide an enriched curriculum for elementary and junior high pupils. And Police Commissioner Lewis Valentine urged blacks to take civil-service exams to qualify for posts as patrolmen. "We need more colored men," he said. "We welcome them." Valentine, who had purged the department in an anticorruption drive before the war, noted that out of the hundreds of officers he had to dismiss, only one was black.[39]

Eventually, in late October, the Savoy Ballroom was permitted to renew its license and reopen.

Among the participants in La Guardia's radio series was Eleanor Roosevelt. But the president's wife subsequently shocked many blacks. Writing in the October issue of *Negro Digest* an article entitled "If I Were a Negro," Mrs. Roosevelt said that, as a black, she would accept advances "though I would not try to bring those advances about more quickly than they were offered."[40]

> If I were a Negro I would take every chance that came my way to prove my quality and ability and if recognition was slow, I would continue to prove myself, knowing that in the end, good performance would be acknowledged.[41]

The editors of the *Amsterdam News*, for one, were upset at Mrs. Roosevelt's attitude. By advising blacks "to continue to plod along fighting to win the war, though recognition is slow, she is putting herself in the same boat with other so-called liberals and 'friends of the Negro' who now go round saying: Forget the injustices meted out to you. Just go ahead, take it on the chin, and fight for the four freedoms." The "tragedy" of statements by her and liberals, the paper said, is that "they don't understand what is happening in the United States." The newspaper wondered "if Mrs. Roosevelt's regrettable article about Negroes was just another attempt by the Administration to curry the favor and support of the Southerners. '44 and the election is, you know, right around the corner. What price democracy!"[42]

TWENTY-ONE

Victory Abroad

You look at me now
And wish to your god that I was dead and gone . . .
And some day I shall look at you.
But I shall not look at you with hate and scorn deep down in my heart
Nor wish to my god that you were dead and gone.
No, I shall look at you, and I shall say to my god:
"Lord, have mercy upon that fellow—
That fellow whose face is not brown."

—Arnold de Mille[1]

The riot in the nation's largest black community—or the prior racial outbreaks in Los Angeles, Detroit, and other cities—notwithstanding, there was still a war to be fought. Winning took precedence.

Although the Roosevelt Administration recognized the political clout of northern blacks, except for rhetoric it continued to ignore the underlying causes of black discontent. And it failed to gauge the increasing aggressiveness the war had spurred. For one thing, by the end of the war, the NAACP had more than doubled its membership, claiming some half a million members in twelve hundred branches.[2] Migration as a result of the war now made blacks influential voters in seventeen northern states that accounted for more than half of the votes in the Electoral College. Many of the states helped Roosevelt win the 1944 national election. Adam Clayton Powell, Jr.'s election to Congress in that same election made him the first black to represent an inner-city district.[3]

The president appointed administrative assistant Jonathan Daniels a special adviser on race relations. Daniels urged, as he did after the Detroit riot, that Roosevelt make "a direct and disciplinary statement to the country . . . a militant one demanding civil obedience from all groups." But the president, then busy with overseeing the American offensive in the South Pacific and, in Europe, the invasion of Italy, returned his memoranda without comment.[4]

By 1944 blacks held 7.5 percent of all jobs in war industries—an improvement but still less than their proportion of the population.[5] Many black women who had been domestic servants got factory jobs, but frequently the work involved the most dangerous ones, handling ammunition, gunpowder, and poisonous chemicals.[6]

Strikes and walkouts related to racial troubles continued to trouble the country. A few days after the Harlem riot, white workers in the mechanical-goods department of the Seiberling Tire and Rubber Company in Toledo, Ohio, refused to work because three black women were assigned to weighing jobs.[7] Thurgood Marshall tried but failed to get the Boilermakers Union to overturn its policy forbidding blacks to join its regular locals.[8] The upgrading of eight black porters to positions as drivers led to a massive transit strike in Philadelphia in August 1944, paralyzing the nation's fourth largest war-production center; Roosevelt was forced to declare an emergency and send in the army to take over the buses and trolleys and run them.

In 1944 alone, the FEPC received five thousand job discrimination complaints, but its death knell had already sounded. Its enemies, Democrats and Republicans opposed to integration of the country's labor force, were able that year to place the agency under the control of Congress rather than the executive branch, and in the following year Congress slashed in half the appropriation to run the agency.[9] The FEPC was dissolved after a filibuster in early 1946 killed an attempt to secure funds to continue its work.[10]

As usual, the rhetoric and actions of southern officials were particularly inflammatory. In the fall of 1943, within weeks after the Harlem riot, Gov. Olin D. Johnston of South Carolina said he was "tired of people agitating social equality of the races in our state." If any outsiders came into South Carolina to "agitate social equality among the races," he said that he would deem it his "duty" to "call upon" the state guard to "help expel them."[11] South Carolina's House of Representatives subsequently adopted a resolution demanding that "henceforth the damned agitators of the North leave the South alone" and reaffirming its "belief in and our allegiance to established white supremacy."[12] The mayor of Barnesville, Georgia, announced that blacks not employed as cooks and nurses or those not in the military service would be arrested. They "must either work, fight or leave this city," he declared.[13] Some seventy miles to the west, in Sandersville, Georgia, the chief of police said that all blacks over the age of sixteen would be required to carry identification badges indicating their name and their work schedule or face arrest.[14] The town of Lawrenceburg, Tennessee, posted a sign at its city limits saying, "NIGGER, READ AND RUN. DON'T LET THE SUN GO DOWN ON YOU HERE. IF YOU CAN'T READ, RUN ANYWAY."[15]

There was progress of a sort in one area: only two blacks were reported lynched in 1944. There had been three lynchings in 1943, five in 1942.[16] Otherwise, there was still a host of problem areas as war became peace. Texas appealed a Supreme Court ruling that had opened Democratic primary elections in Texas to black voters.[17] Florida did not allow white and black students to use the same editions of some textbooks. White and black voters could not enter any polling place in Arkansas in company with one another. South Carolina required racially separate washrooms in its cotton mills, North Carolina in its factories. Four states required separate washrooms in mines. In six states, white and black prisoners could not be chained together. In seven states, tuberculosis patients were separated by race. In eight states, all public recreational places, from parks to pool halls, were segregated. Ten states required separate waiting rooms at bus and train stations. Eleven states required black passengers to ride in the back of buses and streetcars. As many states operated separate schools for the blind. Fourteen states compelled white and black passengers to sit separately on rail trips within their borders. Seventeen states required segregation in public schools; four other states left it to local communities to decide whether to have separate schools. Public schools in the District of Columbia remained segregated.[18]

Incidents at military camps or in towns near bases continued. Black soldiers and white MPs exchanged shots at Brookley Field, near Mobile, Alabama, after the MPs decided to let a white civilian search the blacks' quarters for a suspected robber.[19] A black engineering battalion at an airport on Oahu in the Hawaiian Islands mutinied and refused to work when their black officers were replaced by white officers after the men complained of unfair promotion practices.[20] Four black WACS refused to work at Fort Devens, Massachusetts, saying their assignments were menial and never asked of white WACS.[21] In Mobile, Alabama, where bus drivers were authorized to carry firearms to enforce local laws, a black private was shot and killed when he walked to the wrong section of a bus.[22] Apparently in retaliation for the favored treatment of Italian war prisoners, black soldiers at Fort Lawton, Washington, attacked the POWs, seriously injuring thirty of them.[23] A navy construction battalion that served twenty-one months in the South Pacific went on a two-day hunger strike at Camp Rousseau, west of Los Angeles, in protest over Jim Crow conditions imposed by its commander, a Mississippian.[24]

The most publicized and tragic mutiny occurred in mid-July 1944 at Port Chicago, northeast of San Francisco, after two ships being loaded with ammunition exploded, killing more than two hundred black seamen and injuring more than 230 others. The disaster, the worst homefront accident of the war, accounted for more than 15 percent of all black naval casualties during the war.[25] Forty-four black survivors who balked at resuming the dangerous work were charged with mutiny and given sentences ranging from eight to fifteen years at hard labor and dishonorable discharges.[26]

The Port Chicago disaster prompted some progress. James Forrestal, who became Navy Secretary in the spring of 1944, displayed a totally different attitude about black participation in the navy than his predecessor, Frank Knox. Forrestal had already proposed and Roosevelt had agreed to having blacks make up a tenth of the crews on twenty-five auxiliary ships. The move proved so successful that it was extended to smaller vessels, where blacks and whites worked, ate, and slept together in close quarters. Eventually, two warships manned by all-black crews were commissioned. As a result of Port Chicago, Forrrestal saw to it that white units as well as black ones were assigned to work at the supply base and at other ammunition dumps, and he proposed a number of reforms, including the admission of blacks to the Naval Academy and the end of separate facilities and quotas for blacks who qualified for advanced training. In a revolutionary "Guide to Command of Negro Naval Personnel" that was issued, the navy for the first time stated that it accepted "no theories of racial differences in inborn ability, but expects that every man wearing its uniform be trained and used in accord with his maximum individual capacity determined on the basis of individual performance."[27]

By 1945, although half of the blacks in the navy were still relegated to the stewards' branch, thousands of others were serving as gunners, signalmen, radio operators, machinists, metalsmiths, and electricians—a dramatic turnabout in a service that in 1941 had treated all blacks as servants.[28] Still, Thurgood Marshall complained, "Only after things got *hot* did the navy open up other opportunities to Negroes in other capacities" in units that "somehow or other . . . *happen* to get assigned to the dirtiest, hardest, and most dangerous jobs."[29] And Charles Houston pointed out that there was still not one black lieutenant in the marines and "in places" blacks did "not have as many civil rights as prisoners of war."[30]

In all, during the war, some one million blacks served in all branches of the military—including 165,000 in the navy, 17,000 in the marines, 5,000 in the Coast Guard and 4,000 in the WACS and WAVES.[31] Almost half of them saw service overseas. In addition, 24,000 blacks served in the integrated merchant marine.[32] At the army's peak in 1944, there were 700,000 black GIs., and the number of black officers had risen from the prewar total of only two officers (the three others were chaplains) to more than seven thousand.[33] There were now blacks in almost every branch of the army—in the infantry, in the artillery, in the tank corps, and in paratroop outfits—though, albeit, in still segregated units and still underutilized in actual combat.[34]

Advances aside, white attitudes about blacks were much more difficult to change. Lorenzo Dufau, who served aboard the USS *Mason,* a destroyer escort that was one of the two warships with all-black crews, remembers the entire crew being commended after rescuing tugboats and barges caught in rough seas. But when the *Mason* reached Plymouth, England, and the crew members went on shore leave, they were refused service at a Red Cross canteen. "This is not your canteen," the hostess said. "You go around the corner a couple of blocks." Around the corner was a bomb-damaged building with a pool table, some old magazines, and Kool-Aid and cookies for the men. The Red Cross canteen was serving hot dogs and Coca-Cola. "That hurt me so bad," says Dufau. "I mean, when you're out on that ship at nighttime in war, it doesn't matter what color the crew is, as long as you protect that convoy. But then to get over there, in one of the most bombed-out cities in England, and be told it wasn't our canteen. I never made contributions to the Red Cross because of that experience. When I see a red cross, it brings back memories. It hurts."[35]

Photographer Gordon Parks, who was a war correspondent for the Office of War Information, was assigned to a new all-black aviation squadron, the 332nd Fighter Group. In trying to arrange his trip to accompany the 332nd overseas, he ran into a maze of red tape. Parks was convinced that southern congressmen were seeking to prevent the unit from being "glorified" in the press. He joined the group at Selfridge Field, an air base near Detroit, where he witnessed firsthand the treatment given the airmen by white residents of the area. It was "by far, worse than what they would have received in the countries of America's enemies." For one thing, a local undertaker refused to embalm the body of a black pilot who had crashed in training.[36]

Told that his traveling papers were "out of order," Parks returned to Washington to try to straighten them out. At a bus stop, he met two members of the first black flying unit, the 99th Pursuit Squadron, who had just returned from the fighting in Europe. The squadron was compiling a noteworthy record. By the summer of 1944, when Parks met the two officers, the 99th's pilots had flown more than five hundred combat missions and more than three thousand sorties.[37] (By the end of the war, the squadron flew nearly sixteen hundred missions over North Africa, Italy, and Germany, was credited with shooting down 111 enemy aircraft and destroying 150 on the ground. It was the only escort group that never lost a single bomber to an enemy fighter.[38])

One of the black pilots Parks met, a captain who had been shot down over Austria, held five medals, including the Distinguished Flying Cross and the croix de guerre. Both pilots had completed the required number of combat missions and were eligible to remain stateside and teach, but they had chosen to return to the war zone and were, at that moment, on their way to the Pentagon. But when Parks and the two pilots took seats behind the bus driver, the driver demanded that they go to the back of the bus. The captain refused, saying that they were staying where they were. Finally, a white major sitting opposite them convinced the bus driver to drop the argument.[39]

When Parks finally rejoined the 332nd at Newport News, Virginia, he learned that there had been some gunfire. White paratroopers had beaten a black ground crewman and the base's cinema had tried to keep the 332nd pilots out. The situation had deteriorated so much that the fighter group was issued new traveling orders and left by ship two days earlier than scheduled. But not with Parks; his orders still did not comply, so he again returned to Washington. He could make out the Mall as the helicopter in which he was flying circled the city at dusk:

> It was a beautiful sight, but one coupled with human ugliness. As we dropped lower I could see the tops of stores, theaters and restaurants whose doors were still closed to black people. I thought back to the fighter pilots. They would soon be out to sea sailing toward war and death, ignoring temporarily their differences with the country they were leaving to defend. This was the price for questionable equality.[40]

Walter White made two lengthy trips overseas as a war correspondent for the *New York Post*, one to England, North Africa, Italy, and the Middle East, the other to the Pacific. White's remarks afterwards drew a complaint from Mrs. Roosevelt, who wondered whether his "voicing of bitterness" would "help us solve our extremely difficult questions both in the present and the future." But White said he did not intend to be bitter, only to "tell the truth" as he saw it.[41]

"We have merely transplanted to other lands the American pattern, both good and bad," White told an emergency meeting of the NAACP in Chicago upon his return in early 1944. "Basically, the root of all our difficulties overseas is in insistence on racial segregation."[42]

White found that in England virtually all blacks were serving as "so-called service troops—members of quartermaster, engineer, port battalion and truck units." There was a tendency, he said, "to transform Negro combat units into service units." Certain towns were off limits to black soldiers.[43] He suggested to the War Department more than a dozen ways to improve the race situation. His recommendations included abolishing the "off limits" zones and "odd and even" pass days, the appointment of more black superior officers, biracial MP units, and the formation of black combat units.[44]

But American military authorities insisted that there was no "Negro problem" in England; instead, the problem was a longstanding "American citizen" one, and the solution was "evolution, not revolution."[45] An Inspector General's report said allegations about discrimination were of little merit. Its own inquiry revealed "no serious condition in the racial situation that would tend to impede the war effort to any extent." There was "no evidence of discrimination against the colored troops."[46]

On a later trip in 1944, White arrived in Guam, the major base of supply for the war in the Pacific, just after a Christmas race riot that pitted black engineering and service units against members of the Third Marine Division. Animosities between the two groups came to a head when white marines started running blacks out of Agana, the largest town on the island. On Christmas Eve, a group of blacks who went there on passes were fired upon, and after midnight, marines drove into the black camp, threatening harm. Shortly before noon on Christmas Day, two marines shot and killed a black sailor. That afternoon, a white sailor shot and wounded another black sailor. Around nightfall, a jeep with a machine gun drove past the black camp, firing into it. Blacks immediately jumped into trucks and set out for Agana, but were stopped by MPs and forty-four of them were arrested. The local commander, when he found out that White was a lawyer, asked him to defend the blacks at their courts-martial. White's efforts to save the men failed. All forty-four received prison terms, but the NAACP subsequently appealed the convictions to Forrestal and the White House and had the sentences reversed.

White's story about the incidents on Guam, which a censor promised to cable to the *Post,* carried a dateline of January 20, 1945. But the newspaper never received it, and the story of the clashes was not released until six months later, after White described the incidents on a nationwide radio broadcast.[47]

In the summer of 1944, the War Department issued an order to commanding generals that "all" government transportation—buses, trucks, or other vehicles—be available to military personnel regardless of race. The order, designed to eliminate a major black complaint, covered only federally owned or operated transportation, but it was hailed as "an important step forward in the fight to abolish discrimination." "US Army Bans Jim Crow," ran the headline in the *Baltimore Afro-American*.[48]

Although the War Department issued a number of similar orders designed to improve the treatment of black servicemen, their implementation all too often depended on local commanders. The president had to concede that sometimes commanders resisted rather than comply. He told a special press conference for members of the Negro Newspaper Publishers Association in February 1944:

> It is perfectly true, there is definite discrimination in the actual treatment of the colored engineer troops, and others. . . . The trouble lies fundamentally in the attitude of certain white people—officers down the line who haven't got much more education, many of them, than the colored troops and the Seabees and the engineers for example. And well, you know the kind of person it is. We all do. We don't have to do more than think of a great many people that we know. And it has become not a question of orders—they are repeated fairly often, I think, in all the camps of colored troops—it's a question of the personality of the individual. And we are up against it, absolutely up against it.[49]

Some observers believe that the treatment blacks received in military service contributed to the large number of crimes attributed to them. Statistics not made public until after the war showed in August 1945 that black troops constituted 8 percent of the personnel in the European Theater of Operations, but also 21 percent of American servicemen convicted of crimes. Moreover, 42 percent of those convicted of sex crimes and 35 percent of those convicted of crimes of violence were black GIs.[50]

Despite the experiences that blacks encountered in the military during World War II, it is in the armed services that they have achieved some of their greatest advances, thanks in large part to Harry S Truman, who succeeded Roosevelt on the president's death in April 1945 and ordered the desegregation of the armed forces in 1948. It would have been unthinkable before then that a black man,

Colin L. Powell, could ever become the nation's highest-ranking military officer.

But the war left a bitter taste in the memory of many blacks. The first American hero of the war was a black—Dorie Miller, a steward who, during the Japanese attack on Pearl Harbor, carried his captain to safety and then seized a machine gun and, without any prior weapons training, fired at Japanese aircraft, downing at least one before his ammunition gave out and his ship sank. But the navy at the time did not identify Miller by name. The honor of being known as the war's first hero went instead to a West Point graduate, Colin Kelly, who died three days later. It was only after the *Pittsburgh Courier* spearheaded a drive to find out who the "unidentified Negro messman" mentioned in navy dispatches was that, some three months later, Miller's name was made public.[51] An effort to have him accorded the Congressional Medal of Honor failed.

Similarly, those who fought alongside Sgt. Ruben Rivers campaigned as recently as 1993 to have him awarded, posthumously and belatedly, a Medal of Honor. The twenty-two-year-old sergeant was with one of the few black units to see combat, the 761st Tank Battalion. The renowned unit fought in eastern France for 183 consecutive days without relief in the fall of 1944 as part of Gen. George S. Patton's Third Army. It captured or liberated thirty major towns. The men of the 761st called themselves the Black Panthers, but others called them "Patton's Pets and Eleanor's Niggers."[52] During the drive across France, Rivers's leg was shattered by shrapnel. He was told to evacuate his post, but instead he fought for two days and two nights in the face of a German assault. Rivers died trying to knock out antitank guns that were firing on his unit.

"Nobody wrote about us then," recalls Johnnie Stevens, who served with Rivers in the 761st. "White journalists used to come down after a mission and we'd be sitting licking our wounds. They would ride right past our tanks and start talking to the white soldiers. 'Hey, son, how was it? Where you from?' The next day his name would appear in the papers back home. They never wrote anything about us."[53]

If Miller or Rivers had been honored, it would have been a first for a black serviceman. In all, since it was established in 1862, the Medal of Honor has been awarded to seventy-nine blacks—twenty-four in the Civil War and eighteen in the Indian Wars. But though 353 Medals of Honor were awarded during World War II, not one of the million blacks who were in the armed services during the war received the nation's highest honor, a fact that is indicative both of neglect in recognizing what men like Miller and Rivers did, and of the small part overall that blacks played as combat troops.[54]

Epilogue

We return.
We return from fighting.
We return fighting.

—The Crisis, 1919[1]

The Harlem Riot was a harbinger of the future. Until then, the riots that had broken out across the country, up to and including the Detroit outburst in June 1943, were what sociologists have labeled "communal riots." That is, they were interracial clashes that occurred at the boundaries of expanding black neighborhoods, frequently in the peripheral areas where black and white communites overlapped and their residents came into conflict. Such riots were, as a rule, instigated by whites and had the support, either passive or active, of a city's police force.

But the Harlem Riot was different. It was what the same sociologists call a "commodity riot," an eruption whose main target was white property and stores and, secondarily, the police as symbols of municipal authority. Unlike a communal riot, the commodity riot was an outburst that started within the black community, not at its periphery, and did not involve a confrontation between white and black civilians.[2] The Harlem Riot was, in a sense, rage turned inward, a self-destructive eruption that destroyed the very shops that blacks shopped in and blighted the very streets that they lived on. Its masochistic violence would be repeated two decades later, in an era of peacetime prosperity that most blacks did not enjoy to the extent that whites did. That same rage exploded then in black communities

227

throughout the country, whether in the South, where segregation had become legitimized, or in the North, where de facto segregation was too often practiced. Riots occurred in the Watts section of Los Angeles in 1965; in Chicago, Dayton, and the Hough section of Cleveland in 1966; in 128 cities in the first nine months of 1967 alone, including Detroit, Newark, Cincinnati, Tampa, and Atlanta.[3] Following the assassination of Dr. Martin Luther King, Jr., in April 1968, riots erupted in Harlem, the Bedford-Stuyvesant section of Brooklyn; again in Detroit and Newark; in Toledo, Pittsburgh, Philadelphia, San Francisco, Baltimore, Tallahassee, and Savannah; in Memphis and Nashville, Tennessee, and Jackson, Mississippi; in Boston, Hartford, and Trenton, New Jersey; in Greensboro, Raleigh, Winston-Salem, Charlotte, New Bern, and Durham, North Carolina; and in Washington, D.C.[4] A generation later, the smoldering resentments still flare; in the case of Los Angeles in 1992, they were complicated by the huge influxes of Latino and Asian immigrants into once-black neighborhoods—and aggravated by the greater political sophistication of modern-day urban blacks.

The experience of Harlem in World War II and the chaos of the racial disturbances that enveloped the country then and in the 1960s represented but one of the many threads that led to the civil rights movement. But, despite all the changes the movement has wrought in the past thirty years—the Voting Rights Act; the Civil Rights Act; other antidiscrimination laws, federal, state and local; school integration; affirmative-action legislation to enlist minority representation in private and public enterprises; efforts to reduce poverty in inner cities; the attempts by reformers to bridge the chasm between races —blacks as a whole feel that they are still treated as an underclass in American society.

Some of the landmarks in Harlem of a half-century ago are still recognizable in the mid-1990s. The Hotel Theresa stands at the corner of 125th Street and Seventh Avenue, though its rooms have been converted to offices and apartments. The Apollo Theater on 125th, which had been closed for a while in the 1980s and early 1990s, has reopened. The buildings that housed Blumstein's and Koch's department stores—the names are still emblazoned on them—are now the site of clothing, dry goods, and appliance retailers. Strivers' Row appears a bit seedy, though its residents try to maintain the once-splendid homes; signs warning drivers to slow their horses are still visible on the gates to its stables area. But the Savoy Ballroom was torn down long ago and replaced by a strip of single-story brick shops. An empty, debris-strewn lot marks where the Braddock Hotel stood. The site of the Twenty-eighth Precinct is part of a parking lot for a housing development.

There are new structures—a state office building on 125th Street named for Adam Clayton Powell, Jr., high-rise apartment developments, the impressive Schomburg Center for Research in Black Culture across the street from Harlem Hospital on 135th Street—but they are overwhelmed by their surroundings. For walking through the streets of Harlem, one is struck by the paradox that has haunted the area since blacks first moved there in great numbers and the ghetto that was created became today's slum: the contradiction between the sense of wide-open spaces created by Harlem's broad avenues and low apartment houses—what a lovely section of New York this could be—and the reality, its dirty gutters, littered sidewalks, graffiti-sprayed buildings, and piled-up garbage. In many ways, the riot of 1968 spelled the community's doom. Some apartment houses look bombed out, with gaping holes where windows were, or sometimes sheets of gray steel covering the blank windowspaces. The paint on signs above most stores is peeling, the signs themselves sometimes askew, the stores run-down. Abandoned shops seem to be on every street, interspersed, so it seems, among scores of dilapidated storefront churches with hand-lettered signs announcing their denominations and the names of their ministers. The shelves and cashiers' posts at liquor stores are blocked by walls of thick, bullet-proof plastic. A once-plush apartment house such as 409 Edgecombe Avenue is riddled with darkened hallways and pitted walls, cracked tiles in its lobby, wires dangling in stairwells.

It is like seeing the world turned upside down when taking an M-2 bus that first cuts south through Harlem, then across 110th Street on the northern edge of Central Park before turning down Fifth Avenue. Everything suddenly becomes orderly once the bus turns onto Fifth Avenue. The sidewalks are clean. Uniformed doormen stand guard under the canopies of posh apartment houses. There are no trashcans overflowing with litter here, no garbage strewn along the curbs. The people on the street walk with a sense of purpose.

The contrast with the Harlem the bus has passed through is striking. A desultory atmosphere pervades the streets off its main shopping areas. Too many youngsters and teenagers are walking them when it seems that they should be in school. Men mostly, but sometimes women, too, loiter on brownstone steps or by drab little grocery stores with dusty wares in their dirty windows. They exchange a handshake and a smile when they meet, but then turn somber.

One cannot escape the feeling that the community is neglected, that the city is ignoring it yet again, and that Harlem is under a siege of some sort. And one cannot help wondering what keeps its residents from rising up once more in anger and frustration.

Notes
Bibliography
Index

Notes

Tramp—tramp—tramp—
Along the path of life he goes . . .
Tramp—tramp—tramp—
Slowly, rhythmically,
Tramp—tramp—tramp—
Patiently, uncomplainingly,
Tramp—tramp—tramp!

—Arnold de Mille[1]

Book Epigraph

1. Langston Hughes's poem, "Beaumont to Detroit: 1943," appeared in the *People's Voice*, July 3, 1943.

Prologue

1. Unless otherwise noted, the Prologue is an amalgam of the Aug. 1 and 2, 1943, editions of the *New York Times*, as well as the July 31, 1943, issues of the *Amsterdam News, New York Age,* and *People's Voice.*
2. Evelyn Hunt O'Garro, interview by author, Apr. 27, 1993.
3. Arnold de Mille, interview by author, Apr. 4, 1994.

1. E Pluribus Unum

1. Morris Janowitz, "Patterns of Collective Racial Violence," in *The History of Violence in America: Historical and Comparative Perspectives,* ed. Hugh D. Graham and Ted Robert Gurr (New York: Frederick A. Praeger, 1969), 443.
2. I. N. Phelps Stokes, *New York Past and Present: Its History and Landmarks, 1524–*

1939 (New York: n.p., 1939), 4. The illustration that is reprinted there is entitled "Nieuw Amsterdam Ofte Nue Nieuw Iorx Opt 'T Eylant Man."

3. Roi Ottley and William J. Weatherby, eds., *The Negro in New York: An Informal Social History* (Dobbs Ferry, N.Y.: Oceana, 1967), 2–3.

4. Stokes, *New York Past*, 65–66.

5. Ottley and Weatherby, *Negro in New York*, 4.

6. Christopher Moore, "Unearthing Black History," *District Lines* 9. (spring 1994), 2.

7. Stokes, *New York Past*, 66.

8. Ottley and Weatherby, *Negro in New York*, 5.

9. Stokes, *New York Past*, 66.

10. Ottley and Weatherby, *Negro in New York*, 7.

11. Stokes, *New York Past*, 65. The Jesuit father was Isaac Jogues, a French cleric.

12. Ottley and Weatherby, *Negro in New York*, xvi.

13. Moore, "Unearthing Black History," 2.

14. Ottley and Weatherby, *Negro in New York*, 19.

15. Ibid., 22.

16. Ibid., 21–22.

17. Ibid., 23.

18. Ibid., 24.

19. Ibid., 26.

20. Thomas J. Davis, *A Rumor of Revolt: The 'Great Negro Plot' in Colonial New York* (New York: Free Press, 1985), ix.

21. Stokes, *New York Past*, 71.

22. Davis, *Rumor of Revolt*, ix.

23. Bayard Still, *Mirror for Gotham: New York as Seen by Contemporaries from Dutch Days to the Present* (New York: New York Univ. Press, 1956), 19.

24. Georgette Weir, "Underground Landmark," *Vassar Quarterly*, summer 1993, 30.

25. Moore, "Unearthing Black History," 2.

26. Mary White Ovington, *Half a Man: The Status of the Negro in New York* (New York: Hill and Wang, 1969), 4.

27. Still, *Mirror for Gotham*, 21.

28. Ibid., 35. Patrick M'Robert, who visited New York in 1744, is quoted.

29. Ibid., 25. The doctor was Scottish-trained Dr. Alexander Hamilton, who settled in Annapolis in 1739 and visited New York in 1744.

30. Ibid., 53. The German is not identified. His letter is dated Sept. 11, 1780.

31. Stokes, *New York Past*, 68. The church was in an almost deserted area of upper Manhattan, not far from First Avenue and 125th Street. It was completed in 1667 but abandoned twenty years later in favor of a new site and a better edifice.

32. Still, *Mirror for Gotham*, 69. The traveler quoted is John Lambert, who reached the city on Nov. 24, 1807.

33. Ottley and Weatherby, *Negro in New York*, 61.

34. Still, *Mirror for Gotham*, 76. The notice appeared in the paper on Aug. 20, 1814.

35. Ibid.

36. Ibid., 111–12.

37. Ottley and Weatherby, *Negro in New York,* 62.

38. Ibid.

39. Ibid., 63.

40. Ovington, *Half a Man,* 7. The upstate delegate was John L. Russell of St. Lawrence, the New York City delegate John H. Hunt.

41. Ottley and Weatherby, *Negro in New York,* 63.

42. Still, *Mirror for Gotham,* 106–7.

43. Ibid., 100.

44. Ibid., 89–90.

2. Urban Migrants

1. Jeff Kisseloff, *You Must Remember This: An Oral History of Manhattan from the 1890s to World War II* (New York: Schocken, 1989), 267.

2. Still, *Mirror for Gotham,* 89.

3. Ibid.

4. Ottley and Weatherby, *Negro in New York,* 64–65.

5. Stokes, *New York Past,* 78.

6. Still, *Mirror for Gotham,* 89.

7. Ottley and Weatherby, *Negro in New York,* 76.

8. Ibid., 76–77.

9. *New York Times,* June 15, 1991. A potter's field unearthed in 1991 in the same area contained the remains of former slaves as well as Revolutionary War prisoners of war.

10. Still, *Mirror for Gotham,* 123.

11. Stokes, *New York Past,* 75, 77.

12. Ibid., 79.

13. Ibid., 81.

14. Still, *Mirror for Gotham,* 159.

15. Iver Bernstein, *The New York City Draft Riots: Their Significance for American Society and Politics in the Age of the Civil War* (New York: Oxford Univ. Press, 1990), 283.

16. Ovington, *Half a Man,* 14. The black writer was Samuel R. Scottron.

17. Stokes, *New York Past,* 80.

18. *New York Times,* Apr. 7, 1995.

19. Still, *Mirror for Gotham,* 188–89. The Frenchman was Ernest Duvergier de Hauranne, who arrived in New York in June 1864.

20. Ottley and Weatherby, *Negro in New York,* 123.

21. Bernstein, *Draft Riots,* 66. The *Tribune* edition of Aug. 3, 1864 is quoted.

22. Jervis Anderson, *This Was Harlem: 1900–1950* (New York: Farrar, Straus, Giroux, 1993), 8.

23. Still, *Mirror for Gotham,* 246.

24. Ottley and Weatherby, *Negro in New York,* 134–35.

25. Ovington, *Half a Man,* 21.

26. Still, *Mirror for Gotham*, 217.

27. Ovington, *Half a Man*, 22.

28. Stokes, *New York Past*, 85.

29. Ottley and Weatherby, *Negro in New York*, 166. The girlfriend is identified as May Enoch.

30. *Story of the Riot* (Citizens' Protective League, 1900), 2.

31. Ibid., 4.

32. Ottley and Weatherby, *Negro in New York*, 179.

33. Stokes, *New York Past*, 67.

3. Negro Harlem

1. Deirdre Mullane, ed., *Crossing the Danger Water: Three Hundred Years of African-American Writing* (New York: Doubleday, 1993), 457. The unattributed a poem, entitled "They're Leaving Memphis in Droves," appeared in the *Chicago Defender*.

2. Still, *Mirror for Gotham*, 307.

3. Charles V. Hamilton, *Adam Clayton Powell, Jr.: The Political Biography of an American Dilemma* (New York: Collier, 1991), 62.

4. Dominic J. Capeci, Jr., *The Harlem Riot of 1943* (Philadelphia: Temple Univ. Press, 1977), 32.

5. Claude McKay, *Harlem: Negro Metropolis* (New York: Harcourt Brace Jovanovich, 1968), 16.

6. Larry A. Greene. "Harlem in the Great Depression, 1928–1936" (Ph.D. diss., Columbia Univ., 1979), 5.

7. Still, *Mirror for Gotham*, 307.

8. Ottley and Weatherby, *Negro in New York*, 181.

9. Ovington, *Half a Man*, 25.

10. Ibid., 26.

11. Greene, "Harlem in Great Depression," 11.

12. Ovington, *Half a Man*, 42–43.

13. Ibid., 44.

14. Ibid., 62.

15. Ibid., 48.

16. Ibid., 50.

17. Ibid., 104. The white death rate was 16.6 per thousand in 1908.

18. *New York City Guide* (New York: Random House, 1939), 258.

19. David Levering Lewis, *When Harlem Was in Vogue* (New York: Knopf, 1981), 27.

20. Greene, "Harlem in Great Depression," 10.

21. Ottley and Weatherby, *Negro in New York*, 267.

22. Greene, "Harlem in Great Depression," 5. The density for blacks per acre was 336, for whites 223.

23. Ibid., 1.

24. Ibid., 3.

25. Ibid., 1. The educator was Kelly Miller.

26. Ibid., 8.

27. Anderson, *This Was Harlem*, 185.

28. Ibid., 144. The observer was Wallace Thurman.

29. Mullane., *Crossing*, 479.

30. Anderson, *This Was Harlem*, 185.

31. Mullane, *Crossing*, 480.

32. Anderson, *This Was Harlem*, 299–303. The magazine quoted was the *Saturday Evening Post*.

33. Harold Orlansky, "The Harlem Riot: A Study in Mass Frustration," *Social Analysis*, report No. 1. (New York: n.p., 1943), 25. The study referred to is "Negro Youth at the Crossways" by E. Franklin Frazier, published by the American Council on Education in 1940.

34. Lewis, *Harlem in Vogue*, 127.

35. McKay, *Negro Metropolis*, 27.

36. Anderson, *This Was Harlem*, 320.

37. Ibid., 322–23. Johnson's description was written in 1930.

38. McKay, *Negro Metropolis*, 21.

4. "Nigger Heaven"

1. Anderson, *This Was Harlem*, 218–19. The quoted passage is from Carl Van Vechten's novel, "Nigger Heaven."

2. Walker Smith, interview by author, Apr. 7, 1994.

3. Kisseloff, *You Must Remember*, 265.

4. Foster Palmer, interview by author, Mar. 23, 1994.

5. Allen Worrell, interview by author, Apr. 14, 1993.

6. O'Garro interview.

7. Doris Saunders, interview by author, Apr. 27, 1993.

8. Kisseloff, *You Must Remember*, 281.

9. Sarah Delaney and A. Elizabeth Delany, *Having Our Say: The Delany Sisters' First 100 Years* (New York: Kodansha, 1993), 103.

10. Kisseloff, *You Must Remember*, 265.

11. Capeci, *Harlem Riot*, 144. Capeci says there were 155 black policemen: six were sergeants, one a parole commissioner, and one a surgeon. La Guardia uses the same totals, according to the *New York Times* of Aug. 7, 1943, and notes that the force had only twenty-two more blacks than it had a decade earlier. The figure for the total police force is from *Annual Report, Police Department, City of New York 1943* (New York: New York City Police Department, 1944), 3. The force was understrength in 1943, with only 17,210 officers. In 1942, the total was 17,582. The decline in manpower was a result of the war.

12. *New York Times*, Oct. 10, 1942.

13. St. Clair T. Bourne, interview by author, June 12, 1994. Bourne worked on the *Amsterdam News* from 1937 to his appointment as managing editor of the new *People's Voice* in Feb. 1942.

14. Smith interview.

15. Kisseloff, *You Must Remember,* 270.

16. Ibid., 281.

17. Capeci, *Harlem Riot,* 37.

18. *Negroes of New York* (Work Project Administration research study compiled by the Writers' Program, n.d., Typescript), chap. 18, 8.

19. O'Garro interview.

20. McKay, *Negro Metropolis,* 117.

21. Ottley and Weatherby, *Negro in New York,* 231.

22. Still, *Mirror for Gotham,* 337.

23. Ibid., 338.

24. Capeci, *Harlem Riot,* 37. The writer quoted is Carl Offord.

25. McKay, *Negro Metropolis,* 101.

26. Lewis, *Harlem in Vogue,* 109.

27. Greene, "Harlem in Great Depression," 432.

28. Saunders interview.

29. Worrell interview.

30. Palmer interview.

31. Delany, *Having Our Say,* 137.

32. *New York Times,* Oct. 20, 1942. The six black men did not identify themselves by name.

33. *New York Times,* Apr. 25, 1945. The *Times* quoted the Census Bureau that the number of counties between 1900 and 1940 in which blacks were in the majority had decreased from 286 to 180.

34. Mullane, *Crossing,* 455.

35. Capeci, *Harlem Riot,* 32.

36. Lewis, *Harlem in Vogue,* 34.

37. Capeci, *Harlem Riot,* 32.

38. Ibid., 38. Hamilton's biography of Powell gives the figure as 800 percent.

39. Still, *Mirror for Gotham,* 336.

40. *New York Times,* Nov. 18, 1941.

41. *Negroes of New York,* chap. 18, 4.

42. Ibid., chap. 18, 3.

43. *Census Tract Data on Population and Housing in New York City: 1940* (New York: Welfare Council Committee on 1940 Census Tract Tabulations for New York City, 1942). The precise figures were 7,454,995 for the city as a whole and 458,444 for blacks.

44. *Negroes of New York,* chap. 18, 2.

45. Ibid., chap. 18, 13.

46. Ibid., chap. 18, 3.

47. Anderson, *This Was Harlem,* 244.

48. *Negroes of New York,* chap. 18, 19n. The figures are a total of 75,123 black children under fifteen years of age in the city as a whole, 46,580 of them in Manhattan.

49. Hamilton, *Powell,* 62. The federal funds were to be used for 168 new school buildings.

50. *New York Times,* May 1, 1993. Robert Moses was Park Commissioner then.

51. *Negroes of New York,* chap. 10, 28. The increase was from 4.2 percent in 1919

to 11.7 percent in 1930. In 1938, the number of white children arraigned decreased 38.3 percent.

52. *Negroes of New York*, chap. 10, 29.

53. Ibid., chap. 10, 30.

54. Capeci, *Harlem Riot*, 40.

55. *Negroes of New York*, chap. 18, 4.

56. Ibid., chap. 18, 15. An exception was Sea View Hospital on Staten Island.

57. Ibid. The statistic was for the years 1929–33.

58. McKay, *Negro Metropolis*, 123.

59. *Negroes of New York*, chap. 18, 17–18. The incident involving Mrs. Handy occurred in March 1937.

60. Ibid., chap. 18, 17.

61. McKay, *Negro Metropolis*, 124. The year was 1939.

62. *Negroes of New York*, chap. 18, 16.

63. Ibid., chap. 18, 17.

64. De Mille interview.

65. Virginia Delany Murphy, interview by author, Mar. 23, 1994.

66. Evelyn Long Cunningham, interview by author, Apr. 28, 1994.

67. Kisseloff, *You Must Remember*, 276.

68. Murray Schumach, interview by author, June 12, 1994.

69. C. L. R. James et al., *Fighting Racism in World War II* (New York: Pathfinder, 1980), 57. The *Socialist Appeal*, Feb. 24, 1940, is quoted regarding a November 1939 case.

5. Dress Rehearsal

1. Herbert Aptheker, *A Documentary History of the Negro People in the United States: 1933–1945*, vol. 4 (New York: Citadel Press, 1990), 227. Paul Laurence Dunbar is quoted by James W. Ford in a 1936 article entitled "The National Negro Congress."

2. Joseph Boskin, *Urban Racial Violence in the Twentieth Century* (Beverly Hills, Calif.: Glencoe Press, 1969), 53–55. The story of the 1935 riot is based primarily on an article by Hamilton Basso in the *New Republic* of Apr. 3, 1935.

3. Richard Maxwell Brown, "Historical Patterns of Violence in America," in Graham and Gurr, *History of Violence*, 55.

4. Augustus W. Low, ed., *Encyclopedia of Black America* (New York: McGraw-Hill, 1981), 232.

5. Low, *Encyclopedia*, 233.

6. Mullane, *Crossing*, 461.

7. Low, *Encyclopedia*, 235.

8. James P. Comer, "The Dynamics of Black and White Violence," in Graham and Gurr, *History of Violence*, 448.

9. Hamilton, *Powell*, 57. Dodge contended, "The Reds have been boring into our institutions for a long time."

10. *Negroes of New York*, chap. 18, 27–28.

11. Aptheker, *Documentary History*, 144. From Alain Locke's article, "Harlem: Dark Weather-Vane," published in *Survey Graphic* of Aug. 1936.

12. *Negroes of New York,* chap. 18, 29.

13. Ibid., chap. 18, 27.

14. Ibid., chap. 18, 28.

15. Hamilton, *Powell,* 60.

16. *New York Times,* Aug. 6, 1943. The chairman of the subcommittee, Arthur Garfield Hayes, wrote a letter to the *Times* following the 1943 Harlem riot, pointing up the police's responsibility for the riot.

17. *Negroes of New York,* chap. 10, 34.

18. Ibid., chap. 18, 34.

19. Aptheker, *Documentary History,* 147. Alain Locke quoted La Guardia at the ceremony in his report, "Harlem: Dark Weather-Vane."

20. Ibid., 148.

21. Ibid., 149.

22. Ibid., 182–84. From Langston Hughes's speech, "To Negro Writers," reprinted from Henry Hart, ed., *American Writers' Congress* (New York: International Publishers, 1935).

23. Ibid., 215–16. A. Philip Randolph's "Keynote Address" is reprinted from *The Official Proceedings of the National Congress* (Washington, 1936).

24. Capeci, *Harlem Riot,* 43.

25. Hamilton, *Powell,* 101.

26. Murphy interview. The father mentioned was married to the sister of the owner of Blumstein's store.

27. Capeci, *Harlem Riot,* 37–38.

28. Ovington, *Half a Man,* 119–20.

29. De Mille interview.

30. Aptheker, *Documentary History,* 220–21. From James W. Ford's "The National Negro Congress."

31. Ibid., 168. From John P. Davis's article, "A Black Inventory of the New Deal," originally published in the *Crisis,* May 1935.

32. James et al., *Fighting Racism,* 15.

33. Hamilton, *Powell,* 109.

34. James et al., *Fighting Racism,* 16.

35. Ibid., 15.

36. Ibid., 16.

37. Comer, "Dynamics," 448.

38. Doris Kearns Goodwin, *No Ordinary Time: Franklin and Eleanor Roosevelt: The Home Front in World War II* (New York: Simon and Schuster, 1994), 163.

39. Theodore F. Harris, *Pearl S. Buck: A Biography,* vol. 2, *Her Philosophy as Expressed in Her Letters* (New York: John Day, 1971), 18.

40. Ibid., 14–18.

41. Clayton R. Koppes and Gregory D. Black, "Blacks, Loyalty, and Motion-Picture Propaganda in World War II," *Journal of American History* 73, no. 2 (1986): 383. Clayton's remarks were made in *Opportunity* magazine, Dec. 1941.

42. James et al., *Fighting Racism,* 28. The quotation is from "Why Negroes Should Oppose the War" by J. R. Johnson, a pen name of C. L. R. James. It was first published

in ten installments in the *Socialist Appeal*, Sept. 6-Oct. 3, 1939, and afterward issued as a pamphlet by Pioneer Publishers.

6. The Black Dilemma

1. Mullane, *Crossing*, 488.
2. *Amsterdam News*, July 31, 1943. Roy Wilkins, in his "The Watchtower" column, quotes an article Mrs. Roosevelt wrote for *The New Threshold* magazine of the United States Student Assembly entitled "Abolish Jim Crow."
3. *Amsterdam News*, May 22, 1943.
4. Nat Brandt, *The Congressman Who Got Away with Murder* (Syracuse, N.Y.: Syracuse Univ. Press, 1991), 4–6.
5. Richard Kluger, *Simple Justice* (New York: Vintage, 1977), 511.
6. Alex Haley, introduction to *The Autobiography of Malcolm X* (New York: Ballantine, 1992), 84.
7. Gordon Parks, *Voices in the Mirror: An Autobiography* (New York: Doubleday, 1990), 81.
8. *New York Times*, Mar. 28, 1993.
9. Ibid.
10. Anderson, *This Was Harlem*, 106.
11. *Negroes of New York*, chap. 13, 7–8.
12. Anderson, *This Was Harlem*, 103.
13. Ibid., 103–4. The policy was announced by Postmaster General Albert S. Burleson.
14. *Negroes of New York*, chap. 13, 9.
15. Emmett J. Scott, *The American Negro in the World War* (Emmett J. Scott, 1919), 92.
16. Ibid., 97–98. The Ninety-second Division was then commanded by Gen. C. C. Ballou. The bulletin, No. 35, was issued under the name of Lt. Col. Allen J. Greer, his chief of staff.
17. Ibid., 101.
18. *Negroes of New York*, chap. 13, 13. The term "Stevedores" is from Scott, *American Negro*, 315.
19. Scott, *American Negro*, 440.
20. Ibid., 442.
21. Ibid., 443.
22. Ottley and Weatherby, *Negro in New York*, 200.
23. Goodwin, *No Ordinary Time*, 169–70.
24. Phillip McGuire, *He, Too, Spoke for Democracy: Judge Hastie, World War II, and the Black Soldier* (Westport, Conn.: Greenwood Press, 1988), 2.
25. Ibid., 3.

7. The Battle Before the War

1. Mullane, *Crossing*, 508.

2. August Meier and Elliott Rudwick, "Black Violence in the 20th Century: A Study in Rhetoric and Retaliation," in Graham and Gurr, *History of Violence*, 401.

3. *New York Age*, May 8, 1943.

4. Ottley and Weatherby, *Negro in New York*, 201n.

5. Goodwin, *No Ordinary Time*, 166.

6. Koppes and Black, "Motion-Picture Propaganda," 385. William Allen White headed the committee.

7. Ibid., 386.

8. James et al., *Fighting Racism*, 61. From "Military Policy and the Negroes," the Political Committee, Socialist Workers Party, following a national conference in Chicago, Sept. 27–29, 1940.

9. McGuire, *He, Too, Spoke*, 3.

10. Goodwin, *No Ordinary Time*, 167.

11. McGuire, *He, Too, Spoke*, 3–4.

12. Goodwin, *No Ordinary Time*, 168.

13. Ibid., 169.

14. Walter White, *A Man Called White: The Autobiography of Walter White* (New York: Viking, 1948), 187.

15. McGuire, *He, Too, Spoke*, xii.

16. Graham Smith, *When Jim Crow Met John Bull: Black American Soldiers in World War II Britain* (London: I. B. Tauris, 1987), 26.

17. Ibid., 23.

18. Ibid., 26.

19. Goodwin, *No Ordinary Time*, 328.

20. Ibid., 169.

21. Ibid., 171.

22. Ibid., 172.

8. Prewar Maneuvers

1. Capeci, *Harlem Riot*, 54.

2. Aptheker, *Documentary History*, 408. From Lester B. Granger's "Barriers to Negro War Employment," published in *Annals of the American Academy of Political and Social Science*, Sept. 1942.

3. Goodwin, *No Ordinary Time*, 247.

4. Aptheker, *Documentary History*, 410. From Granger's article.

5. Ibid., 411.

6. Ibid., 410.

7. Ibid., 412.

8. Richard R. Lingeman, *Don't You Know There's a War On?* (New York: G. P. Putnam's Sons, 1970), 163.

9. Aptheker, *Documentary History*, 412. From Granger's article.

10. *New York Times*, Apr. 29, 1941.

11. *New York Times,* Aug. 5, 1941.

12. *New York Times,* Apr. 27, 1941.

13. *New York Times,* Apr. 29, 1941.

14. Edward Dudley, interview by author, Jan. 24, 1994.

15. Lewis, *Harlem in Vogue,* 286.

16. Aptheker, *Documentary History,* 436. From Shirley Graham's "Negroes Are Fighting for Freedom," published in *Common Sense,* Feb. 1943.

17. Goodwin, *No Ordinary Time,* 250.

18. Roy Wilkins, *Standing Fast: The Autobiography of Roy Wilkins* (New York: Viking, 1982), 180.

19. White, *Autobiography,* 190.

20. Wilkins, *Autobiography,* 180.

21. White, *Autobiography,* 189–90.

22. Ibid., 191.

23. Goodwin, *No Ordinary Time,* 251.

24. Ibid., 252.

25. Capeci, *Harlem Riot,* 11.

26. James et al., *Fighting Racism,* 116. From "The March Is Cancelled" by Albert Parker, published in the *Militant* July 5, 1941. Albert Parker was the pen name of George Breitman.

27. Wilkins, *Autobiography,* 180.

28. Goodwin, *No Ordinary Time,* 253.

29. James et al., *Fighting Racism,* 116. From Parker [Breitman] article.

30. Ibid., 118.

31. Ibid., 191–92. From "Randolph Answers Ethridge" by Albert Parker [George Breitman] in *Militant,* Aug. 1, 1942.

32. Ibid., 192.

33. Kluger, *Simple Justice,* 231. The activist was Charles Houston, then a Howard University law professor.

34. *New York Times,* Dec. 1, 1943.

35. Lingeman, *Don't You Know,* 163. The FEPC directive was issued on Nov. 30, 1943.

36. *New York Times,* Nov. 14, 1941.

37. *New York Times,* Nov. 15, 1941.

9. Priorities

1. Meier and Rudwick, "Black Violence," 402.

2. *New York Times,* Feb. 5, 1941. He was Robert P. Braddicks of 225 West 138th Street, a former Harlem bank official connected with the service department of the newspaper *PM.*

3. *New York Times,* Nov. 23, 1941. The court was located in Linden. The women being called were from Rahway. The clerk, Ralph H. Martone, said he was the first district court clerk in New Jersey to use white women and black men on the same jury. He was calling up black women now because of the shortage of men.

4. *New York Times,* July 3, 1941.

5. *New York Times,* July 9, 1941.

6. *New York Times,* Sept. 21, 1941.

7. Aptheker, *Documentary History,* 397. From an anonymously written article, "Jim Crow in the Army Camps," *Crisis,* Dec. 1940.

8. James et al., *Fighting Racism,* 133–35. From "Sixty Soldiers Go AWOL," *Militant,* Sept. 13, 1941.

9. Ibid., 130. From "The Case of Pvt. Ned Turman: He Died Fighting for Democracy," by Albert Parker [George Breitman], *Militant,* Aug. 23, 1941.

10. The following articles are from *Amsterdam News,* Dec. 13, 1941.

11. Aptheker, *Documentary History,* 432n.

12. Smith, *Jim Crow Met John Bull,* 174.

13. White, *Autobiography,* 209.

14. Patrick S. Washburn, "J. Edgar Hoover and the Black Press in World War II " (paper presented to the History Division of the Association for Education in Journalism and Mass Communication, Norman, Okla., Aug. 3–6, 1986), 4, ERIC, ED 271749.

15. White, *Autobiography,* 207.

16. Ibid., 206.

17. *Amsterdam News,* "Another Slant on Negro Press," May 1, 1943. The *New Republic* article being quoted was written by Thomas Sancton and appeared in the Apr. 26, issue.

18. Wilkins, *Autobiography,* 179–80.

19. Ibid., 179.

20. Ibid., 181.

21. Ottley and Weatherby, *Negro in New York,* 203.

22. Ibid., 323.

23. Ibid., 327.

24. Ibid., 342.

25. Ibid., 341–42.

26. *New York Times,* Jan. 11, 1942.

27. Ellen Tarry, *The Third Door: The Autobiography of an American Negro Woman* (New York: David McKay, 1955), 175.

28. Wilkins, *Autobiography,* 184–85.

29. *The Negro Looks at the War: Attitudes of New York Negroes Toward Discrimination Against Negroes and a Comparison of Negro and Poor White Attitudes Toward War-Related Issues* (Extensive Surveys Division, Bureau of Intelligence, Office of Facts and Figures, 1942), iii-vi.

30. Ibid., iv-viii, 1.

31. Ibid., 4–9.

32. Ibid., 20.

33. Anderson, *This Was Harlem,* 290.

34. Ibid., 290–91.

35. Ibid., 290.

36. James et al., *Fighting Racism,* 242. From "Negroes in the Postwar World," by Albert Parker [George Breitman], a Pioneer Publishers pamphlet, June 1943.

37. Ibid., 156. From "Two Ways of Not Skinning the Cat," by Albert Parker [George Breitman], *Militant,* Mar. 28, 1942.

38. Washburn, "Hoover and the Black Press," 5.

39. Capeci, *Harlem Riot*, 47–48.

40. Washburn, "Hoover and Black Press," 7.

41. Ibid., 9.

42. Ibid., 15.

43. Smith, *Jim Crow Met John Bull*, 175.

44. Ibid., 176.

45. Ibid.

46. White, *Autobiography*, 208–9.

47. Ibid., 11.

48. Marvel Cooke, interview by author, May 18, 1994.

49. Bourne interview.

50. Apetheker, *Documentary History*, 418–19. From "Why Should We March?" by A. Philip Randolph, *Survey Graphic*, Nov. 1942.

51. McGuire, *He, Too, Spoke*, 15.

10. The Experience of War

1. James et al., *Fighting Racism*, 324. From "Just a Negro Soldier" by Bill Horton, *Militant*, Nov. 11, 1944.

2. McGuire, *He, Too, Spoke*, 6.

3. Ibid., 17.

4. Palmer interview.

5. *Amsterdam News*, Nov. 6, 1943.

6. Jack Scarville, interview by author, Jan. 14, 1994.

7. Aptheker, *Documentary History*, 488. From "What the Negro Soldier Thinks About This War" by Grant Reynolds, published in three parts in *Crisis*, Sept., Oct., Nov. 1944.

8. Ibid., 490.

9. Ibid., 492.

10. James et al., *Fighting Racism*, 16.

11. William L. O'Neill, *A Democracy at War: America's Fight at Home and Abroad in World War II* (New York: Free Press, 1993), 236.

12. McGuire, *He, Too, Spoke*, 7.

13. Ibid.

14. Smith interview.

15. Aptheker, *Documentary History*, 501. From Grant Reynolds' article "What the Negro Soldiers Thinks About the War."

16. Ibid., 496.

17. Ibid., 497.

18. Ibid.

19. Ibid., 502.

20. Maj. Arthur A. Tritsch (U.S. Army, Ret.), interview by author, Apr. 9, 1994.

21. Palmer interview.

22. Smith, *Jim Crow Met John Bull*, 140–41. The period covered was Nov. 19, 1943, to Feb. 19, 1944, as reported by the Inspector General of the U.S. Army.

23. Ibid., 223.

24. Ibid., 106. Eisenhower confided his views to actress Merle Oberon.

25. Ibid., 103.

26. Ibid., 113.

27. Harry A. Ploski and Warren Marr, II, *The Negro Almanac: A Reference Work on the Afro-American* (New York: Bellwether, 1976), 623. The first lieutenant promoted was Charles F. Gandy.

28. O'Neill, *Democracy at War*, 237.

29. Scarville interview.

30. Ploski and Marr, *Negro Almanac*, 623. The black officer was Lt. Col. Marcus Ray.

31. Scarville interview.

32. McGuire, *He, Too, Spoke*, 72–73. While black personnel never rose above 6.5 percent at any one time, out of 48,603 blue discharges between Dec. 1, 1941 and June 30, 1945, 10,806—or 20.2 percent—were issued to blacks.

33. Ibid., 71–72.

34. Palmer interview.

35. Goodwin, *No Ordinary Time*, 567–68.

36. Palmer interview.

37. Gail Buckley Lumet, *The Hornes: An American Family* (New York: Knopf, 1986), 180–81.

38. *Amsterdam News*, May 22, 1943.

39. Dr. James Jones, interview by author, Jan. 25, 1994.

40. James et al., *Fighting Racism*, 148. From "Blood Is Segregated Too" by Ernest Williams, *Militant*, Jan. 1 and 31 and Feb. 7, 1942. Ernest Williams was the pen name of Myra Lesnik.

41. McGuire, *He, Too, Spoke*, 75. The policy on blood plasma did not change until Dec. 1, 1950.

42. Bourne interview.

43. Robert P. Crease, *Interview with Frankie Manning*, Ernie Smith Jazz Collection, Jazz Oral History Project: "The Swing Era" (Washington, D.C.: National Museum of American History, n.d.), 325.

44. Ibid., 326–28; Frank (Frankie) Manning, interview by author, Dec. 10, 1994.

45. Malcolm X, *Autobiography*, 121–24.

46. *New York Times*, Dec. 6, 1942. The black, Horace J. McMillian, was graduated from Columbus University's College of Pharmacy in the second class of 198 graduates.

47. *New York Times*, Sept. 10, 1942.

48. McGuire, *He, Too, Spoke*, 38.

49. O'Neill, *Democracy at War*, 236.

50. McGuire, *He, Too, Spoke*, 38.

51. O'Neill, *Democracy at War*, 237.

11. A Conditional Surrender

1. William H. Hastie, "On Clipped Wings: The Story of Jim Crow in the Army Air Corps" (New York: National Association for the Advancement of Colored People, 1943), microfilm, 20.

2. Phillip McGuire, "Judge Hastie, World War II, and the Army Air Corps," *Phylon* 42, no. 2 (1981): 158–59.

3. Ibid., 159.

4. McGuire, *He, Too, Spoke,* 30.

5. Ibid., 28.

6. Ibid.

7. *New York Age,* Mar. 27, 1943.

8. James et al., *Fighting Racism,* 216. From "General Davis Is a Busy Man," *Militant,* Dec. 12, 1942.

9. Murphy interview.

10. Ibid.

11. McGuire, *He, Too, Spoke,* 66.

12. Ibid., 57.

13. Ibid., 58.

14. Ibid., 59.

15. Ibid., 67.

16. Ibid.

17. Ibid., 68.

18. Boskin, *Urban Racial Violence,* 58. From Walter White, "Behind the Harlem Riot of 1943," *New Republic,* Aug. 16, 1943.

19. McGuire, *He, Too, Spoke,* 68.

20. The congressman was Andrew J. May.

21. Hastie, "On Clipped Wings," 5.

22. Ibid., 8.

23. Ibid., 5.

24. Ibid., 10.

25. Ibid., 14.

26. McGuire, "Judge Hastie," 160.

27. Hastie, "On Clipped Wings," 17.

28. Ibid., 18.

29. Ibid.

30. Ibid., 19.

31. Ibid., unpaginated 2d page of Introduction.

32. McGuire, "Judge Hastie," 165.

33. *New York Age,* Mar. 20, 1943.

34. McGuire, "Judge Hastie," 165.

35. Ibid., 160.

12. Images

1. Mullane, *Crossing*, 511. Jean Toomer's "Song of the Son" is from his novel, *Cane*. Nathan Eugene (Jean) Toomer was the grandson of Pinckney B. S. Pinchback, who was acting governor of Louisiana during Reconstruction.

2. Aptheker, *Documentary History*, 457. From "Communications Media and Racism" by Walter White, delivered at a conference Oct. 1–3, 1943 held in Los Angeles under the auspices of the Hollywood Writers' Mobilization and the University of California.

3. Koppes and Black, "Motion-Picture Propaganda," 392.

4. *New York Times*, Sept. 23, 1942.

5. *Amsterdam News*, May 15, 1943.

6. Aptheker, *Documentary History*, 116–17. From "Uncle Tom in Hollywood" by Loren Miller, *Crisis*, Nov. 1934.

7. Ibid., 432. From Shirley Graham's "Negroes Are Fighting for Freedom."

8. Koppes and Black, "Motion-Picture Propaganda," 398.

9. *Amsterdam News*, May 8, 1943.

10. McGuire, *He, Too, Spoke*, 55.

11. Koppes and Black, "Motion-Picture Propaganda," 387.

12. Ibid., 390.

13. Ibid.

14. Ibid.

15. Ibid., 389.

16. Ibid., 393.

17. Ibid., 400.

18. Ibid., 404.

19. Ibid., 398.

20. Ibid., 399.

13. Advances and Retreats

1. Mullane, *Crossing*, 495. From Claude McKay's "The Lynching."

2. McGuire, "Judge Hastie," 166–67.

3. James et al., *Fighting Racism*, 17.

4. O'Neill, *Democracy at War*, 215.

5. Lingeman, *Don't You Know*, 164–65.

6. Aptheker, *Documentary History*, 521. From "Full Employment and the Negro Worker" by Willard S. Townsend, *Journal of Negro Education*, July 1944. Townsend was a leading black in the CIO.

7. Ibid., 416. From Granger, "Barriers."

8. *New York Times*, Apr. 11, 1943.

9. Saunders interview.

10. James et al., *Fighting Racism*, 17.

11. Aptheker, *Documentary History*, 521. From Townsend, "Full Employment."

12. Ibid., 417. From Granger, "Barriers."

13. James et al., *Fighting Racism*, 293. From "A Government Study on Hiring," *Militant*, Dec. 18, 1943.

14. Lingeman, *Don't You Know*, 164.

15. James et al., *Fighting Racism*, 170. From "2,000 March in Maryland," *Militant*, May 30, 1942.

16. Ibid., 171. From "Reviving the March on Washington Movement," *Militant*, June 20, 1942.

17. *New York Times*, May 15 and 16, 1942.

18. *New York Times* and *Atlanta Constitution*, Aug. 12, 1942.

19. *New York Times*, Oct. 21, 1942.

20. James et al., *Fighting Racism*, 149. From "Fighting in "Louisiana" by Ernest Williams (Myra Lesnik), *Militant*, Jan. 24, 1942.

21. Ibid., 194–96. From "Racist Terror in the South" by Philip Blake, *Militant*, Aug. 22, 1942.

22. *People's Voice*, Apr. 11, 1942.

23. James et al., *Fighting Racism*, 179. From "Signs of the Times" by Albert Parker [George Breitman], *Militant*, June 20, 1942.

24. *New York Times*, Dec. 26, 1942.

14. Violence on the Home Front

1. Mullane, *Crossing*, 521. From Countee Cullen's "From the Dark Tower."

2. James et al., *Fighting Racism*, 227. From "Women Sue Cleveland Plants" by Albert Parker [George Breitman], *Militant*, Jan. 2, 1943.

3. *New York Times*, Jan. 5, 1943.

4. *Amsterdam News*, May 15, 1943.

5. *New York Times*, Apr. 5, 1943.

6. *Amsterdam News*, May 1, 1943.

7. *New York Age*, Mar. 20, 1943.

8. *Amsterdam News*, May 22, 1943.

9. *New York Age*, Apr. 3, 1943.

10. *New York Age*, Mar. 20, 1943.

11. *New York Age*, Apr. 3, 1943.

12. *People's Voice*, May 1, 1943.

13. *New York Age*, July 19, 1943.

14. *Amsterdam News*, May 15, 1943.

15. *Amsterdam News*, May 22, 1943.

16. Ibid.

17. *New York Age*, July 10, 1943.

18. *Amsterdam News*, May 1, 1943.

19. *Amsterdam News*, May 22, 1943. From Roy Wilkins' "The Watchtower" column.

20. *Amsterdam News*, May 22, 1943.

21. Boskin, *Urban Racial Violence*, 57. From White's "Behind the Harlem Riot."

22. *New York Times*, June 11, 1943.

23. *New York Age,* July 19, 1943.

24. *People's Voice,* Aug. 7, 1943.

25. Goodwin, *No Ordinary Time,* 444.

26. *People's Voice,* Aug. 7, 1943.

27. O'Neill, *Democracy at War,* 249.

28. *New York Times,* Apr. 11, 1943.

29. *Uniform Crime Reports for the United States and Its Possessions,* vol. 14 (Washington, D.C.: Federal Bureau of Investigation, 1943), 52.

30. Ibid., 87.

31. Walter A. Lunden, *War and Delinquency: An Analysis of Juvenile Delinquency in Thirteen Nations in World War I and World War II* (Ames, Iowa: Art Press, 1963), 6.

32. Stuart Cosgrove, "The Zoot-Suit and Style Warfare," *History Workshop* 18 (autumn 1984): 78–79.

33. *New York Times,* June 11, 1943. The busboy's name was Clyde Duncan.

34. *New York Times,* June 20, 1943.

35. Boskin, *Urban Racial Violence,* 48. From "The Zoot-Suit Riots (1943)" by Carey McWilliams, *New Republic,* June 21, 1943.

36. Ibid., 47.

37. Ibid.

38. *New York Times,* June 10, 1943.

39. *New York Times,* June 11, 1943.

40. Ibid.

41. *Uniform Crime Reports,* 96.

42. *Amsterdam News,* May 15, 1943.

43. *New York Times,* June 17, 1943.

44. *New York Times,* July 10, 1943.

45. Thomas Sancton, "The Race Riots," *New Republic,* July 5, 1943, 9.

46. Capeci, *Harlem Riot,* 98.

15. A State of Siege

1. Mullane, *Crossing,* 496. From Claude McKay's "Tiger."

2. O'Neill, *Democracy at War,* 216.

3. *New York Times,* June 27, 1943.

4. O'Neill, *Democracy at War,* 219.

5. Ibid.

6. Goodwin, *No Ordinary Time,* 326–27.

7. White, *Autobiography,* 227.

8. Aptheker, *Documentary History,* 448. From "Detroit Race Riot of 1943" by Earl Brown, *Why Race Riots: Lessons from Detroit,* Public Affairs Pamphlet No. 87.

9. Ibid.

10. Goodwin, *No Ordinary Time,* 446. The assistant was C. E. Rhetts.

11. Boskin, *Urban Racial Violence,* 41. From "The Gestapo in Detroit (1943)," *Crisis,* Aug. 1943.

12. Goodwin, *No Ordinary Time,* 327.

13. Capeci, *Harlem Riot*, 95.

14. O'Neill, *Democracy at War*, 217.

15. *New York Times*, June 27, 1943.

16. Sancton, "Race Riots," 10.

17. *Amsterdam News*, May 1, 1943.

18. James et al., *Fighting Racism*, 182–83. From "The Shameful Walkout at Hudson," *Militant*, June 27, 1942.

19. Goodwin, *No Ordinary Time*, 370.

20. White, *Autobiography*, 225.

21. *People's Voice*, Aug. 7, 1943.

22. White, *Autobiography*, 225.

23. Wilkins, *Autobiography*, 182.

24. Ibid.

25. White, *Autobiography*, 225–26.

26. Sancton, "Race Riots," 9.

27. White, *Autobiography*, 225–26.

28. Boskin, *Urban Racial Violence*, 41. From Marshall's "Gestapo in Detroit."

29. Sancton, "Race Riots," 9.

30. White, *Autobiography*, 226.

31. James et al., *Fighting Racism*, 264. From "Police, Politicians, and the Press" by Philip Blake, *Militant*, July 3, 1943.

32. Boskin, *Urban Racial Violence*, 41–44.

33. *People's Voice*, Aug. 7, 1943.

34. Capeci, *Harlem Riot*, 95.

35. James et al., *Fighting Racism*, 270. From "Roosevelt's Letter" by David Ransom, *Militant*, July 31, 1943. The congressman to whom Roosevelt wrote was Vito Marcantonio, a leader of the American Labor Party who frequently supported communist issues.

36. *New York Times*, July 4, 1943.

37. *New York Times*, July 13, 1943.

38. *New York Times*, July 23, 1943. The reporter was Turner Catledge, later managing editor of the *Times*.

39. *New York Times*, June 29, 1943.

40. Goodwin, *No Ordinary Time*, 447. Her friend was Pauli Murray.

41. Capeci, *Harlem Riot*, 91.

42. Goodwin, *No Ordinary Time*, 447.

43. Sancton, "Race Riots," 12–13.

44. Capeci, *Harlem Riot*, 91.

45. Goodwin, *No Ordinary Time*, 447.

46. Aptheker, *Documentary History* 453. From Brown's "The Detroit Race Riot of 1943."

47. Charles W. Eagles, "Two 'Double V's': Jonathan Daniels, FDR, and Race Relations during World War II," *North Carolina Historical Review* 59 (July 1982): 259.

48. Capeci, *Harlem Riot*, 97.

49. Sancton, "Race Riots," 9.

16. Leaders

1. Mullane, *Crossing*, 543. From Sterling Brown's "Strong Man."
2. Roi Ottley, *New World A-Coming* (New York: Arno Press and The New York Times, 1968) 220. Ottley says Powell had blue eyes; but he is sometimes described as having hazel eyes.
3. Kisseloff, *You Must Remember*, 296.
4. Ottley, *New World*, 220.
5. Ibid., 220–21.
6. Bourne interview.
7. Capeci, *Harlem Riot*, 28. NAACP lobbyist Clarence Mitchell is quoted.
8. Hamilton, *Powell*, 98.
9. Ottley, *New World*, 288–89.
10. Hamilton, *Powell*, 118.
11. McKay, *Negro Metropolis*, 125–27.
12. Hamilton, *Powell*, 119.
13. Ibid., 105.
14. *People's Voice*, Aug. 7, 1943.
15. Hamilton, *Powell*, 175.
16. Capeci, *Harlem Riot*, 22.
17. Ibid., 23.
18. Hamilton, *Powell*, 177.
19. *Negro Looks at the War*, 18.
20. Ibid., 18–19.
21. Bourne interview.
22. Hamilton, *Powell*, 1.
23. Ibid., 3.
24. Ronald H. Bayor, *Fiorello La Guardia: Ethnicity and Reform* (Arlington Heights, Ill.: Harlan Davidson, 1993), 149.
25. Capeci, *Harlem Riot*, 11.
26. Bayor, *La Guardia*, 149.
27. *New York Times*, Sept. 21, 1947.
28. *New York Times*, Oct. 9, 1943. The fight occurred on South Street near Rutgers Slip.
29. *New York Times*, Apr. 16, 1942.
30. *New York Times*, Jan. 9, 1942. The mayor's wife was Marie Fischer. The adopted children were a girl, Jean, and a boy, Eric.
31. *New York Times*, May 27, 1942.
32. Bayor, *La Guardia*, 159.
33. *New York Times*, Oct. 21, 1941.
34. *New York Times*, Jan. 23, 1942.
35. *New York Times*, Dec. 6, 1941.
36. Dominic J. Capeci, Jr., "Walter F. White and the Savoy Ballroom Controversy of 1943," *Afro-Americans in New York Life and History* 5 (July 1981): 25–26.
37. White, *Autobiography*, 3.

38. Ibid., 10.

39. Ibid., 10-11.

40. Lewis, *Harlem in Vogue*, 299.

17. Conflicts

1. Mullane, *Crossing*, 467. From Claude McKay's poem "If We Must Die!"

2. Hamilton, *Powell*, 117.

3. *New York Times*, Nov. 10, 1941.

4. *New York Times*, Jan. 23, 1942.

5. Capeci, *Harlem Riot*, 58.

6. *New York Times*, Nov. 30, 1943.

7. *New York Times*, Feb. 3, 1943.

8. Capeci, *Harlem Riot*, 27.

9. Hamilton, *Powell*, 125.

10. *New York Times*, Apr. 16, 1942.

11. *New York Times*, Jan. 2, 1943.

12. *New York Times*, Jan. 8, 1943. The doctor's name was Henry K. Cudmore. He was 55 years old.

13. *New York Times*, Feb. 18, 1943.

14. *New York Times*, Mar. 15, 1943.

15. *New York Times*, May 2, 1943. The foreign correspondent was Don Iddon of the *Daily Mail* (London).

16. *New York Times*, Mar. 30, 1943.

17. *New York Times*, Dec. 12, 1941.

18. *New York Times*, May 26, 1943. More than two hundred actors petitioned La Guardia through the Actors Equity Association to do something about the attacks on actors, pedestrians, and others.

19. *New York Times*, Jan. 9, 1943.

20. *New York Times*, Apr. 5, 1943. Mrs. David M. Levy is quoted. She was director of the agency.

21. *New York Times*, Apr. 14, 1943. The magistrate was J. Roland Sala of Brooklyn Felony Court.

22. *New York Times*, Apr. 14, 1943.

23. *New York Times*, Feb. 3, 1943.

24. Hamilton, *Powell*, 125.

25. *New York Age*, May 1, 1943.

26. Lewis, *Harlem in Vogue*, 170.

27. *People's Voice*, May 1, 1943.

28. *New York Age*, May 1, 1943.

29. Ernie Smith, *Interview with Norma Miller*, Ernie Smith Jazz Collection, Jazz Oral History Project: "The Swing Era" (Washington, D.C.: National Museum of American History, n.d.), 63.

30. Ibid., 93.

31. Ibid., 145.

32. Ibid.

33. *People's Voice*, May 1, 1943.

34. Capeci, "Walter White and Savoy Ballroom," 17.

35. Malcolm X, *Autobiography*, 131.

36. *People's Voice*, May 8, 1943.

37. *New York Age*, May 1, 1943.

38. *Amsterdam News*, May 8, 1943.

39. *People's Voice*, May 1, 1943.

40. *People's Voice*, May 8, 1943.

41. *Amsterdam News*, May 29, 1943.

42. Capeci, *Harlem Riot*, 17.

43. *People's Voice*, Aug. 7, 1943.

44. Capeci, *Harlem Riot*, 81.

45. *New York Times*, Nov. 16, 1943.

46. *New York Times*, Jan. 20, 1942.

47. *Report of the Police Commissioner to the Mayor, November 20, 1943* (New York: Lewis J. Valentine, 1943), 17.

48. Ibid., 50.

49. Capeci, *Harlem Riot*, 83.

50. *New York Times*, June 28, 1943.

51. White, *Autobiography*, 230.

52. Capeci, *Harlem Riot*, 84.

53. Hamilton, *Powell*, 121–22.

54. Capeci, *Harlem Riot*, 83.

55. Ibid., 85.

56. Ibid., 87–89.

57. Hamilton, *Powell*, 120.

58. Bourne interview.

59. Hamilton, *Powell*, 178.

60. *People's Voice*, July 3, 1943. Powell made the charge in a speech before the City Council.

61. *People's Voice*, July 24, 1943. The "Grand Kligrapp" gave his names as James G. Blanchert.

62. *People's Voice*, July 31, 1943.

63. Hamilton, *Powell*, 122. It is not known where Powell was at the time of the Harlem riot.

18. The People's Voices

1. Mullane, *Crossing*, 497. From Claude McKay's "The White City."

2. Foster Palmer's quote as well as the other italicized quotes in this chapter are from the interviews conducted by the author.

3. All of the above news stories cited are from the *New York Times* of Aug. 1, 1943. Moses's quote is on page 9 of the Sunday Magazine section.

4. The news stories cited are from the July 31, 1943 editions of the *Amsterdam News, New York Age,* and *People's Voice.*

19. The Harlem Riot

1. Arnold Rampersad, *The Life of Langston Hughes: I Dream a World*, vol. 2: 1941–1967 (New York: Oxford Univ. Press, 1988), 76–77.

2. Kisseloff, *You Must Remember*, 282. Nora Mair is quoted.

3. Except as otherwise noted, the events recounted about the Harlem riot are taken from an amalgam of sources: the Aug. 2–8, 1943, issues of the *New York Times*, Aug. 2, 1943, edition of the *New York Post*, and the Aug. 7 and 14, 1943, issues of the *Amsterdam News, New York Age*, and *People's Voice;* interviews with St. Clair Bourne, Marvel Cooke, Evelyn Long Cunningham, Dr. James Jones, Frederick Douglass Mays, Arnold de Mille, Evelyn Hunt O'Garro, Foster Palmer, and Allen Worrell; also, Anderson, *This Was Harlem*, 295–98; Claude Brown, *Manchild in the Promised Land* (New York: Signet, 1965), 12–14; Capeci, *Harlem Riot*, 99–127; Malcolm X, *Autobiography*, 130–32; Orlansky, "Harlem Riot," 3–29; Boskin, *Urban Racial Violence*, White's "Behind the Harlem Riot," 56–61; White, *Autobiography*, 233–40; and Wilkins, *Autobiography*, 183–84.

4. Margie Polite was briefly committed to a medical institution for treatment, then tried and found guilty of disorderly conduct. She was finally released from prison on probation in September. (*New York Times*, Aug. 12 and Sept. 11, 1943.) What happened to Bandy and his mother is not known. He was turned over to the army for disciplinary action, but what his punishment entailed was never disclosed. His mother, Mrs. Roberts, failed to appear for an initial court hearing but was later being held in lieu of $1,000, awaiting trial in Special Sessions Court. No mention is made of her after a news story in the *Times* of Sept. 11, 1943. Prosecutors either decided not to press charges, or she never showed up for trial. Her first name, incidentally, is sometimes given as Florien, but that may be a typographical error.

20. Recriminations

1. Anderson, *This Was Harlem*, 39. "I'm a Jonah Man" by Alexander Rogers was popularized by black entertainer Bert Williams.

2. *New York Times*, Sept. 2, 1943. The damage totals were announced by Matthew J. Eder, secretary of the Uptown Chamber of Commerce, after a survey. Some sources say five persons, not six, were killed.

3. Orlansky, "Harlem Riot," 6.

4. *People's Voice*, Aug. 7, 1943.

5. Ibid.

6. Boskin, *Urban Racial Violence*, 60–61. From White, "Behind the Harlem Riot."

7. White, *Autobiography*, 239.

8. *New York Times*, Aug. 6, 1943.

9. *Amsterdam News*, Aug. 7, 1943. The correspondent was Elmer A. Carter.

10. Capeci, *Harlem Riot*, 122.

11. Rampersad, *Langston Hughes*, 75–76.

12. Orlansky, "Harlem Riot," 28.

13. *New York Times*, Aug. 3, 1943.

14. *New York Times*, Mar. 4, 1943.

15. *New York Times*, Aug. 3, 1943.

16. *New York Times*, Aug. 5, 1943.

17. *New York Times*, Aug. 3, 1943.

18. *People's Voice*, Aug. 14, 1943.

19. *New York Age*, Aug. 7, 1943.

20. Capeci, *Harlem Riot*, 121–22.

21. *Amsterdam News*, Aug. 14, 1943.

22. Capeci, *Harlem Riot*, 173.

23. *People's Voice*, Aug. 7, 1943.

24. Capeci, *Harlem Riot*, 121.

25. James et al., *Fighting Racism*, 283. From "Not Another Detroit," *Militant*, Aug. 7, 1943.

26. Ibid., 286–87. From "Some Faulty Evaluations" by Albert Parker [George Breitman], *Militant*, Sept. 4, 1943.

27. *New York Times*, Jan. 23, 1943.

28. *New York Times*, Aug. 8, 1943. The correspondent quoted is Turner Catledge.

29. *New York Times*, Aug. 8, 1943. The correspondent quoted is Russell B. Porter.

30. *New York Times*, Aug. 3, 1943.

31. Capeci, *Harlem Riot*, 125.

32. *People's Voice*, Aug. 14, 1943.

33. *Amsterdam News*, Aug. 7, 1943.

34. Kluger, *Simple Justice*, 318.

35. Ibid., 256.

36. Ibid., 256–57.

37. Capeci, *Harlem Riot*, 157.

38. Rampersad, *Langston Hughes*, 77.

39. *New York Times*, May 1, 1944.

40. *Amsterdam News*, Nov. 6, 1943.

41. *Amsterdam News*, Nov. 6, 1943.

42. Ibid.

21. Victory Abroad

1. "And Some Day I Shall Look at You" by Arnold de Mille appeared in the *Chicago Defender*, Apr. 10, 1937.

2. Wilkins, *Autobiography*, 189.

3. O'Neill, *Democracy at War*, 240.

4. Eagles, "Two 'Double V's'," 259.

5. O'Neill, *Democracy at War*, 239.

6. Goodwin, *No Ordinary Time*, 370.

7. *New York Times*, Aug. 5, 1943.

8. Kluger, *Simple Justice*, 228.

9. James et al., *Fighting Racism*, 352. From "Death Knell of FEPC" by Louise Simpson, *Militant*, July 21, 1945. Simpson was the Socialist Workers candidate for City Council from Harlem in the 1945 elections.

10. White, *Autobiography*, 193–94.

11. *New York Age*, Aug. 14, 1943.

12. *New York Times*, Mar. 1, 1944.

13. James et al., *Fighting Racism*, 288. From "Four Freedoms at Home" by Albert Parker [George Breitman], *Militant*, Aug. 28 and Sept. 18, 1943.

14. Ibid., 288–89.

15. Wilkins, *Autobiography*, 188.

16. *New York Times*, Dec. 31, 1944.

17. *New York Times*, Apr. 21, 1944.

18. Kluger, *Simple Justice*, 327.

19. Aptheker, *Documentary History*, 531–32. From "Some Mutinies, Riots, and Other Disturbances" by Florence Murray, *Negro Handbook, 1946–1947*.

20. Ibid., 529–30.

21. Ibid., 532.

22. Goodwin, *No Ordinary Time*, 522.

23. Aptheker, *Documentary History*, 534–35. From Murray's "Some Mutinies."

24. Ibid., 536.

25. Goodwin, *No Ordinary Time*, 524.

26. Aptheker, *Documentary History*, 526–28. From Murray's "Some Mutinies."

27. Goodwin, *No Ordinary Time*, 524.

28. Ibid., 627.

29. James et al., *Fighting Racism*, 321. From "Fifty Found Guilty of Navy 'Mutiny'" by Robert Chester, *Militant*, Nov. 11, 1944.

30. Charles F. Houston, "The Negro Soldier," *Nation*, Oct. 21, 1944.

31. Ploski and Marr, *Negro Almanac*, 624.

32. Ibid.

33. Mable M. Smythe, ed., *The Black American Reference Book* (Englewood Cliffs, N.J.: Prentice-Hall, 1976), 65.

34. Goodwin, *No Ordinary Time*, 626.

35. *New York Times Magazine*, May 7, 1955, 94–95.

36. Parks, *Voices*, 82.

37. Ploski and Marr, *Negro Almanac*, 624.

38. Goodwin, *No Ordinary Time*, 424.

39. Parks, *Voices*, 89.

40. Ibid., 91.

41. Smith, *Jim Crow Met John Bull*, 171.

42. Aptheker, *Documentary History*, 483. From Walter White, "White Supremacy and World War II."

43. Ibid., 483–85.

44. Smith, *Jim Crow Met John Bull*, 169.

45. Ibid., 171.

46. Ibid., 169.

47. White, *Autobiography*, 277–86.

48. Goodwin, *No Ordinary Time*, 521–22.

49. Smith, *Jim Crow Met John Bull*, 111.

50. Ibid., 186.

51. Goodwin, *No Ordinary Time*, 329.

52. *New York Times Magazine*, May 7, 1995, 95.

53. Ibid.

54. *New York Times*, Mar. 28, 1993.

Epilogue

1. Mullane, *Crossing*, 465. From "Returning Soldiers," *Crisis*, May 1919.

2. Morris Janowitz, "Patterns of Collective Racial Violence," in Graham and Gurr, *History of Violence*, 418. From chap. 10.

3. Low, *Encyclopedia*, 238–39.

4. Ibid., 239.

Notes

1. "Along the Path of Life He Goes" by Arnold de Mille, *Toledo Press*, Apr. 10, 1937.

Bibliography

1. Mullane, *Crossing*, 501. From "I, Too," by Langston Hughes.

Bibliography

I, too, sing America
I am the darker brother. . . .
They'll see how beautiful I am
And be ashamed—

I, too, am America.

—Langston Hughes[1]

Manuscript Sources

Ernie Smith Jazz Collection.
Jazz Oral History Project: "The Swing Era." National Museum of American
  History, Washington, D.C.

Printed Documents

Annual Report, Police Department, City of New York 1943. New York: New York
  City Police Department, 1944.
Census Tract Data on Population and Housing in New York City: 1940. New York:
  Welfare Council Committee on 1940 Census Tract Tabulations for New
  York City, 1942.
*The Negro Looks at the War: Attitudes of New York Negroes Toward Discrimination
  Against Negroes and a Comparison of Negro and Poor White Attitudes Toward
  War-Related Issues*. Extensive Surveys Division, Bureau of Intelligence,
  Office of Facts and Figures, 1942.
Negroes of New York. Work Projects Administration research study compiled
  by the Writers' Program, n.d. Typescript.

Report of the Police Commissioner to the Mayor, November 20, 1943. New York: Lewis J. Valentine, 1943.

Story of the Riot. Citizens' Protective League, 1900.

Uniform Crime Reports for the United States and Its Possessions. Vols. 12–16. Washington: Federal Bureau of Investigation, 1942–46.

Newspapers and Periodicals

The following newspapers were used extensively, chiefly to recreate the events surrounding August 1, 1943, but as otherwise noted in footnotes: *Amsterdam News, Atlanta Constitution, New York Age, New York Post, New York Times,* and *People's Voice.*

Interviews

Bourne, St. Clair T. Taped interview, May 18, 1994.

Cooke, Marvel. Taped interview, May 18, 1994.

Cunningham, Evelyn Long. Taped interview, Apr. 28, 1994.

De Mille, Arnold. Taped interview, Apr. 4, 1994.

Dudley, Edward. Telephone interview, Jan. 24, 1994.

Jones, Dr. James. Taped interview, Jan. 25, 1994.

Jones, Madison S. Telephone interview, Jan. 19, 1994.

Manning, Frank (Frankie). Telephone interview, Dec. 10, 1994.

Mays, Frederick Douglass. Taped interview, Jan. 14, 1994.

Murphy, Virginia Delany. Taped interview, Mar. 23, 1994.

O'Garro, Evelyn Hunt. Taped interview, Apr. 27, 1993.

Palmer, Foster. Taped interview, Mar. 23, 1994.

Saunders, Doris. Taped interview, Apr. 27, 1993.

Scarville, Jack. Taped interview, Jan. 14, 1994.

Schumach, Murray. Interview with author, June 12, 1994.

Smith, Ernie. Interview with author, Dec. 5, 1994.

Smith, Walker. Taped interview, Apr. 7, 1994.

Tritsch, Maj. Arthur A. Telephone interview, Apr. 9, 1994.

Worrell, Allen. Taped interview, Apr. 14, 1993.

Books

Anderson, Jervis. *This Was Harlem: 1900–1950.* New York: Farrar, Straus, Giroux, 1993.

Aptheker, Herbert. *A Documentary History of the Negro People in the United States: 1933–1945.* Vol. 4. New York: Citadel Press, 1990.

Astor, Gerald. *The New York Cops*. New York: Charles Scribner's Sons, 1971.

Baldassare, Mark, ed. *The Los Angeles Riots: Lessons for the Urban Future*. Boulder, Colo.: Westview Press, 1994.

Bayor, Ronald H. *Fiorello La Guardia: Ethnicity and Reform*. Arlington Heights, Ill.: Harlan Davidson, 1993.

Bernstein, Iver. *The New York City Draft Riots: Their Significance for American Society and Politics in the Age of the Civil War*. New York: Oxford Univ. Press, 1990.

Boskin, Joseph. *Urban Racial Violence in the Twentieth Century*. Beverly Hills, Calif.: Glencoe Press, 1969.

Brandt, Nat. *The Congressman Who Got Away with Murder*. Syracuse, N.Y.: Syracuse Univ. Press, 1991.

Brown, Claude. *Manchild in the Promised Land*. New York: Signet, 1965.

Capeci, Dominic J., Jr. *The Harlem Riot of 1943*. Philadelphia: Temple Univ. Press, 1977.

Davis, Thomas J. *A Rumor of Revolt: The 'Great Negro Plot' in Colonial New York*. New York: Free Press, 1985.

Delany, Sarah, and A. Elizabeth Delaney. *Having Our Say: The Delany Sisters' First 100 Years*. New York: Kodansha, 1993.

Dictionary of American Biography. Vols. 1–21, Supplements 1–8. New York: Charles Scribner's Sons, 1928–1988.

Goodwin, Doris Kearns. *No Ordinary Time: Franklin and Eleanor Roosevelt: The Home Front in World War II*. New York: Simon and Schuster, 1994.

Graham, Hugh D., and Ted Robert Gurr, eds. *The History of Violence in America: Historical and Comparative Perspectives*. New York: Frederick A. Praeger, 1969.

Hacker, Andrew. *Two Nations: Black and White, Separate, Hostile, Unequal*. New York: Charles Scribner's Sons, 1992.

Hamilton, Charles V. *Adam Clayton Powell, Jr.: The Political Biography of an American Dilemma*. New York: Collier, 1991.

Harris, Theodore F. *Pearl S. Buck: A Biography*. Vol. 2; *Her Philosophy as Expressed in Her Letters*. New York: John Day, 1971.

Hawkins, Stuart. *New York, New York*. New York: Wilfred Funk, 1957.

James, C. L. R., George Breitman, Edgar Keemer, and others. *Fighting Racism in World War II*. New York: Pathfinder, 1980.

Kisseloff, Jeff. *You Must Remember This: An Oral History of Manhattan from the 1890s to World War II*. New York: Schocken, 1989.

Kluger, Richard. *Simple Justice*. New York: Vintage, 1977.

Lewis, David Levering. *When Harlem Was in Vogue*. New York: Knopf, 1981.

Lingeman, Richard R. *Don't You Know There's a War On?* New York: G. P. Putnam's Sons, 1970.

Low, Augustus W., ed. *Encyclopedia of Black America*. New York: McGraw-Hill, 1981.

Lumet, Gail Buckley. *The Hornes: An American Family*. New York: Knopf, 1986.

Lunden, Walter A. *War and Delinquency: An Analysis of Juvenile Delinquency in Thirteen Nations in World War I and World War II*. Ames, Iowa: Art Press, 1963.

Malcolm X, with Alex Haley. *The Autobiography of Malcolm X*. New York: Ballantine, 1992.

Mannheim, Hermann. *War and Crime*. London: Watts, 1941.

McDonald, Arthur. *War and Criminal Anthropology*. New Orleans. Reprint of February 1915 article from *Pan-American Magazine*, n.p., n.d.

McGuire, Phillip. *He, Too, Spoke for Democracy: Judge Hastie, World War II, and the Black Soldier*. Westport, Conn.: Greenwood Press, 1988.

McKay, Claude. *Harlem: Negro Metropolis*. New York: Harcourt Brace Jovanovich, 1968.

Monkkonen, Eric H., ed. *Delinquency and Disorderly Behavior*. Westport, Conn.: Meckler, 1991.

Mullane, Deirdre, ed. *Crossing the Danger Water: Three Hundred Years of African-American Writing*. New York: Doubleday, 1993.

New York City Guide. New York: Random House, 1939.

O'Neill, William L. *A Democracy at War: America's Fight at Home & Abroad in World War II*. New York: Free Press, 1993.

Ottley, Roi. *New World A-Coming*. New York: Arno Press and The New York Times, 1968.

Ottley, Roi, and William J. Weatherby, eds. *The Negro in New York: An Informal Social History*. Dobbs Ferry, N.Y.: Oceana, 1967.

Ovington, Mary White. *Half a Man: The Status of the Negro in New York*. New York: Hill and Wang, 1969.

Parks, Gordon. *Voices in the Mirror: An Autobiography*. New York: Doubleday, 1990.

Ploski, Harry A. and Warren Marr, II. *The Negro Almanac: A Reference Work on the Afro-American*. New York: Bellwether, 1976.

Rampersad, Arnold. *The Life of Langston Hughes: I Dream a World*. Vol. 2: 1941–1967. New York: Oxford Univ. Press, 1988.

Roberts, Robert A. *Encyclopedia of Historic Forts: The Military, Pioneer, and Trading Posts of the United States*. New York: Macmillan, 1988.

Schoener, Allon. *Harlem on My Mind: Cultural Capital of Black America 1900–1978*. New York: Dell, 1979.

Scott, Emmett J. *The American Negro in the World War*. Emmett J. Scott, 1919.

Smith, Graham. *When Jim Crow Met John Bull: Black American Soldiers in World War II Britain*. London: I. B. Tauris, 1987.

Smithies, Edward. *Crime in Wartime: A Social History of Crime in World War II.* London: George Allen and Unwin, 1982.

Smythe, Mable M., ed. *The Black American Reference Book.* Englewood Cliffs, N.J.: Prentice-Hall, 1976.

Still, Bayard. *Mirror for Gotham: New York as Seen by Contemporaries from Dutch Days to the Present.* New York: New York Univ. Press, 1956.

Stokes, I. N. Phelps. *New York Past and Present: Its History and Landmarks, 1524–1939.* New York: n.p., 1939.

Tarry, Ellen. *The Third Door: The Autobiography of an American Negro Woman.* New York: David McKay, 1955.

Trottman, Beresford S. B. *Who's Who in Harlem.* New York: Magazine and Periodical Printing and Publishing, n.d.

Valentine, Lewis J. *Night Stick: The Autobiography of Lewis J. Valentine.* New York: Dial Press, 1947.

Von Hentig, Hans. *Crime: Causes and Conditions.* New York: McGraw-Hill, 1947.

White, Walter. *A Man Called White: The Autobiography of Walter White.* New York: Viking, 1948.

Wilkins, Roy. *Standing Fast: The Autobiography of Roy Wilkins.* New York: Viking, 1982.

Articles

Birch, Ian. "After the Blitz Here Comes the Ritz Again Going Back to the Zoots." *History Workshop* 20 (autumn 1985): 76–80.

Capeci, Dominic J., Jr. "Walter F. White and the Savoy Ballroom Controversy of 1943." *Afro-Americans in New York Life and History* 5 (July 1981): 13–32.

Chibnall, Steve. "Whistle and Zoot: The Changing Meaning of a Suit of Clothes." *History Workshop* 20 (Autumn 1985): 56–79.

Cosgrove, Stuart. "The Zoot-Suit and Style Warfare." *History Workshop* 18 (autumn 1984): 77–91.

Eagles, Charles W. "Two 'Double V's': Jonathan Daniels, FDR, and Race Relations during World War II." *North Carolina Historical Review* 59: (July 1982): 252–70.

Koppes, Clayton R., and Gregory D. Black. "Blacks, Loyalty, and Motion-Picture Propaganda in World War II." *Journal of American History* 73, no. 2 (1986): 383–406.

Lawes, Lewis E. "Will There Be a Crime Wave?" *New York Times Sunday Magazine*, Nov. 5, 1944, 16–17, 53.

McGuire, Phillip. "Judge Hastie, World War II, and the Army Air Corps." *Phylon* 42, no. 2 (1981): 157–67.

Moore, Christopher. "Unearthing Black History." *District Lines* 9 (spring 1994): 2–3.

Moses, Robert. "What's the Matter With New York?" *New York Times Sunday Magazine*, Aug. 1, 1943, 8–9, 28–29.

Reynolds, David. "The Churchill Government and the Black American Troops in Britain During World War II." *Transactions of the Royal Historical Society* 35 (1985): 113–33.

Sancton, Thomas. "The Race Riots." *New Republic*, July 5, 1943, 9–13.

Stein, Gertrude. "The New Hope in Our 'Sad Young Men.' " *New York Times Sunday Magazine*, June 3, 1945, 5, 38.

Weir, Georgette. "Underground Landmark." *Vassar Quarterly*, Summer 1993, 30.

Woolf, S. J. "Cops' Cop With a Five-Borough Beat." *New York Times Sunday Magazine*, Nov. 19, 1944, 16, 38–39.

Unpublished Papers

Greene, Larry A. "Harlem in the Great Depression, 1928–1936." Ph.D. diss., Columbia Univ., 1979.

Hastie, William H. "On Clipped Wings: The Story of Jim Crow in the Army Air Corps." New York: National Association for the Advancement of Colored People, 1943. Microfilm.

Orlansky [Orlans], Harold. "The Harlem Riot: A Study in Mass Frustration." *Social Analysis*, report no. 1. New York: n.p., 1943.

Washburn, Patrick S. "J. Edgar Hoover and the Black Press in World War II." Paper presented to the History Division of the Association for Education in Journalism and Mass Communication, Norman, Okla., Aug. 3–6, 1986. ERIC, ED 271749.

Index